D0593912

RICHARD WRIGHT

a primary bibliography

*A
Reference
Publication
in
Afro-American
Studies*

Charles T. Davis, *Editor*
Henry-Louis Gates, Jr., *Associate Editor*

RICHARD WRIGHT

a primary bibliography

CHARLES T. DAVIS
and
MICHEL FABRE

Z
8986.323
.D38
1982

G.K.HALL &CO.
70 LINCOLN STREET, BOSTON, MASS.

INDIANA
UNIVERSITY LIBRARY

JUN 19 1984

NORTHWEST

Copyright © 1982 by Michel Fabre & Charles Davis.

Library of Congress Cataloging in Publication Data

Davis, Charles Till.
  Richard Wright, a primary bibliography.

  Includes indexes.
  1. Wright, Richard, 1908-1960—Bibliography.
I. Fabre, Michel. II. Title.
Z8986.323.D38   [PS3545.R815]   016.813'52   81-13398
ISBN 0-8161-8410-0   AACR2

This publication is printed on permanent/durable acid-free paper
MANUFACTURED IN THE UNITED STATES OF AMERICA

pd
6-19-84

In Memoriam

Charles T. Davis

April 29, 1918 - March 25, 1981

Thou art not dead,
but flown afar,
up hills of endless light
through blazing corridors of suns,
where worlds do swing
of good and gentle men,
of women strong and free.

W. E. B. Du Bois

Contents

The Authors

Michel Fabre is a French citizen. He holds a Ph.D. from the Sorbonne, where he also received his B.A. and M.A. degrees. He has taught at Kings College (London), Wellesley College, Harvard University, and the University of Nanterre (Paris). In 1971 he was appointed Professor of American and Afro-American Studies at the Université Paris III (Sorbonne Nouvelle), where he is now director of the Centre d'Etudes Afro-Américaines et des Nouvelles Littératures en Anglais. His numerous publications include The Unfinished Quest of Richard Wright, which received the Anisfield-Wolf Award in 1973, and a Richard Wright Reader (1978).

Charles T. Davis served most recently as Professor of English and Chairman of Afro-American Studies, Yale University. He was graduated from Dartmouth College (B.A.) and University of Chicago (M.A.), and received his Ph.D. from New York University. Previous to his Yale appointment, Professor Davis taught at the University of Iowa, Harvard, Pennsylvania State University, and Princeton.

During his academic career, he received numerous honors and distinctions, most recently as Master of Calhoun College, Yale University (1973-1980), Richard Wright Memorial Lecturer, Yale (1977), Rockefeller Fellow (1980-81) and Fellow, Yale Humanities Institute (1980-82). He published widely and was noted for his writings on Edward Arlington Robinson and Richard Wright.

Preface

This bibliography of the works of Richard Wright is divided into two main sections, two appendices, and an index.

Published Works by Wright

The first section, "Richard Wright's Published Works," is organized chronologically according to the first year of publication of a given work. Within each year, works are divided by genre into four main categories: Drama, Fiction, Nonfiction, and Poetry. The Fiction category is subdivided into Shorter Writings and Books. The Nonfiction category, also subdivided into Shorter Writings and Books, includes essays, newspaper articles, book reviews, blurbs (for book dust jackets), introductions, published letters, liner notes (for record album covers), miscellaneous writings, and statements. Within each year of the published works section, works are numbered in sequence, without regard to category.

Unpublished Works

The section of "Richard Wright's Unpublished Works" is arranged alphabetically by title or by the made-up title [in brackets] assigned for identification in the James Weldon Johnson Wright Collection. This section is also divided into four categories: Drama (including film, television, and radio scripts), Fiction (Shorter Writings and Books), Nonfiction (including all the nonfiction categories of the published section, plus interviews for which Wright prepared written notes), and Poetry (including song lyrics).

Appendix I

Appendix I, "Translations of Richard Wright's Published Works," is arranged first in alphabetical order by language, then within each language in alphabetical order by the title by which the work is known in English. Reprint information is included. The list of translations is based upon the Index Translationum and upon the copies of texts that Wright and Mrs. Ellen Wright have received from publishers over the years.

Preface

Appendix II

Appendix II, "Material by Others Related to Wright's Published
Works," is a short bibliography of such works residing in the James
Weldon Johnson Wright Collection at Beinecke Library, Yale Univer-
sity. This appendix is arranged alphabetically by titles.

Index

The index includes all the titles of Wright's published and unpublished works, with the entry number in which they first appear.
Also included are the names of any individuals mentioned in the
entries who are connected with Wright's published or unpublished
works.

Cross-References

Within the published works section, cross-references for reprint
information and related works are given in the following form:

Year.Entry number.
For example:
Reprint of 1958.2
Reprinted: 1961.5
See also 1947.4

In the first example, the work is a reprint of a work originally
published in 1958, and may be found in entry 2 under that year. The
second example refers to a work reprinted in 1961 that may be found
in entry 5 of that year. In the third example, the work bears some
relationship to entry 4 in the year 1947. For instance, it may be a
new version of a previous short story.

Publishing Information

A typical entry in the published works section reads as follows:

1   "Silt." New Masses 24, no. 9 (24 August):19-20.
     [1935-37]

The entry includes the title or made-up title [in brackets] of the
work; the title of the anthology or periodical (if any) in which the
work appears; the name or names of the editor(s); appropriate publishing information; and the assumed date written, if known [in
brackets]. A brief description of the work follows, if necessary.

Information on manuscripts related to a published work follows
the initial entry for that work. A typical manuscript entry includes
the following: the form of the manuscript (typescript, autograph,
or carbon); the number of unnumbered leaves and of numbered leaves;
the nature of the manuscript (draft, galley proof, notes, etc.) and a
brief description; a working title, if it differs from Wright's final

title; the location of the manuscript, or the James Weldon Johnson
call number, if located in that collection at the Beinecke Library,
Yale University, New Haven, Connecticut.

Special Problems

   Some of the manuscripts in the James Weldon Johnson Collection,
especially ideas for plays or novels, are restricted, and information
about them in this bibliography is limited. These manuscripts may be
examined only by special permission.

   In spite of careful checking by research assistants, some works
cannot be located and have been marked "unverified" [in brackets].
All other entries have been located in the JWJ Wright Collection, the
Sterling Library at Yale, the National Union Catalogue, the Index
Translationum, the New York Public Library, and so forth.

   Volume numbers of periodicals have been used when available.
Some foreign periodicals and little magazines do not use volume numbers, or use them for some years and not others.

   Daily Worker articles, mostly written while Wright was a re-
porter for the newspaper in 1937, sometimes bear Wright's byline,
sometimes his "Harlem Bureau" byline, and sometimes no byline. These
last articles are presumed to be written by Wright because of their
content and because they are part of Wright's collection of clippings.
A few of these could not be verified, either in the Daily Worker
repository at Yale University's Sterling Library or at the New York
Public Library. Page and column numbers are given for the late New
York edition, unless "early edition" is specified.

Mary Lang McFarland
Darby Tench

Introduction

This descriptive bibliography of the works of Richard Wright is
the most comprehensive and most substantial effort undertaken to date
to establish an accurate Wright canon. Its completeness depends
greatly upon the Richard Wright Archive, now resting in the James
Weldon Johnson Collection of Afro-American Literature at the Beinecke
Library, Yale University. It also reflects work invested in bibliog-
raphies published earlier. In 1965 Michel Fabre collaborated with
Edward Margolies in a pioneering bibliography. He published a more
complete bibliography in New Letters in 1972, and he brings the experience from preparing these publications to this volume, his third
effort in the field.

No general bibliography like this one can make the claim of being
definitive. There is always the possibility that a Wright manuscript
might turn up in a publisher's office or in an abandoned trunk in
Chicago, New York, or Paris. But that possibility seems unlikely
when one considers the care expended upon discovering, checking,
classifying, and describing the items listed here.

The authors provide data on successive American and English editions, including reprints and extracts. They offer, in addition,
descriptions of drafts and early or variant versions that record
departures from the published Wright texts. Also made available is
information on translations. The objective of the volume is to en-
able a scholar to reconstruct the genesis of each work and to trace
its textual history, including its appearance in languages other than
English. Clearly, no general bibliography can provide every detail
of the transformation of a text. Nothing will take the place of
private research into the incorporation of multiple and complex revisions. But what is provided here is a necessary and indispensable
starting point for Wright scholars, who may be expected to approach
the canon with varying levels of commitment and knowledge.

The rich resources of the Richard Wright Archive require a comment, since many references in the bibliography come from the Archive.
Beinecke Library has a version of all works by Wright appearing in
other public collections, with one important exception. This is a

set of page proofs of Native Son (with manuscript revisions), presently located in the Fales Collection at the New York University Library. The Wright Archive at Yale contains the bulk of the successive drafts and versions of Wright's published works and nearly all of his unpublished works. Though the manuscripts and typescripts of published texts are available for consultation, the unpublished documents are not. The examination of these materials requires written authorization from Richard Wright's widow, Mrs. Ellen Wright, and/or approval by the Committee on the Wright Archive at the Yale University Library. In the interest of completeness, mention must be made of a few deliberate omissions in this bibliography of items extant in the Archive. Absent from the listing are a small number of typescripts made at Wright's request from already published essays, introductions, and reviews, as well as a few typescripts made by Fabre from barely legible manuscripts.

The bibliography also omits a comprehensive listing of Wright's correspondence. This is a task that remains for other hands. To be found here are only letters published in newspapers or periodicals. Though private collections possess only a few manuscripts of Wright's works, the bulk of his letters now rest primarily in the files of his agent and his publishers. A collection of about five hundred letters to Edward C. Aswell, Wright's editor at Harper and Brothers, written between 1940 and 1957, is now at the Princeton University Library. Efforts to discover additional recipients and repositories of Wright's correspondence continue. Meanwhile, a collection of Wright's letters, prepared and edited by Michel Fabre and Edward Margolies, awaits publication at Harper and Row.

The authors of this bibliography hope that the book will bring new insights to the general reader, as well as accurate information for the Wright scholar. There is, first of all, the excitement of viewing in detail the whole professional career of Richard Wright. Some readers will be impressed by small discoveries: references to the generally unknown poems published in Midland Left in February 1935, or to the comments prepared for exhibitions in Paris. Others may be surprised by the strong commitment to poetry, an interest that reflects the framework of his creative life, as Wright moves from revolutionary verse to haiku. All may be amazed at the vast store of nonfiction writing, of literary, political, and social criticism, as well as a staggering number of articles on the passing scene written for the Daily Worker. Much of Wright's nonfiction attained publication at least once, but a considerable amount of his fiction, including finished or nearly finished pieces, never appeared in published form. No doubt, the labor of Wright scholars will be necessary to place many of these works within a context that guarantees maximum accessibility for general readers. The prospect now exists for the publication of several volumes of uncollected and unpublished writings. These projects should allow all students of Wright to achieve new insights into the art and mind of one of the most exciting writers of our time.

Introduction

This volume represents one form of basic research that needed to be done on Wright. There are other kinds of necessary scholarship. A work that directly complements this one is a bibliography of secondary sources undertaken by Keneth Kinnamon with the help of Joseph Brown, Michel Fabre, and Craig Werner, to be published by G. K. Hall. What began as a modest project expanded into a comprehensive listing of over eight thousand items, largely because of Kinnamon's insistence that the bibliography should become more far-ranging and inclusive. The result is an indispensable tool for the student of Wright's literary reputation, and it has, among other things, supplied a sense of urgency for a description of the Wright canon that would be equally thorough and comprehensive. These two works stand by a third, The Unfinished Quest of Richard Wright (1973) by Michel Fabre, which offers biographical data and commentary on the genesis of individual works.

The authors gratefully express their indebtedness to Rutherford D. Rogers, Yale University Librarian, and to Donald Gallup, Elizabeth Wakeman Dwight Curator of the Yale Collection of American Literature in Beinecke Library, who made available in photostat the card catalogue of the Wright Archive, which was relied on heavily in preparing this book. The work of the librarians at the James Weldon Johnson Collection was indispensable. Mrs. Joan Binder deserves special mention, because she prepared the catalogue for the Archives from 1975 to 1978, working with the library staff under the direction of Donald Gallup and with the collaboration of Michel Fabre.

Mrs. Ellen Wright allowed access to her library; Edward Margolies freely offered his experience as a pioneering Wright bibliographer; John Reilly permitted consultation of his records of Wright manuscripts in other libraries in the United States; Rebecca and David McBride corrected inaccuracies in the Fabre bibliography of 1972. All deserve our thanks, as do Yale students Charles Perry, Vincent Peterson, Joseph Conway, Inajo Davis, David Berreby, Stuart Taylor, and Randall C. Reeves. Research assistants Mary Lang McFarland and Darby Tench provided an invaluable service in giving a final shape to the bibliography, eliminating inconsistencies in fact and form, supervising research, and proofreading the entire manuscript at its various stages. Typists Gwen Williams and Sharon Adams worked with diligence, accuracy, and patience with everyone on the project. We acknowledge our debt, too, to the Program in Afro-American Studies at Yale, which provided warm cooperation and material and spiritual support. Finally, we thank our editors at G. K. Hall for their intelligent suggestions and unflagging interest.

Richard Wright's Published Works

1924

FICTION

Shorter Writings

1   "The Voodoo of Hell's Half Acre." Jackson (Miss.) Southern
    Register, circa Spring.
    No complete version available.

1931

FICTION

Shorter Writings

1   "Superstition." Abbott's Monthly Magazine 2 (April):45-47,
    64-66, 72-73. [1930]
    Signed Richard N. Wright.

1934

POETRY

1   "Child of the Dead and Forgotten Gods." The Anvil 2, no. 5
    (March-April):30. [1933]

2   "Everywhere Burning Waters Rise." Left Front 1, no. 4
    (May-June):9.

3   "I Have Seen Black Hands." New Masses 11, no. 13 (26 June):
    16. [1933]
        Reprinted: 1941.28; 1949.20; 1964.11; 1969.35; 1970.63;
    1971.36; 1978.25.

1934

4   "A Red Love Note." Left Front 1, no. 3 (January-February):3.
     [1933]

5   "Rest for the Weary." Left Front 1, no. 3 (January-February):
     3. [1933]

6   "Strength." The Anvil 2, no. 5 (March-April):20. [1933]

                                 1935

NONFICTION

Shorter Writing

Essay

1   "Joe Louis Uncovers Dynamite." New Masses 17, no. 2
     (8 October):18.
          Reprinted: 1969.19; 1970.33; 1978.10.

POETRY

2   "Ah Feels It in Mah Bones." International Literature 4
     (April):80. [1934]

3   "Between the World and Me." Partisan Review 2 (July-August):
     18-19. [1934]
          Reprinted: 1935.4; 1946.25; 1949.18; 1963.9; 1967.9;
     1968.17; 1970.57-60; 1973.3; 1978.23.

4   "Between the World and Me." In Proletarian Literature in the
     United States. Edited by Granville Hicks et al. New York:
     International Publishers, pp. 202-3.
          Reprint of 1935.3.

5   "I Am A Red Slogan." International Literature 4 (April):35.
     [1934]

6   "Live and Rise." Midland Left, no. 2 (February):13-14.

7   "Obsession." Midland Left, no. 2 (February):14.

8   "Red Leaves of Red Books." New Masses 15, no. 5 (30 April):6.

9   "Spread Your Sunrise." New Masses 16, no. 1 (2 July):26.
     [1934]

1936

FICTION

Shorter Writing

1   "Big Boy Leaves Home." In The New Caravan. Edited by Alfred
    Kreymborg et al. New York: Norton, pp. 124-58. [1935]
        Included in Uncle Tom's Children. Reprinted: 1938.1;
    1969.2; 1970.5-6; 1971.3-4; 1972.1. See also Uncle Tom's
    Children--Five Long Stories, 1940.12.

    Typescript (carbon): 48 numb. leaves.
    Late draft, with a few MS corrections (on pp. 19, 23, 33,
    37).
    Chicago Public Library, Cleveland Hall Biography.

    Same (carbon), uncorrected.

NONFICTION

Shorter Writings

Essay

2   "Two Million Black Voices." New Masses 18, no. 9
    (25 February):15.
        Report of the first National Negro Congress in Chicago.

Book Review

3   "A Tale of Folk Courage." Partisan Review and Anvil 3
    (April):31.
        Review of Black Thunder, by Arna Bontemps.

Introduction

4   Foreword to Illinois Labor Notes 4, no. 3 (March):2.
        Foreword to the special issue devoted to the National
    Negro Congress in Chicago.

    Typescript (original): 1 leaf.
    Written for special National Negro Congress issue for
    distribution to delegates at the Congress.
    JWJ Wright Misc. 377.

    Typescript (original) and autograph MS: 1 leaf.
    Outline and notes.
    JWJ Wright Misc. 471a.

1936

Letter

5   "In Defense of Meyer Levin." Partisan Review and Anvil 3
    (June):30.
        Letter to the editor defending progressive writer Meyer
    Levin, who had been labeled a reactionary in an article
    published by the magazine.

Miscellaneous

6   "Richard Wright." In The New Caravan. Edited by Alfred
    Kreymborg et al. New York: Norton, p. 663.
        Short biographical notice on himself.

POETRY

7   "Hearst Headline Blues." New Masses 19, no. 7 (12 May):14.

8   "Old Habit and New Love." New Masses 21, no. 12 (15 December):
    29.

9   "Transcontinental." International Literature 5 (January):
    52-57. [1935]

                              1937

FICTION

Shorter Writings

1   "Silt." New Masses 24, no. 9 (24 August):19-20. [1935-1937]
        Title was later changed to "The Man Who Saw the Flood."
    Reprinted: 1946.6; 1969.4; 1971.9-11. See also 1961.5.

    "Silt."
    Typescript (carbon): 7 numb. leaves.
    Early copy, with a few MS corrections. First published in
    the New Masses 24 (24 August 1937) with his original title.
    JWJ Wright 142.

    "Silt."
    Another typescript (carbon): 8 numb. leaves.
    Incorporating above corrections.
    JWJ Wright 143.

    Carbon of above, with revised title pasted in.
    JWJ Wright 144.

                               4

1937

NONFICTION

Shorter Writings

Daily Worker Articles, with Wright or Harlem Bureau byline

2   Richard Wright. "Negro Writers Launch Literary Quarterly."
    8 June, p. 7, cols. 3-4.

3   Harlem Bureau. "Negro Ministers' Union to Push Race Progress."
    9 June, p. 3, cols. 3-4.

4   Harlem Bureau. "Rally for Ethiopia is Backed by C. P."
    10 June, p. 2, cols. 4-5.

5   Harlem Bureau. "PWA Houses are Opened in Harlem." 17 June,
    p. 5, col. 3.

6   Harlem Bureau. "Party Leaders Honor Negro Woman Leader."
    22 June, p. 5, cols. 3-4.

7   Harlem Bureau. "Harlem to Protest Scottsboro Verdict."
    30 June, p. 3, cols. 4-5.

8   Harlem Bureau. "Protest Job Discrimination Against Negro."
    30 June, p. 5, col. 4.

9   Harlem Bureau. "Scottsboro Meetings Set in Harlem." 2 July,
    p. 3, col. 6.

10 Harlem Bureau. "Harlem WPA Staffs Stage Death Watch."
    2 July, p. 5, cols. 1-2.

11 Harlem Bureau. "WPA Slashes Are Bar to Harlem Homes."
    8 July, p. 4, cols. 7-8.

12 Harlem Bureau. "WPA Layoffs Wipe Out Jobs of Negroes."
    10 July, p. 5, col. 6.

13 Harlem Bureau. "Harlem Rallies to Aid Nine Scottsboro Boys."
    10 July, p. 5, cols. 4-5.

14 Harlem Bureau. "Harlem Maps Fight Against WPA Slashes."
    13 July, p. 5, col. 3.

1937

15 Harlem Bureau. "Negro Union Painters Seek Higher Wages."
    14 July, p. 3, col. 7.

16 Harlem Bureau. "Harlem Baby Denied Medical Care Dies."
    14 July, p. 4, col. 8.

17 Harlem Bureau. "Butcher Slugs Negro Youth Asking Change."
    14 July, p. 5, col. 1.

18 Harlem Bureau. "Harlem Merchants Will Close to Protest Relief
    Slash." 15 July, p. 1, cols. 2-3; p. 4, cols. 1-2.

19 Richard Wright. "Butcher Who Attacked Negro Boy is Fired."
    15 July, p. 2, cols. 5-6.

20 Harlem Bureau. "WPA March to Protest Scottsboro Verdict."
    17 July, p. 1, cols. 4-5; p. 4, col. 7.

21 Harlem Bureau. "Bar Negro Relief After Pink Slip Cuts."
    20 July, p. 1, col. 1.

22 Harlem Bureau. "Negro Women Will Picket Italian Consul."
    20 July, p. 3, col. 6.

23 Harlem Bureau. "Store Clerks Demand End of Jim Crow."
    20 July, p. 3, col. 2.

24 Harlem Bureau. "Women Picket Italy's Consulate Tomorrow."
    22 July, p. 4, cols. 1-2.

25 Harlem Bureau. "Fla. Lynching Draws Harlem Protest Action."
    22 July, p. 5. [Unverified]

26 Harlem Bureau. "Harlem ILD, CP Hold Protest on Scottsboro."
    22 July, p. 8, col. 5.

27 Harlem Bureau. "100 Negro, White Women Picket Italian Con-
    sulate." 24 July, p. 5, cols. 3-4.

28 Harlem Bureau. "Pickets Ask Negro Hiring in Movie House."
    25 July. [Unverified]

29 Harlem Bureau. "Harlem Party to Protest Japan's Action."
    27 July, p. 2, col. 6.

30 Harlem Bureau. "Torchlight March Called August 7 by Harlem
    Group." 27 July, p. 2, col. 7.

1937

31   Harlem Bureau. "Harlem Spurs Scottsboro Boys Fight."
      30 July, p. 3, col. 3.

32   Harlem Bureau. "Harlem to Hold Peace Parade on Wednesday."
      31 July, p. 3, col. 2.

33   Harlem Bureau. "Got Raw Deal on WPA Says Negro Actor."
      1 August, p. 3. [Unverified]

34   Harlem Bureau. "Harlem C. P. to Hear Report by Jack Stachel."
      2 August, p. 3, col. 6.

35   Richard Wright. "Negro, with 3-Week-Old Baby, Begs Food on
      Streets." 4 August, p. 3, cols. 3-4.

36   Harlem Bureau. "Harlem Viewed Peace Caravan Last Evening."
      5 August, p. 3, col. 4.

37   Harlem Bureau. "Harlem Rallies Behind March for WPA Jobs."
      7 August, p. 2. [Unverified]

38   Harlem Bureau. "Harlem Cop Compelled to Apologize for Abuse."
      8 August. [Unverified]

39   Richard Wright. "CP Leads Struggle for Freedom, Stachel
      Says." 9 August, p. 2, cols. 7-8.

40   Harlem Bureau. "Negro Charges Discrimination by AFL Heads."
      11 August, p. 3, col. 2.

41   Harlem Bureau. "Scottsboro Fight Pushed at Harlem Rally."
      11 August, p. 3, col. 3.

42   Harlem Bureau. "Communist Head Speaks at Sidewalk Univer-
      sity." 12 August, p. 3, cols. 5-6.

43   Harlem Bureau. "Harlem Office Opened by ILD." 12 August,
      p. 5, col. 1.

44   Richard Wright. "Huddie Ledbetter, Famous Negro Folk Artist,
      Sings the Songs of Scottsboro and His People." 12 August,
      p. 7, cols. 3-7.

45   Richard Wright. "Communist Leader Warns on Harlem Tiger
      Stooges." 13 August, p. 4, cols. 4-5.

46   Harlem Bureau. "Harlem Plans to Send 25 on WPA March."
      13 August, p. 4, col. 6.

1937

47   Harlem Bureau. "ALP Seeks New Schools for Harlem."
     14 August, p. 3, col. 3.

48   Harlem Bureau. "Harlem Crowd Shows Feeling on Chiseling."
     16 August, p. 5, col. 6.

49   Richard WRight. "What Happens at a Communist Party Branch
     Meeting in the Harlem Section?" 16 August, p. 6,
     cols. 4-6.

50   Harlem Bureau. "Negro Union to Celebrate Twelfth Year."
     17 August, p. 4, col. 4.

51   Harlem Bureau. "Negro Group Attacks RR Jim Crow Policy."
     17 August. [Unverified]

52   Richard Wright. "Pullman Porters to Celebrate 12th Year of
     Their Union." 19 August, p. 3, cols. 2-5.

53   Harlem Bureau. "Race Tolerance Lecture Scheduled Here on
     Tuesday." 19 August, p. 3, col. 6.

54   Harlem Bureau. "Negro Congress to Convene in Phila."
     21 August, p. 2, cols. 4-5.

55   Richard Wright. "Scottsboro Boys on Stage Is Opposed."
     21 August, p. 2, col. 2.

56   Harlem Bureau. "Record of Nat'l Negro Congress." 21 August,
     p. 2, col. 3.

57   Harlem Bureau. "WPA Official Charged with Negro Bias."
     23 August, p. 3, col. 7.

58   Harlem Bureau. "Low-Cost Rent in Harlem Too High for Many."
     23 August, p. 3, col. 8.

59   Harlem Bureau. "Harlem Party to Hear Berry on 18th Anniver-
     sary." 24 August, p. 2, col. 7.

60   Harlem Bureau. "Negro Unions Plan Campaign on Education."
     24 August, p. 5, col. 5.

61   Richard Wright. "'Opportunity for Soviet Youth Unlimited,'
     Says Negro Musician." 24 August, p. 6, cols. 4-6.

62   Harlem Bureau. "Statement on Scottsboro is Made by Group."
     27 August, p. 2, col. 3.

1937

63   Harlem Bureau. "Famous Negro Leaders Guide Congress Action."
      27 August, p. 4, col. 2.

64   Richard Wright. "Born A Slave, She Recruits 5 Members for
      Communist Party." 30 August, p. 3, cols. 4-5.

65   Harlem Bureau. "Harlem to Get Scottsboro Defense Group."
      30 August, p. 5, col. 5.

66   Harlem Bureau. "Fight Parties in Harlem." 30 August, p. 8,
      cols. 6-7. [Early edition]

67   Harlem Bureau. "Retail Clerks to Continue Picketing."
      2 September, p. 3, col. 3.

68   Harlem Bureau. "Harlem Plans Big Party Building Drive."
      2 September, p. 5, col. 4.

69   Richard Wright. "Harlem Women Hit Boost in Milk Price."
      3 September, p. 1, cols. 3-5.

70   Harlem Bureau. "Negro Congress Directives are Issued."
      3 September, p. 4, col. 4.

71   Harlem Bureau. "Harlem to Denounce Terror in West Indies."
      4 September, p. 3, cols. 4-5.

72   Harlem Bureau. "African Leader Here to Discuss Home Issues."
      4 September, p. 3, col. 6.

73   Richard Wright. "Insect-Ridden Medicine Given in Hospital."
      4 September, p. 5, col. 5.

74   Harlem Bureau. "Negro Women Attacked in IRT Subway."
      5 September, p. 5. [Unverified]

75   Harlem Bureau. "Negro Baiting WPA Supervisor Out in the
      Cold." 5 September. [Unverified]

76   Richard Wright. "Mrs. Holmes and Daughters Drink From the
      Fountain of Communism." 7 September, p. 5, cols. 1-2.

77   Harlem Bureau. "Harlem Women Picket Milk Co. Tomorrow."
      8 September, p. 3, col. 7.

78   Harlem Bureau. "Harlem Rent Strike Ends; Tenants Win."
      8 September, p. 3, col. 8.

1937

79   Harlem Bureau. "Amter to Open East Harlem Drive In Talk."
      9 September, p. 2, col. 1.

80   Harlem Bureau. "Harlem to Launch Fund Drive Tonight."
      9 September, p. 3, cols. 4-5.

81   Harlem Bureau. "African Negro Under Court Marshal [sic] Law,
      Says Head." 9 September, p. 3, col. 6.

82   Harlem Bureau. "Porters Meet Sunday to Mark Victory Pact."
      10 September, p. 4, col. 3.

83   Harlem Bureau. "Scores Picket Borden's, Protesting High
      Prices." 11 September, p. 5, cols. 5-6.

84   Harlem Bureau. "Lower Harlem Rally Spurs Party Drive."
      11 September, p. 5, col. 4.

85   Harlem Bureau. "Upper Harlem Rally to Hear Party History."
      11 September, p. 5, col. 7.

86   Richard Wright. "'Horseplay' at Lafayette Fun for Children
      and Grown-Ups Alike." 11 September, p. 7, cols. 5-6.

87   Harlem Bureau. "Picket Milk Firm Against Price Rises."
      11 September, p. 5, col. 3. [Early edition]

88   Harlem Bureau. "Porters Have Closed Shop . . ." 13 September,
      p. 3, cols. 4-5.

89   Harlem Bureau. "Harlem Stores Sign CIO Union Pact."
      14 September, p. 3, col. 3.

90   Harlem Bureau. "East Harlem Party Building Drive Mapped."
      14 September, p. 3, col. 5.

91   Harlem Bureau. "Amter Speaks at Big Rally in 'Little
      Italy.'" 16 September, p. 3, col. 8.

92   Harlem Bureau. "24 Negro Families Begin Rent Strike."
      16 September, p. 5, cols. 4-5.

93   Harlem Bureau. "Scottsboro Rallies to be Held Tonight."
      17 September, p. 4, col. 5.

94   Harlem Bureau. "Scottsboro Drive Pushed." 18 September,
      p. 5, col. 7.

95   Harlem Bureau. "Scottsboro Mother Talks Monday Night."
20 September, p. 2, col. 8.

96   Harlem Bureau. "East Harlem C. P. Recruits 40 Members."
20 September, p. 5, col. 6.

97   Richard Wright. "Harlem Spanish Women Come Out of the
Kitchen." 20 September, p. 5, cols. 6-8.

98   Harlem Bureau. "Harlem Group Pushes Aid for China."
22 September, p. 2, col. 8.

99   Harlem Bureau. "Negro Woman Beaten by Harlem Merchant."
22 September, p. 5, cols. 6-7.

100   Harlem Bureau. "8 Harlem Leaders Join China Rally."
23 September, p. 2, col. 1.

101   Richard Wright. "10,000 Negro Vets in N.Y. Silent, But
They're Talking up at Home." 23 September, p. 4,
cols. 2-5.

102   Harlem Bureau. "Harlem Rally For China on Sept. 27."
24 September, p. 2, col. 2.

103   Harlem Bureau. "Scottsboro Drive Pushed in Harlem."
24 September, p. 4, col. 2.

104   Harlem Bureau. "Harlem C. P. to Open Educational Forum."
25 September. [Unverified]

105   Harlem Bureau. "Negro Pastor Assails Tokio Aggression."
25 September, p. 2, col. 6.

106   Richard Wright. "Big Harlem Rally For China Tonight."
27 September, p. 4, col. 4.

107   Richard Wright. "American Negroes in Key Posts of Spain's
Loyalist Forces." 29 September, p. 2, cols. 1-3.

108   Richard Wright. "Randolph Urges Parley Between CIO-AFL
Unions." 30 September, p. 3, cols. 6-7.

109   Richard Wright. "Bates Tells of Spain's Fight for Strong
Republican Army." 1 October, p. 2, cols. 1-3.

110   Harlem Bureau. "C. P. Nominee Withdraws to Aid A.L.P."
2 October, p. 4, col. 5.

1937

111   Harlem Bureau. "Harlem Unions Back Nat'l. Negro Congress."
      4 October, p. 5, cols. 4-5.

112   "Amter Speaks October 8 at Harlem Rally." 4 October, p. 5,
      col. 6.

113   Harlem Bureau. "Scottsboro Drive Gains in Harlem."
      5 October, p. 8, col. 3.

114   Harlem Bureau. "Harlem Center for Children Opens October 10."
      5 October, p. 8, col. 3.

115   Harlem Bureau. "Scottsboro Mother Sees Son in Jail."
      6 October, p. 5, col. 7.

116   Richard Wright. "Negro Youth on March, Says Leader."
      7 October, p. 3, col. 6.

117   "Lower Harlem To Hear Amter Talk Tonight." 7 October, p. 4,
      col. 3.

118   Richard Wright. "Opening of Harlem Project Homes Shows How
      Slums Can be Wiped Out in New York." 8 October, p. 5,
      cols. 2-5.

119   "Socialists Back Negro Congress." 8 October, p. 5, col. 1.

120   Harlem Bureau. "Mother, Three Children Are Evicted in
      Harlem." 9 October, p. 5, cols. 5-6.

121   Harlem Bureau. "Tim Holmes to Speak at Harlem Forum."
      9 October, p. 5, col. 8. [Early edition]

122   Harlem Bureau. "Heights Leads in Campaign for Press."
      11 October, p. 4, col. 8.

123   Harlem Bureau. "Hathaway and Amter Speak at Jewish Rally."
      11 October, p. 2, col. 3.

124   Harlem Bureau. "Negro Gets Job as City Buyer of All Chemi-
      cals." 12 October, p. 2, col. 3.

125   Harlem Bureau. "Mrs. Roosevelt to Speak in Harlem
      October 22." 12 October, p. 2, col. 8.

126   Harlem Bureau. "Schedule [sic] Talk by Browder in Spanish
      Harlem." 13 October, p. 4, col. 3.

127   Harlem Bureau. "She Lay Dying, But They Would Not Give Her
      Aid." 13 October, p. 5, cols. 7-8.

128   Harlem Bureau. "Harlem Plans Scottsboro Defense Rally."
      13 October, p. 5, col. 7.

129   Harlem Bureau. "Hotel Workers to Back Negro Conference."
      13 October, p. 5, col. 7.

130   Harlem Bureau. "See Biggest Negro Parley Since Days of
      Reconstruction." 14 October, p. 5, cols. 2-3.

131   Harlem Bureau. "National Negro Congress to Open Tomorrow
      Morning." 14 October, p. 5, col. 1-3.

132   "Scottsboro Meeting in Brooklyn Friday." 14 October, p. 8,
      cols. 4-5.

133   Harlem Bureau. "Scottsboro Drive Backed by Candidate."
      15 October, p. 5, col. 3.

134   "Public Libraries Need Books." 15 October, p. 9, col. 2.

135   Richard Wright. "Negro Tradition in the Theater."
      15 October, p. 9, cols. 4-6.

136   "Harlem Rent Strike Gains New Supports." 17 October.
      [Unverified]

137   Harlem Bureau. "Harlem Rent Strikers Win in Court Fight."
      19 October, p. 5, col. 8.

138   Harlem Bureau. "Ford to Give Negro Congress Report Friday."
      19 October, p. 5, col. 7.

139   Richard Wright. "Harlem, Bronx Sign Competition Pact."
      19 October, p. 5, col. 1.

140   "Juanita Hall to Sing." 20 October, p. 7, col. 7.

141   Richard Wright. "Harlem Negro Leaders Back Mayor for Liberal
      Views." 20 October, p. 4, cols. 2-4.

142   Harlem Bureau. "Browder Talks in East Harlem." 21 October,
      p. 1, col. 3.

143   Harlem Bureau. "Ask Aid for Scottsboro Defense Drive."
      21 October, p. 4, col. 6.

1937

144   "Browder to Speak in Harlem Tomorrow." 21 October, p. 4.
      [Unverified]

145   Harlem Bureau. "Patterson Talks Friday in Harlem."
      21 October, p. 5, col. 2.

146   Harlem Bureau. "YCL Supports Harlem C. P. Daily Drive."
      21 October, p. 5, col. 6.

147   Harlem Bureau. "Ford Speaks Tonight at Harlem Rally."
      22 October, p. 2. [Unverified]

148   Richard Wright. "Browder Warns of Growth of Fascism in Latin
      America." 23 October, p. 5, cols. 1-2.

149   Richard Wright. "New Negro Pamphlet Stresses Need for U.S.
      People's Front." 25 October, p. 3, cols. 1-2.

150   Harlem Bureau. "Scottsboro Parley in Harlem Tonight."
      25 October, p. 4, cols. 1-2.

151   Harlem Bureau. "100 Women To Score Gijon Massacre."
      26 October, p. 2, col. 2.

152   Harlem Bureau. "Harlem Women to Get Advice on Meat Buying."
      26 October, p. 5, cols. 4-5.

153   Harlem Bureau. "Parley Maps Scottsboro Campaign."
      26 October, p. 5, col. 6.

154   Harlem Bureau. "Scottsboro Drive Pushed by Harlem C. P."
      29 October, p. 4, col. 8.

155   Richard Wright. "Harlem Leaders Rap Amsterdam News' Stand
      for Mahoney." 29 October, p. 7, cols. 4-5.

156   Harlem Bureau. "Fifty Fascists Attack Women's Picket Line."
      30 October, p. 2, cols. 4-5.

157   "Mayor Signs Scottsboro Petition." 31 October. [Unverified]

158   Harlem Bureau. "Plan to Push Scottsboro Campaign."
      1 November, p. 7, col. 6.

159   "Picket Lines Win Withdrawal of All Goods Made in Japan."
      1 November, p. 8, cols. 7-8.

1937

160   Richard Wright. "Harlem Vote Swings Away From Tiger."
      2 November, p. 3, cols. 6-7.

161   Richard Wright. "Negro Leaders Hail Victory of A.L.P. at New
      York Polls." 4 November, p. 5, cols. 1-2.

162   Harlem Bureau. "Stachel to Speak Friday in Harlem."
      5 November, p. 2, col. 6.

163   Harlem Bureau. "Negro Schoolboy Attacked by Teacher."
      5 November, p. 5, cols. 5-6.

164   Harlem Bureau. "Harlem Concert to Mark Soviet Union
      Festival." 6 November, p. 2, col. 7.

165   Harlem Bureau. "Plan to Aid Negroes in West Indies."
      6 November, p. 3, col. 6.

166   Harlem Bureau. "Tenants Plan Big League in Harlem."
      6 November, p. 3, col. 3.

167   Harlem Bureau. "Harlem Sentiment Seen Favoring Boycott of
      Borden." 6 November, p. 5. [Unverified]

168   Richard Wright. "A.L.P. Assemblyman Urges State Control of
      Price of Milk." 8 November, p. 1, cols. 1-2.

169   Harlem Bureau. "Scottsboro Mother to Lead Protest."
      8 November, p. 2, col. 7.

170   Harlem Bureau. "Stachel Sounds Call for Unity of Unions in
      Harlem Address." 8 November, p. 3, cols. 7-8.

171   Harlem Bureau. "Tenants Push Fight on High Harlem Rents."
      8 November, p. 4. [Unverified]

172   Harlem Bureau. "Sharecropper Friends to Hold Savoy Dance."
      9 November, p. 4, col. 1.

173   Harlem Bureau. "Negroes Form Committee to Aid Spain."
      12 November, p. 2, col. 6.

174   Harlem Bureau. "Call Parley to Aid West Indian Negroes."
      12 November, p. 2, cols. 7-8.

175   Harlem Bureau. "Scottsboro Sunday Tomorrow in New York
      Baptist Churches." 13 November, p. 4, cols. 5-6.

1937

176   Harlem Bureau. "Scottsboro Drive Backed by State CP."
      15 November, p. 3, col. 6.

177   Harlem Bureau. "Negroes Win Back Jobs on WPA Theatre."
      15 November, p. 4, col. 2.

178   Harlem Bureau. "Scottsboro Mother to Lead Delegation."
      15 November, p. 5, cols. 4-5.

179   Harlem Bureau. "Patterson Speaks on USSR November 18 at
      Harlem Forum." 16 November, p. 2, col. 3.

180   Harlem Bureau. "Scottsboro Delegation is Chosen."
      17 November, p. 3, col. 4.

181   Harlem Bureau. "Harlem Community Organizer to Speak on Drive
      Tonight." 17 November, p. 4, col. 7.

182   Harlem Bureau. "Harlem Rent Strikers Win Agreement."
      17 November, p. 5, col. 6.

183   Harlem Bureau. "Anti-Lynching Delegation Delays Trip."
      18 November, p. 2, col. 2.

184   Richard Wright. "ALP Assemblyman in Harlem Hails Unity of
      Labor at Polls." 18 November, p. 2, cols. 7-8.

185   Harlem Bureau. "Baby Carriage Parade to Protest Milk Gouge."
      20 November, p. 1, cols. 6-7.

186   Harlem Bureau. "Harlem Leaders Hit Tory Filibuster on Anti-
      Lynch Bill." 20 November, p. 3, cols. 7-8.

187   "Rep. O'Connell Urges Democracies to Unite in Fight on
      Fascism." 22 November, p. 4, col. 4.

188   "YCL Session Opens November 26 in Brooklyn." 22 November,
      p. 4, col. 7.

189   Harlem Bureau. "Memorial for Milton Herndon Next Sunday."
      22 November, p. 4, col. 8.

190   Harlem Bureau. "Negro Tenants Win Rent Cuts in 8 Houses."
      23 November, p. 4, col. 8. [Unverified]

191   Harlem Bureau. "2 Scottsboro Boys Leave on National Tour."
      24 November, p. 2, col. 2.

1937

192 Harlem Bureau. "Few Harlem Tables Weighted by Turkey."
26 November, p. 4, cols. 4-5.

193 Harlem Bureau. "Ford Replies to Negro Pastor in Discussion
of Fascist Peril." 26 November, p. 5, cols. 1-3.

194 Harlem Bureau. "Honor Herndon at Harlem Rally Sunday."
27 November, p. 2, col. 5.

195 Harlem Bureau. "Negro Congressman to Speak Sunday in Harlem
Church." 27 November, p. 5, col. 5.

196 Richard Wright. "Walter Garland Tells What Spain's Fight
Against Fascism Means to the Negro People." 29 November,
p. 2, cols. 3-6.

197 Harlem Bureau. "Anti-Lynching Bill Will Pass, Says Mitchell."
29 November, p. 4, col. 2.

198 Harlem Bureau. "Pickets Force Stores to Ban Japan Goods."
30 November, p. 1, col. 3.

199 Harlem Bureau. "Boycott is Spreading in Harlem's Stores."
2 December, p. 1, cols. 6-7.

200 Harlem Bureau. "Assemblymen From Harlem to Map Plans."
4 December, p. 5, col. 1.

201 Harlem Bureau. "Weisbecker Strike Strong in Harlem."
4 December, p. 3, col. 5.

202 Richard Wright. "'He Died by Them'--Hero's Widow Tells of
Rescue of Negroes." 6 December, p. 1, cols. 4-5.

203 Harlem Bureau. "YCL Pushes Scottsboro Defense Fight."
6 December, p. 3, cols. 5-6.

204 Richard Wright. "Harlem, East Side Honor Hero Who Died in
Rescue of Negroes." 7 December, p. 4, cols. 6-7.

205 Harlem Bureau. "Harlem Pays Tribute to Truckdriver Who
Rescued Negro Children in Fire." 8 December, p. 3,
cols. 5-8.

206 Harlem Bureau. "Scottsboro Group Warns on T. S. Harten."
8 December, p. 4, col. 1.

1937

207   Harlem Bureau. "12 Harlem Shops Sign to Ban Fascist Goods."
       9 December, p. 3, cols. 5-6.

208   Harlem Bureau. "Probe of Negro Conditions Opens December 13."
       9 December, p. 5, col. 7.

209   "Sen. Barkley Warns U.S. of War Makers." 13 December, p. 1,
       col. 1.

210   Harlem Bureau. "Domestics Score Abuse of Negroes."
       13 December, p. 3, col. 6.

211   "Huge Negro Death Rate Shown in Niagara Frontier Surveys."
       13 December, p. 23, cols. 6-7.

212   Harlem Bureau. "Red Caps to Meet Jan. 14 in Chicago."
       13 December, p. 3.

213   Richard Wright. "Gouging, Landlord Discrimination Against
       Negroes Bared at Hearing." 15 December, p. 6, cols. 4-6.

214   "Two Cops Slay Negro Boy--'Ran When Questioned.'"
       16 December, p. 1, col. 4.

215   Harlem Bureau. "Utilities Admit Bars to Negro on Jobs."
       16 December, p. 4, cols. 7-8.

216   Harlem Bureau. "Plan Memorial For Heroic Truck Driver."
       18 December, p. 4, col. 3.

217   Harlem Bureau. "300 at Harlem ERB Sit in to Demand Rent,
       Food Budgets." 18 December, p. 4, cols. 5-6.

218   Harlem Bureau. "Berry to Lead Forum in Congress Discussion."
       18 December, p. 4, col. 1.

219   Harlem Bureau. "Pickets Ask Somervell Ouster for Negro
       Firings." 21 December, p. 4, cols. 4-5.

220   Harlem Bureau. "From Spain's Loyalist Trenches Larry Foy Asks
       About Harlem's Fight Against Fascism in the U.S."
       23 December, p. 2, cols. 3-6.

221   Richard Wright. "James W. Ford Celebrates 44th Birthday--
       Leads Progressives in Harlem Community." 23 December,
       p. 4, cols. 2-5.

1937

222   Harlem Bureau. "Negro, Who Escaped Lynch Mob in South,
       Ordered to Return by Harlem Relief Officials." 27 Decem-
       ber, p. 3, cols. 6-8.

223   Richard Wright. "Santa Claus Has a Hard Time Finding Way to
       Harlem Slums." 27 December, p. 4, cols. 6-8.

224   Richard Wright. "'Every Child is a Genius'--Art Young's
       Famous Line Finds Realization in Harlem's New Community Art
       Center." 28 December, p. 7, col. 3.

Essays

225   "Blueprint for Negro Writing." New Challenge 2 (Fall):53-65.
          Reprinted: 1971.18-19; 1976.1; 1978.8.

       "The Direction of Negro Writing in America."
       Typescript (original): 18 numb. leaves.
       First draft, with author's corrections.
       Chicago Public Library.

       Typescript (carbon), signed: 21 numb. leaves.
       Early version, with author's MS corrections and title,
       "Blueprint for Negro Literature." With carbons of leaves
       20, 21 laid in. This version published in Amistad.
       JWJ Wright Misc. 285.

       "Blueprint for Negro Literature."
       Second copy of original draft, with MS corrections.
       N.Y. Public Library, Schomburg Coll. C2.

       Another typescript (original): 10 numb. leaves.
       Copy prepared by Michel Fabre for Amistad from typescript
       in Chicago Public Library.
       JWJ Wright Misc. 286.

       Carbon of above.
       JWJ Wright Misc. 287.

226   "The Ethics of Living Jim Crow, an Autobiographical Sketch."
       In American Stuff: WPA Writers' Anthology. New York:
       Viking Press, pp. 39-52.
          Incorporated in Black Boy. [1936]. Reprinted:
       1940.14; 1941.12; 1944.6; 1945.7; 1960.15; 1967.6; 1968.6;
       1970.17-25; 1971.20; 1972.5.

1937

Book Reviews

227   "Between Laughter and Tears." New Masses 25, no. 2
      (5 October):22, 25.
          Review of These Low Grounds, by Waters E. Turpin, and
      Their Eyes Were Watching God, by Zora Neale Hurston.

228   "A Sharecropper's Story." New Republic 93 (1 December):109.
          Review of I Was a Sharecropper, by Harry Harrison Kroll.

POETRY

229   "We of the Streets." New Masses 23, no. 4 (13 April):14.
      [1936]

                              1938

FICTION

Shorter Writings

1   "Big Boy Leaves Home." In Uncle Tom's Children: Four
     Novellas. New York: Harper, pp. 2-70.
         Reprint of 1936.1.

2   "Bright and Morning Star." New Masses 27, no. 7 (10 May):
     97-99, 116-24. [1937]
         Reprinted: 1939.1-2; 1940.3-4; 1941.4-5; 1949.1-2;
     1965.2; 1966.1; 1968.1; 1969.3; 1971.5. See also Uncle
     Tom's Children--Four Novellas, 1938.9.

     Typescript (original): 1 leaf.
     First leaf only, with his title. Material not used in the
     story as published.
     JWJ Wright 952.

3   ["Bright and Morning Star"] Utrennyaya zvezda. Translated by
     N. Daruzes. Moscow: Pravda, 48 pp.

4   "Down By the Riverside." In Uncle Tom's Children: Four
     Novellas. New York: Harper, pp. 73-166. [1936]
         Reprinted: 1940.5; 1942.2; 1971.6. See also Uncle
     Tom's Children--Four Novellas, 1938.9.

     Typescript (original): 39 leaves.
     Early working draft, with extensive revisions. Hand
     stamped by John J. Trounstine, Wright's agent.
     JWJ Wright 954.

1938

Another typescript (original): 56 numb. leaves.
Incomplete, intermediate draft, lacking conclusion of
story. With MS revisions.
JWJ Wright 955.

Another typescript (original): 48 numb. leaves.
Final draft, with a few corrections.
JWJ Wright 956.

5   "Fire and Cloud." Story Magazine 12 (March):9-41. [1936]
        Was awarded the Story Magazine Prize in December 1937.
    Reprinted: 1938.6-7; 1940.6; 1941.6; 1970.10-11; 1978.2.
    See also Uncle Tom's Children - Four Novellas, 1938.9.

    Typescript (original): 36 leaves.
    Working draft, with extensive MS revisions.
    JWJ Wright 957.

    Another typescript (original): 65 numb. leaves.
    With a few MS corrections.
    JWJ Wright 958.

    Page proofs: leaves 9-41.
    With a few MS corrections.
    For publication in Story 12 (March 1938):68.
    JWJ Wright 375a.

6   "Fire and Cloud." In O'Henry Memorial Award Prize Stories of
    1938. Edited by Harry Hansen. New York: Doubleday,
    Doran & Co., pp. 19-81.
        Reprint of 1938.5.

7   "Fire and Cloud." In Uncle Tom's Children: Four Novellas.
    New York: Harper, pp. 220-317.
        Reprint of 1938.5.

8   "Long Black Song." In Uncle Tom's Children: Four Novellas.
    New York: Harper, pp. 169-217. [1936]
        Reprinted: 1940.7; 1955.2; 1970.12; 1971.8; 1978.3.
    See also Uncle Tom's Children--Four Novellas, 1938.9.

    Typescript (original): 35 leaves.
    Working draft, with extensive MS revisions. Incomplete
    copy, lacks leaves 2-14. With brief notes for a dramatiza-
    tion laid in, 1 leaf.
    JWJ Wright 962.

    Another typescript (original): 14 leaves.
    Partial working draft, with MS corrections.
    JWJ Wright 963.

1938

Another typescript (original): 1 leaf, 37 numb. leaves.
Final draft, including section deleted from story as pub-
lished.
JWJ Wright 964.

Books

9   Uncle Tom's Children: Four Novellas. New York: Harper,
    317 pp.
       Includes "Big Boy Leaves Home" (pub. 1937), "Down by the
    Riverside" [1936], "Long Black Song" [1936], and "Fire and
    Cloud" (pub. 1938). Reprinted: 1939.3. See also
    1940.12-13.

    Typescript (original): 1 leaf, 7 numb. leaves.
    With author's extensive MS corrections. Chicago, June
    1936. Note included in first edition as published by
    Harper, 1939.
    JWJ Wright 949.

    Another typescript (original): 3 numb. leaves.
    Another version, with MS corrections.
    JWJ Wright 950.

    Typescript (photocopy): 1 leaf.
    Title leaf from setting copy, bearing signed inscription
    "To be sold only for the cause of Loyalist Spain 3/18/38."
    MS in private collection.
    JWJ Wright 951.

10 [Uncle Tom's Children] A Csiu Csiangi Pokol. Translated by
    Gyorgy Buky. Budapest: Legrady, 159 pp.

11 [Uncle Tom's Children] Deti Djadi Toma: "Big Boy pokidayet
    dom" ["Big Boy Leaves Home"], translated by V. Toper; "Na
    beregu reki" ["Down by the Riverside"], translated by
    Y. Kalshinkova; "Tuchi y plamya" ["Fire and Cloud"], trans-
    lated by T. Ozerkaya; "Utrennyaya zvezda" ["Bright and
    Morning Star"], translated by N. Daruzes. Internatsional-
    naya literatura, no. 7, pp. 3-85.

NONFICTION

Shorter Writings

Daily Worker Articles, with Wright Byline

12 "Why the Eyes of the People Turn to the Ring for the Title
    Bout at Yankee Stadium Tonight." 22 June, p. 1, cols. 3-6.

1938

[The role of the artist in America.]
Typescript (original): 2 leaves.
Draft of an article on the role of the writer and artist in
the United States after 1929. On verso of second leaf are
MS notes for an article on the Joe Louis-Max Schmeling
prize fight, 1938, published in the Daily Worker, 22 June
1938.
JWJ Wright Misc. 750.

13   "And Oh! Where Were Hitler's Pagan Gods?" 24 June, p. 1,
     cols. 1-2.

Essays

14   "About the War in Spain." In Writers Take Sides. New York:
     League of American Writers, pp. 36-37.

15   "High Tide in Harlem." New Masses 28 (5 July):18-20.
     On Joe Louis's victory over Schmeling.

16   "How Uncle Tom's Children Grew." Columbia University Writers'
     Bulletin 2 (May):15-17.

17   "Portrait of Harlem." In New York Panorama. Edited by New
     York W.P.A., New York: Random House, pp. 132-51. [1937]
         Unsigned.

     MS in N.Y. Public Library.

     Typescript (carbon): 37 leaves.
     Final draft, with a few MS corrections. Dated 25 February
     1938.
     Private collection.

     Related material:
     [Federal Writers Project editorial conference.]
     Typescript (original and carbon): 15 [i.e., 18] numb.
     leaves.
     Script for discussion of the work of the Federal Writers
     Project, broadcast by WNYC, 13 April 1938. With Wright's
     comments on racial surveys and The New York City Guide and
     his MS corrections of text. Other participants are Gordon
     Kingman, James Magraw, Harry L. Shaw, Jr., Donald Thompson,
     and Manly Wade Wellman.
     JWJ Wright Misc. 338.

Richard Wright's Published Works

1938

Book Review

18 "Adventure and Love in Loyalist Spain." New Masses 26, no. 11
    (8 March):25-26.
    Review of The Wall of Men, by William Rollins, Jr.

    Typescript (carbon): 3 numb. leaves.
    A review of The Wall of Men, by William Rollins, Jr.
    JWJ Wright Misc. 651.

Letter

19 "Reader's Right: Writers Ask Break for Negroes." New York
    Post, 5 April, p. 20.
    Letter to the editor.

1939

FICTION

Shorter Writings

1 "Bright and Morning Star." In Best American Short Stories,
   1939. Edited by Edward J. O'Brien. Boston: Houghton
   Mifflin, pp. 374-415.
   Reprint of 1938.2.

2 "Bright and Morning Star." In Fifty Best American Short
   Stories (1914-1939). Edited by Edward J. O'Brien. Boston:
   Houghton Mifflin, pp. 810-50.
   Reprint of 1938.2.

Books

3 Uncle Tom's Children: Four Novellas. Foreword by Paul
   Robeson. London: Gollancz, 286 pp.
   Reprint of 1938.9.

4 [Uncle Tom's Children] Deti Djadi Toma. Translated by
   A. Snejdera. Introduction by Isidor Schneider. Moscow:
   Goslitizdat, 224 pp.

1940

NONFICTION

Shorter Writing

Essay

5   "Can We Depend Upon Youth to Follow the American Way?"
     Bulletin of America's Town Meeting on the Air 4 (24 April):
     15-17.
          Participation in panel discussion.

POETRY

6   "Red Clay Blues." New Masses 32, no. 6 (1 August):14.
          Written in collaboration with Langston Hughes. Re-
     printed: 1978.26; 1979.3.

1940

FICTION

Shorter Writings

1   "Almos' a Man." Harper's Bazaar, 74 (January):40-41.
     [1934-37]
          Revised last two chapters of an unpublished novel,
     "Tarbaby's Dawn." Story later revised and title changed to
     "The Man Who Was Almost a Man." Reprinted: 1940.2;
     1941.3; 1944.2-3; 1945.1-2; 1946.1; 1955.1; 1961.1; 1965.1;
     1967.1; 1969.1; 1970.2-4; 1971.1-2. See also 1960.1.

     "Almos' a Man" ["Initiation"].
     Typescript (original): 21 numb. leaves.
     Early version, with MS corrections.
     JWJ Wright 148.

     Carbon of above: 21 numb. leaves.
     See MS for "Tarbaby's Dawn," unpublished.
     JWJ Wright 149.

2   "Almos' a Man." In O'Henry Award Prize Stories of 1940.
     Edited by Harry Hansen. New York: Doubleday, Doren & Co.,
     pp. 289-305.
          Reprint of 1940.1.

1940

3   "Bright and Morning Star." In American Issues. Edited by
    Carlos Baker and Willard Thorp. Chicago: Lippincott.
    Reprint of 1938.2.

4   "Bright and Morning Star." In Uncle Tom's Children: Five
    Long Stories. New York: Harper, pp. 321-84.
    Reprint of 1938.2.

5   "Down by the Riverside." In Uncle Tom's Children: Five Long
    Stories. New York: Harper, pp. 73-166.
    Reprint of 1938.4.

6   "Fire and Cloud." In Uncle Tom's Children: Five Long Sto-
    ries. New York: Harper, pp. 220-317.
    Reprint of 1938.5.

7   "Long Black Song." In Uncle Tom's Children: Five Long
    Stories. New York: Harper, pp. 169-217.
    Reprint of 1938.8.

Books

8   Native Son. Introduction by Dorothy Canfield Fisher. New
    York: Harper, 359 pp.
        Later rewritten with Paul Green as a play. Reprinted:
    1940.9-10; 1942.4-5; 1943.1; 1950.3; 1957.2; 1959.4;
    1961.11; 1964.6; 1966.4; 1969.9. See also 1941.1.

    Typescript (original): 250 leaves.
    Developmental material, extensively revised and corrected,
    including autograph sections. With miscellaneous leaves
    and fragments laid in, 151 leaves, and with working notes,
    35 leaves.
    JWJ Wright 813.[1-3]

    Another typescript (original): 1 leaf, 474 numb. leaves.
    Working draft of an intermediate version, with author's MS
    corrections and revisions, some pasted in, others laid in,
    5 leaves.
    JWJ Wright 814.[1-4]

    Another typescript (original): 63 leaves.
    Partial copy of a later working draft, with MS revisions.
    JWJ Wright 815.

    Carbon of above: 556 leaves.
    Complete copy of later working draft, incorporating pre-
    vious revisions, and with additional typed corrections.
    JWJ Wright 816.[1-5]

1940

Setting typescript (original): 20 leaves, 566 numb. leaves.
With MS editorial markings.
New York Public Library. Schomburg Collection.
JWJ Wright 817.[1-3]

Galley proofs: 1 leaf, 134 numb. leaves.
With miscellaneous proof sheets. Dated 20 September 1939.
JWJ Wright +818.

Page proofs, revised as of 1 December 1939. About one
third of the pages contain textual variations from first
edition.
New York University, Fales Collection.

Related Material:
Typescript: 1 leaf.
Outline and description of Native Son.
Princeton University Library. Story Magazine Files.

[Plans for work.]
Typescript (original): 3 leaves.
Plan for work on his novel, Native Son, submitted to the
Guggenheim Foundation.
JWJ Wright Misc. 517.

[Native Son publication announcement.]
Typescript (carbon): 2 leaves.
Describes contents of novel.
JWJ Wright Misc. 485.

[Letter to Mike Gold.]
Typescript (original): 9 numb. leaves.
Draft of a reply to comments and articles about Native Son
in the New Masses.
JWJ Wright Misc. 460.

9   Native Son. Toronto: Munson, 359 pp.
          Reprint of 1940.8.

10   Native Son. London: Gollancz, 410 pp.
          Reprint of 1940.8.

11   Native Son excerpt. In "Negro Housing in Chicago," by Horace
          Cayton. Social Action, 15 April, pp. 14-16.
          See 1940.8.

12   Uncle Tom's Children: Five Long Stories. Toronto: Munson,
          384 pp.
               Includes four stories originally found in Uncle Tom's
          Children--Four Novellas, plus "Bright and Morning Star."
          Reprinted: 1940.13. See also 1938.9.

1940

13 Uncle Tom's Children: Five Long Stories. London: Gollancz,
     384 pp.
     Reprint of 1940.12.

NONFICTION

Shorter Writings

Essays

14 "The Ethics of Living Jim Crow." In Uncle Tom's Children:
     Five Long Stories. New York: Harper, pp. ix-xxx.
     Reprint of 1937.226.

15 "How 'Bigger' Was Born." Saturday Review 22 (1 June):4-5,
     17-20.
     A nearly complete text of Wright's March 1940 lecture.
     See 1940.16; 1942.7. See also 1940.28.

     "How 'Bigger' Was Born."
     Typescript (original): 47 leaves.
     "First draft," with author's MS corrections and revisions,
     some on versos of leaves.
     JWJ Wright +167.

     Another typescript (original): 3 leaves.
     Intermediate working draft, with author's extensive MS
     revisions.
     His title: "The Birth of Bigger."
     JWJ Wright 168.

     Another typescript (original): 32 numb. leaves.
     Second draft, with author's MS revisions, some pasted in.
     JWJ Wright 169.

     Setting typescript (original): 4 leaves, 33 numb. leaves.
     Third draft, with MS corrections and editorial markings.
     JWJ Wright 170.

     Another typescript (original): 61 leaves.
     Fourth draft, incorporating corrections made in setting
     typescript.
     JWJ Wright 171.

     Carbon of above: 31 leaves.
     JWJ Wright 172.

16 ["How 'Bigger' Was Born."] "The Birth of Bigger Thomas."
     Negro Digest 6 (September-October):23-28.
     Condensed version. See 1940.15.

17 "I Bite the Hand that Feeds Me." Atlantic Monthly 155 (June):
    826-28.
        Reply to a review of Native Son by David L. Cohn in the
    May 1940 issue of Atlantic Monthly. Reprinted: 1942.9;
    1970.30-31; 1978.9.

    [Notes on "The Negro Novel: Richard Wright," by David L.
    Cohn].
    Advance proofs: 3 leaves.
    With extensive MS notes by Richard Wright for "I Bite the
    Hand that Feeds Me."
    JWJ Wright Misc. 418.

    Typescript (original): 12 pp.
    Early draft of Wright's reply to David L. Cohn's review of
    Native Son in Atlantic Monthly (May 1940), with extensive
    MS notes and corrections.
    JWJ Wright Misc. 413.

    Another typescript (original): 12 numb. leaves.
    Second draft, with extensive MS corrections and additions.
    JWJ Wright Misc. 414.

    Another typescript (original): 13 numb. leaves.
    Third draft, with extensive MS corrections.
    JWJ Wright Misc. 415.

    Setting typescript (original): 11 numb. leaves.
    With MS editorial markings and extensive deletions.
    JWJ Wright Misc. 416.

    Carbon of above: 15 numb. leaves.
    JWJ Wright Misc. 417.

    Corrected author's proofs, with deletions by editor.
    Private collection.

Book Reviews

18 "As Richard Wright Sees Autobiographies of Langston Hughes
    and W. E. B. Du Bois." Chicago News, 4 December, p. 40.
        Review of The Big Sea, by Langston Hughes, and Dusk at
    Dawn, by W. E. B. Du Bois.

    Typescript (original): 1 leaf.
    Early short draft of review.
    JWJ Wright Misc. 656.

    Another typescript (original): 3 leaves.
    Working draft. With his title: "Two Negro Autobiogra-
    phies."
    JWJ Wright Misc. 657.

1940

19   "Forerunner and Ambassador." New Republic 103 (24 October):
      600-1.
         Review of The Big Sea, by Langston Hughes.

      Carbon typescript: 1 leaf.
      JWJ Wright Misc. 671.

20   "Inner Landscape." New Republic 103 (5 August):195.
         Review of The Heart Is a Lonely Hunter, by Carson
      McCullers.

      Typescript (original): 3 leaves.
      Working draft of review.
      Working title: "Bleak Landscape."
      JWJ Wright Misc. 688.

      Another typescript (carbon): 2 leaves.
      Incomplete copy; lacks first leaf.
      Final version.
      JWJ Wright Misc. 689.

21   "Lynching Bee." New Republic 102 (11 March):351.
         Review of Trouble in July, by Erskine Caldwell.

22   "Richard Wright Reviews James Weldon Johnson's Classic,
      Black Manhattan." Chicago News, 22 May, p. 17.

      Typescript (original): 1 leaf.
      His title: "How Will We Treat the Negro if the War
      Starts?"
      JWJ Wright Misc. +716.

Introduction

23   Introduction to Special Laughter, by Howard Nutt.   Prairie
         City, Ill.: Press of James Decker, pp. ix-xii.
            In the form of a letter, dated Spring 1940.

      Typescript (original): 5 leaves.
      Early working draft, with MS corrections and revisions and
      with typed and MS notes laid in, 5 leaves. Dated 6 Decem-
      ber 1940.
      JWJ Wright Misc. 435.

      Another typescript (original): 6 numb. leaves.
      Intermediate working draft, with MS revisions. Dated
      1 December 1940, Brooklyn, N.Y.
      JWJ Wright Misc. 436.

1941

Another typescript (carbon): 6 numb. leaves.
Later version, published in shortened form by James A.
Decker, Prairie City, Ill. (1940).
JWJ Wright Misc. 437.

Another typescript (carbon): 5 leaves.
Another copy of above version.
JWJ Wright Misc. 438.

Letters

24   "Letter to Bruce Kaputska." The Kaputskan 1 (Fall):17.
     [August]
          MS in Private Collection.

25   "Rascoe Baiting." American Mercury 50 (July):376-77.
          Letter to the Editor. Reply to a review of Native Son
     by Burton Rascoe in the May 1940 issue of American Mercury.
     Reprinted: 1970.34; 1978.13.

Pamphlet

26   Pamphlet on Theodore Ward. New York: Negro Playwright's
     Company, p. 3. [Unverified]

Statement

27   "Statement in Support of Browder and Ford." Daily Worker,
     30 September, p. 5, cols. 3-6.

Books

28   How Bigger Was Born. New York: Harper, 39 pp.
          Complete version. See 1940.15.

POETRY

29   ["Red Clay Blues"] "Pyesnya o Krasnoi Zemle." Translated by
     M. Zeukevitch. Internatsionalnaya Literatura, no. 1:
     86.

1941

DRAMA

1   Native Son: The Biography of a Young American; A Play in Ten
     Scenes, by Paul Green and Richard Wright. New York:
     Harper, 148 pp. [1940-1941]

31

1941

Later revised by Paul Green alone. Reprinted: 1941.2.
See also 1970.1.

Typescript (original): 147 leaves.
First rough working draft.
Includes correction notes.
JWJ Wright 834.

Another typescript (original): 97 leaves.
Another version.
JWJ Wright +835.

Another typescript (original): 88 leaves.
Another copy of above version, with MS notes and directions
for staging.
JWJ Wright 837.

Setting typescript (carbon): 127 leaves.
With MS editorial markings, as published by Harper (1941).
JWJ Wright 838.

Carbon of above: 100 leaves.
Acts I and II only, with MS notes.
JWJ Wright 839.

Galley proofs: 5 leaves.
Incomplete set of an unpublished version.
Scenes 9 and 10 only.
JWJ Wright 840.

New York Public Library (NN NCOF +): 96 leaves, 29 leaves.
Native Son, Scene 9. Private Collection.
Galleys: 5 leaves.

Typescript (carbon): 9 numb. leaves, 17 leaves.
Includes a draft of Scene 8 from an early version, an incomplete draft of Scene 9, and a draft of Scene 10 with
extensive MS revisions, some laid in.
JWJ Wright 841.

Another typescript (carbon): 27 leaves.
Old version of Act III, with a typed letter, signed, from
Wright's agent Paul Reynolds returning MS from Harper's.
With typed and autographed notes on reactions to the script
and suggestions for revisions, etc., 44 leaves.
JWJ Wright 842.

Related Material:
[Comment on the production.]
Typescript (original): 1 leaf.
Draft of a statement complimenting Orson Welles, the
Mercury Theatre group, and Bern Bernard on the production

1941

of Native Son. With MS corrections. Written on verso of
St. James Theatre announcement of the cast.
JWJ Wright 843.

Another typescript (carbon): 1 leaf.
JWJ Wright 844.

[Interview.]
Typescript (original): 5 leaves.
Wright's responses only. With MS corrections. On the
development of the play script and the stage production,
etc.
JWJ Wright 845.

[Introductory remarks.]
Typescript (original): 1 leaf.
JWJ Wright 846.

[Tribute to Canada Lee.]
Typescript (original): 2 leaves.
Praising Lee's portrayal of Bigger Thomas in Native Son.
JWJ Wright Misc. 784.

See "What Do I Think of the Theatre?" 1941.16.

"The Problem of the Hero" [unpublished play].
Based on a conversation with Paul Green concerning the
dramatization of Native Son.
JWJ Wright Misc. 631-632.

2   Native Son: The Biography of a Young American; A Play in Ten
    Scenes.   In The Burns Mantle Best Plays and the Yearbook of
    the Drama in America. Edited by B. Mantle. Vol. 24. New
    York: Dodd, Mead, pp. 29-63.
        Reprint of 1941.1.

FICTION

Shorter Writings

3   "Almos' a Man." In Best American Short Stories, 1941.
    Edited by J. O'Brien. Boston: Houghton Mifflin,
    pp. 356-71.
        Reprint of 1940.1.

4   "Bright and Morning Star." In The Negro Caravan. Edited by
    Sterling Brown et al. New York: Dryden Press, pp. 106-36.
        Reprint of 1938.2.

1941

5   Bright and Morning Star. New York: International Publishers,
    48 pp.
        With Wright's letter to International Publishers and a
    foreword by James W. Ford. Reprint of 1938.2.

6   "Fire and Cloud." In American Scenes. Edited by William
    Kozlenko. New York: John Day, pp. 51-57.
        Radio adaptation by Charles H. O'Neill. Reprint of
    1938.5.

Books

7   [Native Son] Sangre Negra. Translated by Pedro Lemona.
    Buenos Aires: Sudamericana, 572 pp.
        Condensed version in Omnibook (Buenos Aires),
    (February 1946):1-49.

8   [Native Son] Sohn dieses Landes. Translated by Klaus
    Lambrecht. Zurich: Humanitas Verlag, 503 pp.

9   [Native Son] "Syn Ameriki." Translated by Y. Kalashinkova.
    Internatsionalnaya Literatura, no. 1:3-44; no. 2:4-153.

10 Native Son excerpts. P.M. Magazine, 7 May, p. 12.
        Includes scenes of watching the plane and imitating
    whites.

11 Native Son excerpts. In The Democratic Spirit. Edited by
    Bernard Smith. New York: Knopf, pp. 819-28.
        Includes scene where Bigger watches the plane, plays
    with Gus.

NONFICTION

Shorter Writings

Essays

12 "The Ethics of Living Jim Crow." In The Negro Caravan.
    Edited by Sterling Brown et al. New York: Dryden Press,
    pp. 1050-60.
        Reprint of 1937.226.

13 ["How Bigger Was Born"] "Kak rodilsya Bigger." Translated by
    Y. Kalashinkova. Internatsionalnaya Literatura, no. 3:
    145-56.

1941

14   "Not My People's War." New Masses 39, no. 13 (17 June):8-9,
     12.
         Reprinted: 1941.15.

15   "Not My People's War." In Magazine Abstracts. Vol. 7.
     Washington, D.C.: U.S. Division of Intelligence, Office of
     Government Reports, p. 70.
         Reprint of 1941.14.

16   "What Do I Think of the Theatre?" New York World-Telegram,
     2 March, p. 20.
         On the stage adaptation of Native Son.

     Typescript (original): 2 leaves.
     Working draft, with MS corrections.
     JWJ Wright Misc. 792.

     Another typescript (carbon): 3 numb. leaves.
     JWJ Wright Misc. 793.

Blurb

17   On Let My People Go, by Henrietta Buckmaster. New York:
     Harper.
         Dust jacket notes.

Introductions

18   Foreword to Morris V. Schappes, Letters From the Tombs. New
     York: Schappes Defense Committee, pp. v-vi.

     Typescript (original): 1 leaf.
     Working draft, with MS corrections.
     JWJ Wright Misc. 385.

19   "Letter to International Publishers." In Bright and Morning
     Star. New York: International Publishers, p. 1.
         An introduction to the short story published in booklet
     form. See 1941.5.

20   [Prefatory note to Playbill for Native Son.] St. James
     Theatre, New York, March, p. 1.

Letter

21   "Greetings." New Masses, 38, no. 9 (18 February):26.
         Extract of a letter encouraging the magazine.

1941

Liner Notes

22 "King Joe" ["Joe Louis Blues"]. New York Amsterdam Star News,
    18 October, p. 16.
        Lyrics for OKEH Record no. 6475 [3 October], by
    Bregman, Vocco & Conn [1942], set to music by Count Basie.
    Reprinted: 1971.24; 1979.3.

    Typescript (original): 1 leaf.
    Working draft, with extensive MS corrections and additions.
    With his MS and typed notes laid in, 6 leaves.
    JWJ Wright Misc. 595.

    "King Joe."
    Another typescript (carbon): 1 leaf.
    Private Collection.

23 "Note on Jim Crow Blues." Preface to Josh White's Keynote
    Phonograph Album no. 107, "Southern Exposure."

    Typescript (original): 2 leaves.
    With MS corrections.
    JWJ Wright Misc. 494.

Statements

24 "US Negroes Greet You." Daily Worker, 1 September, p. 7,
    cols. 1-2.
        Statement sent to International Literature following the
    Nazi attack upon the Soviet Union. Reprinted: 1941.25.

25 ["US Negroes Greet You"] "I Support the Soviet Union." Soviet
    Russia Today, September, p. 29.
        Reprint of 1941.24.

Books

26 Twelve Million Black Voices: A Folk History of the Negro in
    the United States. Photo direction by Edwin Rosskam. New
    York: Viking Press, 152 pp.
        Reprinted: 1941.27; 1947.24; 1978.22.

    Typescript and autographed MS: 116 leaves.
    Developmental notes and background material.
    JWJ Wright 919.

    Typescript (original): 1 leaf, 2 numb. leaves.
    First draft, with author's MS additions and with revised
    passages laid in, 2 leaves, and a title leaf.
    JWJ Wright 920.

Another typescript (original): 3 leaves, 3 numb. leaves.
Intermediate draft, incorporating above revisions. With
preliminary material.
JWJ Wright 921.

Another typescript (original): 3 leaves.
Incomplete draft; lacking first leaf.
JWJ Wright 922.

Another typescript (carbon): 2 leaves, 3 numb. leaves.
Final draft, including preliminary material. Additional
drafts appear in complete MS.
JWJ Wright 923.

Typescript (original): 7 numb. leaves.
Early draft of "Our Strange Birth" section. Based on his
autograph MS (folder no. 913).
His title: "The Strange Birth."
JWJ Wright 924.

Another typescript (original): 12 numb. leaves.
"First rough working draft." With author's extensive MS
revisions and additions.
JWJ Wright 925.

Another typescript (original): 12 numb. leaves.
Retyped copy of above MS, incorporating revisions and with
additional corrections.
JWJ Wright 926.

Carbon of above: 12 numb. leaves.
Lacks additional corrections.
JWJ Wright 927.

Another typescript (carbon): 14 numb. leaves.
Another draft, with extensive MS revisions.
JWJ Wright 928.

Carbon of above: 14 numb. leaves.
Without revisions.
JWJ Wright 929.

Another typescript (original): 25 leaves.
Intermediate draft, with author's MS revisions. Consists
mostly of individual paragraphs on each leaf.
JWJ Wright 930.

Another typescript (original): 14 numb. leaves.
Later draft, with additional MS revisions and with some
corrected leaves laid in, 3 leaves.
JWJ Wright 931.

1941

Typescript (original):   45 leaves.
First rough draft of "Inheritors of Slavery." With extensive MS revisions, some pasted in, others laid in. With
miscellaneous notes typed in.
JWJ Wright 932.

Another typescript (original):   69 leaves.
Early working draft, written mostly as individual para-
graphs on each leaf.
JWJ Wright 933.

Another typescript (original):   32 leaves.
Miscellaneous leaves, with extensive corrections and
revisions.
JWJ Wright 934.

Typescript (original):   58 leaves.
Early draft of "Death on the City Pavements." Mostly
individual paragraphs on each leaf. With MS corrections
and additions and with miscellaneous material laid in,
4 leaves.
JWJ Wright 935.

Another typescript (original):   12 numb. leaves.
First rough working draft, with author's MS additions and
corrections.
JWJ Wright 936.

Another typescript (original):   41 leaves.
Partial draft of final sections of the chapter, with extensive MS deletions and revisions. Leaves numbered 64-84,
90-98. With miscellaneous leaves laid in, 3 leaves.
JWJ Wright 937.

Another typescript (carbon):   13 numb. leaves.
Another partial draft (labeled "First rough working draft"),
with MS corrections. Leaves also numbered 61-73.
JWJ Wright 938.

Typescript (original) and autograph MS: 13 leaves.
"First rough working draft" of "Men in the Making," with
author's extensive corrections and revisions. Leaves numbered 86-98.
JWJ Wright 939.

Another typescript (original):   16 leaves.
Another "First rough working draft," with MS corrections,
mostly written as individual paragraphs on each leaf.
JWJ Wright 940.

1941

Another typescript (original): 13 leaves.
Corrected copy of above draft, with additional MS correc-
tions. Leaves numbered 86-98, with a revised leaf laid in.
JWJ Wright 941.

Another typescript (original): 10 numb. leaves.
Another corrected copy of above draft, with extensive MS
revisions and deletions. Leaves numbered 86-95. Carbons
of this draft appear in complete MS (folder no. 915).
JWJ Wright 942.

Another typescript (original): 7 leaves.
Intermediate version incorporates revisions made above and
includes miscellaneous leaves deleted from that draft, with
some MS corrections. Leaves numbered 86-92.
JWJ Wright 943.

Another typescript (original): 6 leaves.
Another draft based on intermediate version and consisting
of questions and replies. Provides material for final
revisions. With a few MS corrections.
JWJ Wright 944.

Another typescript (carbon): 5 leaves.
Working draft of final version, with MS revisions based on
replies to questions posed above.
JWJ Wright 945.

Another typescript (original): 6 leaves.
Another draft of final version, incorporating above re-
visions, and with a few additional corrections.
JWJ Wright 946.

[Complete copy].
Autograph MS: 72 leaves.
Early draft.
JWJ Wright 913.

Typescript (original): 81 leaves.
First draft based on above MS, dated January 1941. With
author's extensive MS revisions and additions, some on
versos of leaves.
JWJ Wright 914.

Another typescript (carbon): 5 leaves, 97 numb. leaves.
Intermediate draft, lacks revisions made in later drafts of
individual chapters. Original chapter 4 filled with individual working drafts (folder no. 942).
JWJ Wright 915.

1941

Another typescript (original): 55 leaves.
Later version, lacking chapter 3 and foreword. With a few
MS corrections. Leaves numbered 1-49, 86-91.
JWJ Wright 916.

[Complete copy].
Setting typescript (original): 6 leaves, 91 numb. leaves.
With extensive MS and typed corrections and MS editorial
markings. With acknowledgments for photographs laid in,
7 leaves.
JWJ Wright 917.

Galley proofs: 27 numb. leaves.
JWJ Wright 918.

See "Twelve Million Black Voices: A Picture Story,"
1942.10; and "Where Do We Go From Here," U.72.
Unpublished.

27   Twelve Million Black Voices. Toronto: Macmillan, 152 pp.
     Reprint of 1941.26.

POETRY

28   "I Have Seen Black Hands." In The Negro Caravan. Edited by
     Sterling Brown et al. New York: Dryden Press, pp. 407-8.
     Reprint of 1934.3.

1942

DRAMA

1   Native Son excerpt. In Scenes for Student Actors. Edited by
    Frances Cosgrove. New York: Samuel French, pp. 14-15.

FICTION

Shorter Writings

2   "Down by the Riverside." In This America. Edited by Joseph
    D. Karn and Irwin Griggs. New York: Macmillan, pp. 770-
    821.
       Reprint of 1938.4.

3   "The Man Who Lived Underground." Accent 2 (Spring):170-76.
    [1941]
       Excerpts from a novel, largely different from the cor-
    responding passages in the novella in Cross Section (1944).
    Reprinted: 1946.5; 1956.2. See also 1944.5.

1942

"The Man Who Lived Underground" [short version].
Typescript (original): 155 leaves.
Working draft, extensively revised.
JWJ Wright 212.

Another typescript (original): 46 leaves.
Working draft of part one only. With author's extensive MS
revisions.
JWJ Wright 213.

Another typescript (original): 83 leaves.
Later draft of a condensed version, derived from preceding
drafts. With MS corrections and revisions, and with miscellaneous deleted pages and fragments, 15 leaves.
JWJ Wright 214.

Typescript (carbon): 72 numb. leaves.
Working draft of version published in Cross Section (1944).
With author's extensive MS corrections and with miscel-
laneous leaves, including originals of above typescript,
and others from final draft laid in, 19 leaves.
JWJ Wright 215.

Another typescript (original): 70 numb. leaves.
Final draft, incomplete, incorporating revisions of pre-
ceding draft (folder no. 214). Lacks final episode.
Published in Cross Section (1944) and in Eight Men.
JWJ Wright 216.

Carbon of preceding draft.
JWJ Wright 217.

Typescript: 77 numb. leaves.
Some MS revisions.
Princeton University Library, Story Magazine Files.

Typescript (carbon): 14 leaves.
Leaves 149 [sic; 139]-46, 161-67 removed from intermediate
draft (folder no. 205), with author's MS deletions.
(See JWJ Wright 205).
JWJ Wright 218.

Books

4   Native Son. New York: Grosset & Dunlap, 361 pp.
        Reprint of 1940.8.

5   Native Son. New York: Harper, 361 pp.
        Reprint of 1940.8.

1942

6   <u>Native Son</u> excerpt. <u>The People's Voice</u>, 14 February-14 April.
Serial publication of part of the novel.

NONFICTION

<u>Shorter Writings</u>

Essays

7   "How Bigger Was Born." In <u>Native Son</u>. New York: Harper;
(Grosset & Dunlap), pp. i-li.
This is the first publication of the essay together with
the novel. Reprinted: 1947.8; 1968.7; 1969.18; 1970.26-29;
1971.21; 1972.7. See also 1940.28.

8   "How Bigger Was Born." In <u>This is My Best</u>. Edited by Whit
Burnett. Philadelphia: Blackiston, pp. 448-58.
With an introductory note by Wright. Reprint of 1942.7.

9   "I Bite the Hand That Feeds Me." In <u>Highways of College Com-
position</u>. Englewood Cliffs, N.J.: Prentice-Hall. [Un-
verified]
Reprint of 1940.17.

10   "Twelve Million Black Voices--A Picture Story." <u>Coronet</u> 15
(April):76-92.
Original introduction (p. 77) and verse captions to
accompany photos and extracts from <u>Twelve Million Black
Voices</u>.

Twelve Million Black Voices [preface to condensed version
in <u>Coronet</u>].
Typescript (original): 2 leaves.
With author's MS corrections.
JWJ Wright 947.

Another typescript (carbon): 2 numb. leaves.
JWJ Wright 948.

11   "What You Don't Know Won't Hurt You." <u>Harper's Magazine</u> 186
(December):58-61.
Fictionalized Chicago memories later incorporated into
the MS of <u>American Hunger</u>. Reprinted: 1946.13; 1957.10;
1966.10. See also: 1977.1.

Typescript (carbon): 7 numb. leaves.
Early version of his experiences at Michael Reese Hospital,
written in Chicago (before 1937).
His title: "What They Don't Know Won't Hurt 'em."
JWJ Wright Misc. 799.

1942

Autograph MS: 14 leaves.
Working draft.
JWJ Wright Misc. 800.

Typescript (original): 15 numb. leaves.
Another working draft, with MS corrections and deletions.
With his early title: "What They Don't Know Won't Hurt
'em."
JWJ Wright Misc. 801.

Another typescript (original): 9 numb. leaves.
Later working draft, with MS corrections. With some
deleted leaves laid in, 4 leaves, including a leaf with
rough suggestions for last paragraph by Frederick Allen.
JWJ Wright Misc. 802.

Another typescript (carbon): 12 numb. leaves.
Final draft.
JWJ Wright Misc. 803.

12   "Why I selected 'How Bigger Was Born.'" In This is My Best.
      Edited by Whit Burnett. Philadelphia: Lippincott, p. 448.
      [July 1942]

Introductions

13   Introduction to Never Come Morning, by Nelson Algren. New
      York: Harper, pp. ix-x.

      Autograph MS: 3 leaves.
      With his MS notes laid in, 1 leaf, and his MS corrections.
      JWJ Wright Misc. 426.

      Typescript (original): 3 leaves.
      Working draft, with MS corrections.
      JWJ Wright Misc. 427.

      Another typescript (original): 2 numb. leaves.
      Later draft, with a few MS corrections.
      JWJ Wright Misc. 428.

14   Introduction to No Day of Triumph, by Jay Saunders Redding.
      New York: Harper, p. 1.

Letter

15   "To Sender Garlin." Daily Worker, 13 February, p. 7,
      cols. 4-5.
          Letter dated 10 February asking for more consideration
      for readers' opinions.

1942

Books

16   Twelve Million Black Voices excerpt.   "Men in the Making."
      Negro Quarterly 2 (Summer):123-27.

                              1943

FICTION

1   Native Son. Stockholm: Jan Vorlag, 371 pp.
             Reprint of 1940.8.

NONFICTION

Pamphlet

2   "The Negro and the Parkway Community House."   Chicago, 4 pp.
             Pamphlet written in April 1941 at the request of Horace
     Cayton, director of this Chicago institution.

     Typescript (original):   4 numb. leaves.
     Early working draft of essay.   With extensive MS correc-
     tions and additions.
     JWJ Wright Misc. 486.

     Another typescript (original):   4 numb. leaves.
     Intermediate draft with MS corrections.
     JWJ Wright Misc. 487.

     Another typescript (carbon):   4 numb. leaves.
     Final version with his title: "Concerning the Negro and
     the Parkway Community House."
     JWJ Wright Misc. 488.

                              1944

DRAMA

1   Native Son.   In The Burns Mantle Best Plays of 1942-43.
             Edited by B. Mantle.   Vol. 26.   New York: Dodd, Mead,
     pp. [?]-60.
             Summaries and excerpts.   See 1941.1.

                               44

1944

FICTION

Shorter Writings

2   "Almos' a Man." In Anthology of Negro Literature. Edited by
     Sylvester Watkins. New York: Modern Library, pp. 3-16.
     Reprint of 1940.1.

3   "Almos' a Man." Negro Story 1 (May-June):51-60.
     Reprint of 1940.1.

4   ["Big Boy Leaves Home"] "Le départ de Big Boy." With a
     Preface by Paul Robeson. Translated by Marc Blanzat and
     Marcel Duhamel. L'Arbalète (Lyon), no. 9 (August):239-66.

5   "The Man Who Lived Underground." In Cross Section. Edited by
     Edwin Seaver. New York: L. B. Fischer, pp. 58-102.
        This novelette is the second section of the novel, an
     excerpt of which appeared in Accent in 1942. Reprinted:
     1945.5; 1956.1-2; 1961.4; 1968.3; 1970.13; 1971.13; 1978.4.
     See also 1942.3; 1960.4; 1968.3; 1969.8.

     "The Man Who Lived Underground" [long version].
     Typescript (original): 419 leaves.
     First draft, with extensive MS corrections and revisions.
     Alternate leaves numbered.
     JWJ Wright 201.[1-2]

     Another typescript (original): 217 leaves.
     Working draft, with extensive MS typed revisions. Leaves
     numbered 1-269, with revised material laid in. Title leaf
     stamped by Paul Reynolds.
     JWJ Wright 202.

     Typescript (original): 7 leaves.
     Working draft, opening episode only, with author's MS
     revisions.
     JWJ Wright 203.

     Another typescript (original): 257 leaves.
     Working draft, with extensive MS corrections and revisions,
     some pasted in and other miscellaneous revised material
     laid in, 32 leaves. Dated July-December 1941.
     His title: "Secret Song."
     JWJ Wright 204.

     Another typescript (carbon): 230 leaves.
     Intermediate working draft, dated July-December 1941. With
     author's MS corrections and revisions and with his MS notes

1944

and lists of corrections, 9 leaves. Leaves [140]-46,
161-67 were removed for publication as excerpts from The
Man Who Lived Underground, Accent (Spring 1942):170-76.
JWJ Wright 205.

Carbon copy: 243 leaves.
With a few MS and typed corrections. Leaves numbered
1-239, with title and section leaves added.
JWJ Wright 206.

Another typescript (carbon): 207 leaves.
Another intermediate working draft, with author's MS cor-
rections and revisions, some laid in, others pasted in.
With critical comments and suggestions for emendations by
Wright's editor, 118 leaves. Title leaf stamped by Paul
Reynolds.
JWJ Wright 207.[1-2]

Another typescript (original): 2 leaves, 199 leaves.
Late draft, with extensive MS revisions and corrections in
parts 2 and 3.
Princeton University Library, Sylvia Beach Collection.
JWJ Wright 208.

Another typescript (original): 56 leaves.
Incomplete draft, incorporating revisions in preceding
draft.
JWJ Wright 209.

Another typescript (original): 8 leaves.
Working draft of another version of opening episode of
part one, with author's MS corrections.
JWJ Wright 210.

Another typescript (original): 4 leaves.
Another version of opening episode of part one, with
author's MS corrections.
Title: "Secret Song."
JWJ Wright 211.

NONFICTION

Shorter Writings

Essays

6   "The Ethics of Living Jim Crow." In Anthology of Negro Liter-
      ature. Edited by Sylvester Watkins. New York: Modern
      Library, pp. 390-402.
           Reprint of 1937.226.

1944

7 "I Tried to Be a Communist." <u>Atlantic Monthly</u> 159 (August):
   61-70; (September):48-56.
   Part of the second section of "American Hunger," the
   original manuscript of <u>Black Boy</u>. Reprinted: 1949.10;
   1950.6; 1959.6; 1970.32. See also <u>American Hunger</u>, 1977.1.

   "Biography of a Bolshevik."
   Autograph and typed MS: 33 numb. leaves.
   Notes on David Poindexter and Louis Campbell used for "I
   Tried to Be a Communist."
   JWJ Wright Misc. 274.

8 "Richard Wright Describes the Birth of <u>Black Boy</u>, an Autobiography Destined to Disturb White Egotism." <u>New York
   Post</u>, 30 November, p. B6.

   Typescript (original): 1 leaf.
   Early working draft, with MS additions and corrections.
   JWJ Wright Misc. 743.

   Another typescript (original): 1 leaf.
   Partial working draft, with MS corrections and additions.
   JWJ Wright Misc. 744.

   Another typescript (original): 4 numb. leaves.
   Intermediate draft, with MS corrections.
   His title: "Stumbling Upon a Book."
   JWJ Wright Misc. 745.

   Another typescript (carbon): 4 numb. leaves.
   Final draft entitled, "Stumbling Upon a Book."
   JWJ Wright Misc. 746.

Blurb

9 On <u>The Winds of Fear</u>, by Hodding Carter. New York: Farrar.
      Dust jacket notes.

   Autograph MS: 1 leaf.
   Early draft of comment.
   JWJ Wright Misc. 292.

   Typescript (original): 1 leaf.
   Another draft, with MS corrections.
   JWJ Wright Misc. 293.

   Another typescript (carbon): 1 leaf.
   With a typed letter, signed, (draft) to Philip Wylie sub-
   mitting his MS. Letter includes additional comments on
   Carter's book and on Wylie's <u>Generations of Vipers</u>.
   JWJ Wright Misc. 294.

1944

Book

10   Twelve Million Black Voices excerpt. "Men in the Making."
     In Modern Writing. Edited by Willard Thorp. New York:
     American Book Co., pp. 377-81.

1945

FICTION

Shorter Writings

1   "Almos' a Man." In Half a Hundred Tales. Edited by Charles
    Grayston. Philadelphia: Blackiston, pp. 516-27.
    Reprint of 1940.1.

2   "Almos' a Man." In Modern American Short Stories. Edited by
    Bennett Cerf. New York: World Publishing Co., pp. 302-17.
    Reprint of 1940.1.

3   "Early Days in Chicago." In Cross Section. Edited by Edwin
    Seaver. New York: L. B. Fischer, pp. 306-42. [1942-1943]
    Part of a second section of American Hunger MS. Re-
    printed: 1950.1; 1961.3; 1970.7-9; 1971.7. See also
    American Hunger, 1977.1.

    Typescript (original and carbon): 45 numb. leaves.
    Story extracted from Wright's "American Hunger" (1944).
    JWJ Wright 155.

    Carbon of above.
    With new title pasted on.
    JWJ Wright 156.

    Another typescript (carbon): 43 numb. leaves.
    JWJ Wright 157.

4   ["Fire and Cloud"] "Le feu dans la nuée." Translated by
    Marcel Duhamel. Les Temps Modernes 1, no. 1 (October):
    22-47; no. 2 (November):291-312.

5   "The Man Who Lived Underground." In Short Stories of 1945.
    Edited by Bennett Cerf. New York: World Publishing Co.,
    pp. 342-53.
    Cross Section version. Reprint of 1944.5.

1945

NONFICTION

Shorter Writings

Essays

6   "American Hunger." Mademoiselle 21 (September):164-65,
        299-301. [1942-1943]
            This is only a small part of the second section of
        "American Hunger," which was left out of Black Boy. Re-
        printed in American Hunger. See 1977.1.

7   "The Ethics of Living Jim Crow." In A Primer for White Folks.
        Edited by Bucklin Moon. New York: Doubleday, pp. 252-62.
        Reprint of 1937.226.

Blurbs

8   On A Street in Bronzeville, by Gwendolyn Brooks. New York:
        Harper & Bros.
            Dust jacket flap.

        Typescript (original): 1 leaf.
        Draft of comment.
        JWJ Wright Misc. 291.

9   "Don't Wear Your Sunday Best Every Day."
            A 140-word advertisement for war bonds on dust jacket,
        back flap, of Black Boy. See 1945.22.

        Typescript (original): 1 leaf.
        First draft of a statement supporting the purchase of war
        bonds, with MS corrections.
        JWJ Wright Misc. 363.

        Another typescript (original): 1 leaf.
        Working draft, with MS corrections. On Wright's stationery.
        JWJ Wright Misc. 364.

        Another typescript (original): 1 leaf.
        Later draft on Wright's stationery.
        JWJ Wright Misc. 365.

        Another typescript (carbon): 1 leaf.
        JWJ Wright Misc. 366.

        Related Material:
        [War Bonds.]
        Typescript (original): 1 leaf.
        Draft of a statement supporting the defense savings

1945

campaign. With MS corrections. With a typed letter,
signed, (Xerox) from the United States Treasury Department
thanking Wright.
JWJ Wright Misc. +789.

10 On Who Walk the Earth, by Dorsha Hayes. New York: Harper.
   Back dust jacket.

Autograph MS: 2 leaves.
Comment for dust jacket, with MS corrections and MS notes.
JWJ Wright Misc. 295.

Typescript (original): 1 leaf.
Leaf bears two versions, both with Wright's MS corrections.
JWJ Wright Misc. 296.

Book Reviews

11 "Alger Revisited, or My Stars! Did We Read That Stuff?" P.M.
   Magazine (16 September):m8.
      Review of Horatio Alger's Struggling Upward and Other
   Stories.

Autograph MS: 2 leaves.
First draft.
JWJ Wright Misc. +652.

Typescript (original): 3 numb. leaves.
Working draft, with MS corrections.
JWJ Wright Misc. 653.

Another typescript (original): 3 numb. leaves.
Later draft, with MS corrections and title: "American
Capitalism's Greatest Propagandist: Horatio Alger, Jr."
JWJ Wright Misc. 654.

Another typescript (carbon): 3 numb. leaves.
Final draft.
JWJ Wright Misc. 655.

12 "Gertrude Stein's Story is Drenched in Hitler's Horrors."
   P.M. Magazine (11 March):m15.
      Review of Wars I Have Seen, by Gertrude Stein. Re-
   printed: 1978.12.

Typescript (original): 3 leaves.
First draft of review. With MS revisions and corrections,
and his MS notes laid in, 10 leaves.
His working title: "Gertrude Stein Executes the 19th
Century."
JWJ Wright Misc. 672.

1945

Another typescript (original): 6 numb. leaves.
Intermediate draft, with MS corrections.
His title: "Gertrude Stein Kills the 19th Century."
JWJ Wright Misc. 673.

Another typescript (original): 5 numb. leaves.
Later draft, with extensive MS revisions.
JWJ Wright Misc. 674.

Another typescript (original): 4 numb. leaves.
Another late draft, with MS corrections.
JWJ Wright Misc. 675.

Another typescript (original): 4 numb. leaves.
Final draft, dated 20 February 1945.
JWJ Wright Misc. 676.

13   "A Non-Combat Soldier Strips Words for Action." P.M. Magazine
     (24 June):m16.
         Review of The Brick Foxhole, by Richard Brooks.

[Version A.]
Typescript (original): 1 leaf.
Working draft of early version of Wright's review of
Richard Brooks's The Brick Foxhole. With MS corrections.
JWJ Wright Misc. 705.

Another typescript (original): 1 leaf.
Another working draft, with extensive MS corrections.
JWJ Wright Misc. 706.

Another typescript (original): 1 leaf.
A later draft, with a few MS corrections.
JWJ Wright Misc. 707.

Another typescript (carbon): 2 leaves.
Final draft, dated 23 March 1945.
JWJ Wright Misc. 708.

Another typescript (original): 2 leaves.
Final draft, marked "copy."
JWJ Wright Misc. 709.

[Version B.]
Typescript (original): 1 leaf.
Working draft of another version of his review of Richard
Brooks's The Brick Foxhole, with MS additions and correc-
tions. Version contains more descriptive material of the
plot.
JWJ Wright Misc. 710.

1945

Another typescript (original): 2 leaves.
Another working draft, with extensive MS revisions.
JWJ Wright Misc. 711.

Another typescript (original): 5 leaves.
Later working draft, with revisions laid in.
JWJ Wright Misc. 712.

Another typescript (original): 1 leaf.
First leaf only of final draft.
JWJ Wright Misc. 713.

Carbon of above.
Final draft, complete, dated 29 May 1945.
JWJ Wright Misc. 714.

Another typescript (carbon): 1 leaf.
Incomplete, first leaf only.
JWJ Wright Misc. 715.

14 "Two Novels of the Crushing of Men, One White, One Black."
P.M. Magazine, (25 November,):m7-m8.
      Review of Focus, by Arthur Miller, and If He Hollers Let
Him Go, by Chester Himes.

Autograph MS: 9 leaves.
Early working draft of review.
JWJ Wright Misc. 728.

Another autograph MS: 15 leaves.
Expanded working draft, with MS corrections.
JWJ Wright Misc. 729.

Typescript (original): 9 leaves.
With extensive MS corrections and a leaf from another
version laid in.
JWJ Wright Misc. 730.

Introduction

15 Introduction to Black Metropolis, by St. Clair Drake and
Horace R. Cayton. New York: Harcourt-Brace, pp. xvii-
xxxiv.

Typescript (original): 2 numb. leaves.
Early version, with MS corrections.
JWJ Wright 48.

Another typescript (original): 2 leaves.
Another working draft, with MS revisions and corrections.
JWJ Wright 49.

Another typescript (original):   25 numb. leaves.
Intermediate draft, with extensive MS revisions.
JWJ Wright 50.

Another typescript (original):   24 numb. leaves.
Final working draft, with MS and typed revisions, some
pasted in.   Dated July 1945.   With miscellaneous leaves
deleted during revision, 14 leaves.
JWJ Wright 51.

Setting typescript (original):   25 numb. leaves.
With MS editorial markings, dated July 1945.
JWJ Wright 52.

Carbon of above.
With some MS corrections.
JWJ Wright 53.

Another carbon of above.
JWJ Wright 54.

Related material:
[Notes.]
Autograph and typed MS: 32 leaves.
Including notes and questions for a critical discussion of
the scope and impact of the book.
JWJ Wright 55.

[Lecture.]
Typescript (original):   27 numb. leaves.
Draft based on his introduction to Black Metropolis.   With
MS corrections and revisions.
JWJ Wright 56.

Another typescript (carbon):   50 [i.e., 52] numb. leaves.
Final draft.
JWJ Wright 57.

"Contemporary Negro Life in the United States."
Typescript (original):   9 leaves.
Incomplete copy of a lecture to an unidentified group of
writers, prepared for a broadcast [?] in Quebec, Canada.
Material closely related to his introduction to Black
Metropolis.
JWJ Wright Misc. 357.

See preface to Black Metropolis (1960), U.95.

1945

Letters

16   "Una carta de Richard Wright a Antonio Frasconi." Los
     Infrahumanos (Montevideo, Uruguay) 2-3.

17   "Una carta de Richard Wright a Antonio Frasconi." Marcha
     (Mexico) 6, no. 269 (2 February):15.

18   "D'une lettre de Richard Wright." Labyrinthe, no. 15
     (December):7.
     Letter to Antonio Frasconi.

19   "Richard Wright and Antonio Frasconi: An Exchange of Let-
     ters." Twice a Year, nos. 12-13:256-61. [November 1944]
     Reprinted: 1948.11; 1978.14.

     Typescript (original): 3 leaves.
     First draft, with MS corrections of his reply to a letter
     from Frasconi.
     JWJ Wright Misc. 739.

     Another typescript (original): 3 numb. leaves.
     Second draft, with MS corrections.
     JWJ Wright Misc. 740.

     Another typescript (original): 6 numb. leaves.
     Third draft, with MS corrections.
     His title: "A Letter to Uruguay."
     JWJ Wright Misc. 741.

     Another typescript (carbon): 6 leaves.
     Final draft, dated 19 November 1944.
     JWJ Wright Misc. 742.

Panel Discussion

20   "Is America Solving Its Race Problem?" America's Town Meeting
     of the Air Bulletin 11 (24 May):6-7.
          Wright's participation in panel discussion.

     Typescript (original): 4 leaves.
     Early version of an address prepared for a broadcast of
     "America's Town Meeting," 24 May 1945 (The Blue Network
     Co.).
     JWJ Wright Misc. 246.

     Another typescript (original): 3 leaves.
     Shorter draft of above, with MS corrections.
     JWJ Wright Misc. 247.

1945

Typescript (original): 2 leaves.
Early working draft of a second version, with extensive MS
corrections. Includes alternative versions of opening
paragraph (2 leaves).
JWJ Wright Misc. 248.

Another typescript (original): 4 numb. leaves.
Intermediate draft of second version, with extensive MS
corrections and revised leaves. With deleted originals of
leaves 2 and 3, extensively revised, laid in.
JWJ Wright Misc. 249.

Another typescript (original): 3 numb. leaves.
Another intermediate working draft, with MS corrections and
notes.
JWJ Wright Misc. 250.

Another typescript (original): 2 leaves.
Later working draft, with MS corrections.
JWJ Wright Misc. 251.

Another typescript (original): 3 numb. leaves.
Final draft.
JWJ Wright Misc. 252.

Two carbons of above.
JWJ Wright Misc. 253-254.

[Broadcast version.]
Typescript (original): 4 numb. leaves.
Broadcast version of Wright's remarks delivered at Town
Hall's America's Town Meeting.
JWJ Wright Misc. 255.

[Press Release.]
Typescript (mimeograph copy): 3 numb. leaves.
Press release, "News from Town Hall," for address prepared
for a panel discussion on the broadcast of Town Hall's
"America's Town Meeting," 24 May 1945, Radio Station WJ2,
New York. With Wright's extensive MS notes and with press
releases of speeches prepared by other panel members:
Congressman Jerry Voorhis, Elmer Carter (with Wright's MS
notes), and Senator Irving Ives, 9 leaves.
JWJ Wright Misc. 256.[1-2]

21   "Is America Solving Its Race Problem?" Negro Digest 3
       (August):42-44.
           Condensed extract of panel discussion. See 1945.20.

1945

<u>Books</u>

22 Black Boy: A Record of Childhood and Youth. New York:
  Harper, 258 pp. [1942-1943]
   Represents first section of autobiography. Includes
  "The Ethics of Living Jim Crow." Reprinted: 1945.23-25;
  1947.16-17; 1950.18; 1951.9; 1961.15; 1966.11; 1969.21;
  1970.35. See also 1977.1.

  "American Hunger."
  Notes, drafts, and proofs for the autobiographical work
  completed in 1944, of which the greater part was published
  in Black Boy. For material related solely to the final
  section as published in 1977, see American Hunger, 1977.1.

  "American Hunger" [organization notes].
  Typescript and autograph MS: 27 leaves.
  Includes identifications of characters, ideas for episodes,
  titles, etc.
  JWJ Wright 1.

  "Black Confession."
  Autograph MS: 104 leaves.
  First draft, incomplete.
  JWJ Wright 2.

  Typescript (original): 4 leaves, 669 numb. leaves.
  Working draft, with MS and typed revisions, some laid in,
  others on versos of leaves.
  With his title, "Black Confession."
  JWJ Wright 3.[1-5]

  Another typescript (original): 29 leaves.
  Draft of leaves 376-404, deleted from above version for
  revisions, as marked.
  JWJ Wright 4.

  "American Hunger" [early drafts].
  Typescript (original) and autograph MS: 148 leaves,
  177 leaves.
  Preliminary working versions, extensively revised and
  corrected, based on his "Black Confession." Includes two
  drafts of chapter 1, portions of Chapters 2, 3, 8, and 9,
  and other miscellaneous typed fragments and leaves deleted
  from other chapters. This version contains actual names
  of individuals affiliated with the Communist Party, which
  were disguised in later versions.
  JWJ Wright 5[1-2].

  "American Hunger" [intermediate drafts].
  Typescript (original) and autograph MS: 283 leaves,
  65 leaves.

1945

Another working draft, incorporating previous revisions and with additional extensive MS revisions. With miscellaneous fragments from deleted passages and with subtitle "The Horror and the Glory."
JWJ Wright 6[1-2].

"American Hunger" [later draft].
Typescript (original): 478 leaves.
With extensive MS deletions and revisions, some pasted in.
JWJ Wright 7[1-2].

Setting typescript (original): 501 leaves.
With MS editorial markings and some MS corrections.
JWJ Wright 8[1-2].

Carbon of above: 527 leaves.
With typed and MS revisions (some laid in). Leaves 1-44 lacking.
JWJ Wright 9[1-2].

[Chapter 14.]
Typescript (original): 3 leaves.
First draft of a conclusion for chapter 14, prepared for publication of Black Boy.
JWJ Wright 10.

Another typescript (original): 4 leaves.
Working draft, incorporating revisions of first draft, with additional corrections pasted in.
JWJ Wright 11.

Another typescript (original): 4 leaves.
Another working draft, with MS revisions.
JWJ Wright 12.

Another typescript (carbon): 4 leaves.
Setting typescript with MS editorial markings.
JWJ Wright 13.

Another typescript (carbon): 4 leaves.
Copy marked "Exhibit A. Revised version to set from if Book Club [i.e., Book-of-the-Month Club] takes it."
JWJ Wright 14.

[Adaptation.]
Typescript (carbon): 26 numb. leaves.
Condensed version prepared for publication in Coronet, with answer to Wright on behalf of the adaptors, forwarding script (1 leaf).
JWJ Wright 15.

[Black Boy synopsis.]
Setting typescript (original): 2 leaves.
With MS editorial markings. Dated 1 November 1944; pre-
pared for publication by the Book-of-the-Month Club.
JWJ Wright 18.

Page proof: 1 leaf.
JWJ Wright 19.

Plate proofs: 20 leaves.
Revised proofs for the Book-of-the-Month Club edition of
Black Boy, adapted from proofs of American Hunger.
JWJ Wright 25.

Other plate proofs in several private collections.

"American Hunger."
Galley proofs: 14 leaves, 107 numb. leaves.
Author's proof, dated 25-26 April 1944, includes page
proofs of preliminary leaves.
JWJ Wright 20.

Another set: 107 leaves.
Marked "duplicate proof," dated 6 April 1944.
JWJ Wright 21.

Another set: 107 leaves.
Dated 26 April 1944.
JWJ Wright 22.

Page proofs: 130 leaves.
Dated 8 May-31 July 1944.
JWJ Wright 23.

Plate proofs: 53 leaves.
With MS editorial markings and some MS additions.
JWJ Wright +24.

Related material:
[Black Boy and Reading.]
Autograph MS: 1 leaf.
Outline notes for an interview statement on the background
of Black Boy.
JWJ Wright Misc. 275.

Typescript (original): 4 numb. leaves.
Early working draft, with extensive MS corrections.
JWJ Wright Misc. 276.

Another typescript (original): 1 leaf.
Another working draft, with MS corrections.
JWJ Wright Misc. 277.

Another typescript (original): 3 numb. leaves.
Intermediate working draft, with extensive MS corrections.
JWJ Wright Misc. 278.

Another typescript (original): 1 leaf.
Incomplete intermediate draft, first leaf only.
JWJ Wright Misc. 279.

Another typescript (original): 1 leaf.
Later working draft, incorporating earlier revisions and
with additional MS corrections.
JWJ Wright Misc. 280.

Another typescript (original): 2 numb. leaves.
Late draft, with some MS corrections and notes.
JWJ Wright Misc. 281.

23   Black Boy. London: Gollancz, 194 pp.
        Reprint of 1945.22.

24   Black Boy. Toronto: Munson, 228 pp.-
        Reprint of 1945.22.

25   Black Boy. 10th ed. New York: World Publishing Co.
        Reprint of 1945.22.

1946

FICTION

Shorter Writings

1   "Almos' a Man." In A Treasury of Short Stories. Edited by
        Bernardine Kielty. New York: Simon & Schuster,
        pp. 829-39.
        Reprint of 1940.1.

2   ["Early Days in Chicago"] "Débuts à Chicago." Translated by
        J. B. Pontalis. Les Temps Modernes, nos. 11-12 (August-
        September):464-97.

3   ["Long Black Song"] "Complainte noire." Translated by Marcel
        Duhamel. Samedi-Soir, 1 June, p. 3; 8 June, p. 3.

4   ["The Man Who Killed a Shadow"] L'homme qui tua une ombre."
        Les Lettres Françaises, 4 October, pp. 1, 10.

1946

5   "The Man Who Lived Underground." In Accent Anthology. Edited
    by Kerker Quinn and Roger Shattuck. New York: Harcourt,
    Brace, pp. 342-50.
    Reprint of 1942.3.

6   "Silt." In The Second Armchair Companion. Edited by A. L.
    Furman. New York: Lantern Press, pp. 41-47.
    Reprint of 1937.1.

NONFICTION

Shorter Writings

Essays

7   "American Hunger" excerpt. "Un Américain affamé." Translated
    by René Lalou. Gavroche, 31 October, pp. 1-2.

8   "Dans le monde entier, je sais reconnaître un nègre du Sud"
    [No matter where in the world I meet him, I can recognize
    a Southern Negro]. Paris-Matin, 27 June, p. 2. "Pas de
    nègre au wagon-restaurant" [No Negroes in the dining car].
    Paris-Matin, 30 June, p. 2. "Dans le Sud, lorsqu'un Noir
    parle à un Blanc, sa voix grimpe de deux octaves" [In the
    South, when a Black talks to a white man, his voice climbs
    two octaves on the scale]. Paris-Matin, 2 July, p. 2.
    Translated by Jacques de Montsalais.
        Three installments of an article in French, later pub-
    lished in English as "How Jim Crow Feels." See 1946.9.

9   "How Jim Crow Feels." True Magazine (November):25-27, 154-56.
        First published in French in three installments in
    Paris-Matin, 27 June-2 July. On Wright's trip to Mexico
    and the South in the summer of 1940. Reprinted: 1947.9.

    Typescript (carbon) and autograph MS: 3 leaves.
    First draft of an essay on his travels to Mexico and the
    South in 1940.
    His title: "Jim Crow across the United States."
    JWJ Wright Misc. 407.

    Another typescript (original): 6 leaves.
    With MS corrections.
    JWJ Wright Misc. 408.

1946

10 "A Paris les GI Noirs ont appris à connaître et à aimer la
    liberté" [In Paris, Black G.I.'s have learned to know and
    like freedom]. Samedi-Soir, 25 May, p. 2.
    Unpublished in English.

    Autograph MS: 8 leaves.
    Working draft (in English) of his first impression of
    Paris.
    JWJ Wright Misc. 225.

11 "Psychiatry Comes to Harlem." Free World 12 (September):
    49-51.
    On the founding of the Lafargue Clinic by Frederick
    Wertham and others. Reprinted: 1946.12.

    Typescript (original): 6 numb. leaves.
    Working draft, with extensive MS corrections and additions
    and with MS notes laid in, 2 leaves.
    JWJ Wright Misc. 640.

    Another typescript (original): 9 numb. leaves.
    Later draft, with a few MS corrections.
    JWJ Wright Misc. 641.

12 ["Psychiatry Comes to Harlem"] "Psychiatry Goes to Harlem."
    Twice a Year, nos. 14-15 (Fall-Winter):349-54.
    Reprint of 1946.11.

13 "What You Don't Know Won't Hurt You." In Social Insight
    Through Short Stories. Edited by Josephine Strode. New
    York: Harper, pp. 279-85.
    Reprint of 1942.11.

Blurbs

14 "A Steinian Catechism." Notes on Brewsie and Willie, by
    Gertrude Stein. New York: Random House. Comments on back
    of dust jacket.

    Typescript (original): 1 leaf.
    Working draft of comment for advertisement of Gertrude
    Stein's Brewsie and Willie (1946).
    JWJ Wright Misc. 320.

    Another typescript (original) signed: 1 leaf.
    Another version, with MS notes, 2 leaves.
    JWJ Wright Misc. 321.

1946

15   On <u>Count Me Among the Living</u>, by Ethol (Kossa) Saxton.   New
      York: Harper.
           Dust jacket comment.

      Autograph MS: 1 leaf.
      Comment for dust jacket, with Wright's MS corrections.
      JWJ Wright 301.

      Typescript (original):   1 leaf.
      Another draft, with MS corrections.
      JWJ Wright 302.

      Typescript (original):   1 leaf.
      Draft for blurb, with MS corrections.
      Private collection, <u>New Anvil Magazine</u>.

16   On <u>One Small Voice</u>, by Marianne Oswald.   New York: Harper.
           Comments on back of dust jacket.

      Autograph MS: 1 leaf.
      First draft of a dust jacket comment, published by Harper
      (1946).
      JWJ Wright Misc. 303.

      Typescript (original):   1 leaf.
      Second draft, with Wright's MS corrections.
      JWJ Wright Misc. 304.

      Another typescript (original):   1 leaf.
      Final draft, with a few MS corrections.
      JWJ Wright Misc. 305.

      Two carbons of above: 1 leaf.
      JWJ Wright Misc. 306-307.

      Related Material:
      [On Marianne Oswald's <u>One Small Voice</u>.]
      Typescript (original) and autograph MS: 4 leaves.
      Suggestions for a lecture program, with an outline of
      chapters.
      JWJ Wright Misc. 508.

17   On <u>Wasteland</u>, by Jo Sinclair.   New York: Harper.
           Dust jacket comment.

      Typescript (original):   1 leaf.
      Dust jacket comment.
      JWJ Wright Misc. 314.

      Another typescript (carbon):   1 leaf.
      JWJ Wright Misc. 315.

1946

18   On Age of Assassins, by Philippe Soupault.   New York: Knopf,
      315 pp.
           Dust jacket comment.

      Autograph MS: 1 leaf.
      Dust jacket comment, with Wright's MS corrections.
      JWJ Wright Misc. 318.

      Typescript (original):   1 leaf.
      With MS corrections.
      JWJ Wright Misc. 319.

      Typescript (original):   1 leaf.
      Signed, 23 April 1946.
      Private collection.

Book Reviews

19   "American G.I.'s Fears Worry Gertrude Stein."   P.M. Magazine
      (26 July):m15-16.
           Review of Brewsie and Willie, by Gertrude Stein, in the
      form of a letter to Roger Pipett.

      Autograph MS: 2 leaves.
      With a few MS corrections.
      JWJ Wright Misc. 724.

      Typescript (original):   2 leaves.
      Final draft.
      JWJ Wright Misc. 725.

      Advance galleys: 70 leaves (bound).
      With MS notes throughout.
      JWJ Wright Misc. 726.

20   "Wasteland Uses Psychoanalysis Deftly."   P.M. Magazine
      (17 February):m8.
           Review of Wasteland, by Jo Sinclair (pseudonym for Ruth
      Seid).

      Autograph MS: 5 pp.
      First draft of review.   With MS notes laid in, 2 leaves.
      JWJ Wright Misc. 734.

      Another autograph MS: 2 numb. leaves.
      Another early draft, with a few MS corrections.
      JWJ Wright Misc. 735.

      Typescript (original):   5 leaves.
      Intermediate working draft, with extensive MS corrections
      and revisions.
      JWJ Wright Misc. +736.

1946

> Another typescript (original): 3 numb. leaves.
> Another intermediate draft, with author's MS corrections.
> His title: "The Inner Landscape of a Jewish Family."
> JWJ Wright Misc. 737.
>
> Another typescript (carbon): 4 numb. leaves.
> Final draft on Wright's stationery.
> JWJ Wright Misc. 738.

21 "Why I Chose 'Melanctha' by Gertrude Stein." In I Wish I'd
   Written That. Edited by Eugene J. Woods. New York:
   McGraw-Hill, p. 254.
   Review of "Melanctha," by Gertrude Stein.

Books

22 Black Boy. Stockholm: A/B Ljus Forlag, 228 pp.

23 Black Boy excerpt. Gavroche (Paris), 12 September, pp. 1, 6.
   Translation of excerpt published in Coronet.

24 [Black Boy] Mi Vida de Negro. Translated by Clara Diament.
   Buenos Aires: Sudamericana, 396 pp.

POETRY

25 "Between the World and Me." In The Partisan Reader (1934-
   1944). Edited by William Phillips and Philip Rahv. New
   York: Dryden Press, pp. 218-19.
   Reprint of 1935.3.

1947

FICTION

Shorter Writings

1 ["Almos' a Man"] "Presque un homme." Translated by Andrée
  Valette and Raymond Schwab. Samedi-Soir, 19 April, p. 6.

Books

2 [Native Son] Nigger. Translated by Johan Borgen. Oslo:
  Gyldendal, 540 pp.

3 [Native Son] Syn Cerneho Lidu. Translated and with a "Postface" by Alois Humplik. Prague: Horizont, 361 pp.

1947

4   [Native Son] Un Enfant du Pays. Translated by Hélène
     Bokanowski and Marcel Duhamel. Paris: Albin Michel,
     512 pp.

5   [Native Son] Zoon van Amerika. Translated by A. W. Ebbinge-
     van Nes. The Hague: U.M.

6   Native Son excerpt. "Un Enfant du Pays." La Gazette des
     Lettres (Paris), 23 August, p. 4.
     Excerpt on the killing of Mary, prepublication piece
     from translation of Native Son.

7   [Uncle Tom's Children] Les Enfants de l'Oncle Tom. Translated
     by Marcel Duhamel. With an introduction by Paul Robeson.
     Paris: Albin Michel, 250 pp.
          Includes "Le feu et la nuée" ["Fire and Cloud"], "Le dé-
     part de Big Boy" ["Big Boy Leaves Home"], and "Long chant
     noir" ["Long Black Song"].

NONFICTION

Shorter Writings

Essays

8   "How Bigger Was Born." In Literature for Our Time. Edited by
     Leonard Stanley Brown. New York: Holt, pp. 326-33.
     Reprint of 1942.7.

9   "How Jim Crow Feels." Negro Digest 5 (January):44-53.
     Condensed version. Reprint of 1946.9.

10   "Niam N'goura or Présence Africaine's Raison d'Etre."
     Présence Africaine (Paris), no. 1 (November-December):
     184-92.
          An adaptation, done in collaboration with Thomas Diop,
     of Alioune Diop's editorial in the same issue (pp. 7-14).

     Autograph MS: 22 pp.
     Notes for a translation and adaptation of statement of
     aims of Présence Africaine.
     JWJ Wright Misc. 493.

11   "Urban Misery in an American City: Juvenile Delinquency in
     Harlem." Twice a Year, nos. 14-15 (Fall 1946-Winter 1947):
     339-45. [1945-1946]

     Typescript (original): 44 numb. leaves.
     Sketch of a concluding chapter for an essay on

65

1947

rehabilitation of emotionally deprived black children from
Harlem at the Wiltwyck School. Some selections incorpo-
rated into his "Urban Misery in an American City--Juvenile
Delinquency in Harlem."
His working title: "Harlem is Human."
JWJ Wright Misc. 347.

Carbon copy.
JWJ Wright Misc. 348.

"Urban Misery in an American City."
N.Y. Public Library, Schomburg Collection.

Typescript (original): 10 leaves.
Draft of an early version in letter form, with author's
extensive corrections and revisions. Essay endorses work
of the Wiltwyck School (N.Y.) and incorporates partial text
of "The Children of Harlem."
JWJ Wright Misc. 786.

Another typescript (original): 16 numb. leaves.
Working copy marked "first draft," with MS corrections and
incorporating corrections made in preceding MS. His title:
"The Children of Harlem."
JWJ Wright Misc. 787.

Another typescript (original): 13 numb. leaves.
Working draft of a revised version, with MS corrections.
JWJ Wright Misc. 788.

12   "A World View of the American Negro." Twice a Year, nos. 14-
15 (Fall 1946-Winter 1947):346-48.
First published as "Lettre sur le problème noir aux
U.S.A." in Les Nouvelles Epîtres (Paris), Lettre 32, with
facsimile of 20 June 1946 autograph letter by Wright.

Typescript (original): 4 numb. leaves.
Working draft, with author's MS corrections.
JWJ Wright Misc. 810.

Manuscript (original): sent to Les Nouvelles Epîtres;
4 numb. leaves on Wright's stationery.
Dated 1 July. With signed copy of printed French translation of above and signed copy of facsimile dated
20 June 1946.
Private collection.

Blurb

13   On <u>The End Is Not Yet</u>, by Fritz von Unruh. New York: Storm
       Publishers, 540 pp.
             Dust jacket comments using part of Wright's review "A
       Junker's Epic Novel on Militarism." See 1947.15.

       Typescript (original): 1 leaf.
       Working draft of dust jacket comment.
       With a few MS corrections.
       JWJ Wright Misc. 326.

       Another typescript (original): 1 leaf.
       Another draft, with MS corrections.
       JWJ Wright Misc. 327.

       Another typescript (carbon): 1 leaf.
       Private collection.

Book Reviews

14   "E. M. Forster Anatomizes the Novel." <u>P.M. Magazine</u>
       (16 March):m3.
             Review of <u>Aspects of the Novel</u>, by E. M. Forster.

       Typescript (original): 1 leaf.
       Fragment from his review of Forster's <u>Aspects of the Novel</u>.
       JWJ Wright Misc. 669.

       Carbon copy.
       JWJ Wright Misc. 670.

15   "A Junker's Epic Novel on Militarism." <u>P.M. Magazine</u> (4 May):
       m3.
             Review of <u>The End Is Not Yet</u>, by Fritz von Unruh.

       Autograph MS: 4 leaves.
       Early draft, with MS corrections.
       JWJ Wright Misc. 690.

       Typescript (original): 8 leaves.
       Another version, with MS deletions and notes.
       JWJ Wright Misc. 691.

<u>Books</u>

16   <u>Black Boy</u>. New York: World Publishing Co. (Forum Book),
       289 pp.
             Reprint of 1945.22.

1947

17 Black Boy. London: Gollancz (Reader's Union), 286 pp.
    Reprint of 1945.22.

18 "Black Boy." Translated by Marcel Duhamel and Andrée Picard.
    Les Temps Modernes (Paris) 2, nos. 16 (January) to 21
    (June):577-609, 806-45, 980 ff., 1430 ff., 1642 ff.
    Prepublication serialized version of most of Black Boy.

19 Black Boy excerpt. In American Authors Today. Edited by Whit
    Burnett and Charles Slatkin. New York: Ginn & Co.,
    pp. 189-97.

20 Black Boy (Jeunesse Noire). Translated by Marcel Duhamel and
    Andrée R. Picard. Paris: Gallimard, 264 pp.

21 [Black Boy] Ich Negerjunge. Translated by Harry Rosbaud.
    Zürich: Steunberg Verlag, 306 pp.

22 [Black Boy] Negerjongen. Translated by J. van Dietsch.
    Leiden: Sijthoff, 236 pp.

23 [Black Boy] Svart Ungdom. Translated by Johan Borgen. Oslo:
    Gyldendal, 257 pp.

24 Twelve Million Black Voices. London: Drummond, 157 pp.
    Reprint of 1941.26.

1948

FICTION

Shorter Writings

1 ["Bright and Morning Star"] "Claire étoile du matin." Translated by Boris Vian. Présence Africaine (Paris), no. 2
   (January):299-316.

2 ["Down by the Riverside"] "Là-bas près de la rivière." Translated by Boris Vian. L'Age Nouveau, no. 27 (April):6-40.

Book

3 [Native Son] Paura. Translated by Camillo Pellizi. Lugano,
   Switzerland: Ghilda del Libro, 584 pp.

1948

NONFICTION

Shorter Writings

Essays

4   ["How Bigger Was Born"] "Naissance d'un roman nègre." Trans-
     lated by Andrée Valette and Raymond Schwab. La Nef (Paris)
     5, no. 44 (July):43-64.

5   ["The Literature of the Negro in the United States"] "Littéra-
     ture noire américaine." Les Temps Modernes 3, no. 35
     (August):193-220.
     Early version, never published in English. See 1957.9.

6   "Richard Wright nous présente Black Boy" [Richard Wright Pre-
     sents Black Boy]. L'Ordre (Paris), 14 January, p. 3.
     Later became introduction to "American Hunger," in
     Mademoiselle. See 1948.17; 1977.1.

Blurb

7   On The Path of Thunder, by Peter Abrahams. New York: Harper.
     Comments on back of dust jacket.

     Typescript (original): 1 leaf.
     First draft.
     JWJ Wright Misc. 288.

Introductions

8   "Evidence de l'art nègre." [November]
          Introduction to a pamphlet for an African art exhibition
     at Librairie Palmes, Paris, p. [1].

9   "Introductory Note to The Respectful Prostitute by Jean-Paul
     Sartre." Art and Action, A Book of Literature, the Arts
     and Civil Liberties: Twice a Year, no. 10 (10th Anniver-
     sary Issue):14-16.

     Typescript (original): 2 leaves.
     Early version of his comments on La Putain Respectueuse.
     JWJ Wright Misc. 447.

     Typescript (original): 2 leaves.
     Working draft, with a few MS corrections.
     JWJ Wright Misc. 448.

1948

Another typescript (original): 3 numb. leaves.
Draft, with MS corrections.
JWJ Wright Misc. 449.

Another typescript (original): 3 numb. leaves.
Final draft.
JWJ Wright Misc. 450.

Another typescript (carbon): 3 numb. leaves.
JWJ Wright Misc. 451.

"Reactions to the Script of La Putain Respectueuse by Jean-
Paul Sartre."
Typescript (original): 5 numb. leaves.
With corrections.
JWJ Wright Misc. 642.

10   Richard Wright présente Le Musée Vivant" [Richard Wright Pre-
sents Le Musée Vivant]. Le Musée Vivant 12 (November):1.
Introduction to a special issue on African art, prepared
by Madeleine Rousseau.

Letters

11   "Richard Wright and Antonio Frasconi: An Exchange of Letters."
Présence Africaine, no. 5 (April):780-84.
Reprint of 1945.19.

12   "Two Letters to Dorothy Norman." In Art and Action. Edited
by Dorothy Norman. New York: Twice a Year Press,
pp. 65-73.
Includes letters dated 28 February 1948 (pp. 65-71) and
9 March 1948 (pp. 72-73), both from Paris, on the state of
things in Europe.

Speech

13   "L'humanité est plus grande que l'Amérique et la Russie"
[Mankind is larger than the United States or the USSR].
Franc-Tireur (Paris), 16 December, p. 4.
Speech given at a Rassemblement Démocratique Révolution-
naire congress on 10 December 1948, in Paris. Unpublished
in English.

Original typescript: 6 leaves.
Working draft, with author's corrections.
JWJ Wright 409.

Another typescript (original): 5 numb. leaves.
Later draft, with MS corrections.
JWJ Wright 410.

Richard Wright's Published Works

1949

Books

14   [Black Boy] Ben-Kusim.   Translated by Noah Stern.   Tel-Aviv:
     Am'Oved, 278 pp.

15   [Black Boy] Black Boy.   Translated by Nils Holmberg.
     Stockholm: Bonnier, 256 pp.

16   [Black Boy] Musta Poika.   Translated by Eeva Kangasmaa.
     Turku: Aura, 374 pp.

17   [Black Boy] Negro Chele.   Translated by Nikhil Sen.   Calcutta:
     Modern Publishers, 358 pp.

18   [Black Boy] Ragazzo Negro.   Translated by Bruno Fonzi.   Turin:
     Einaudi, 359 pp.

19   [Twelve Million Black Voices] Wir Neger in Amerika.   Trans-
     lated by Anita Hüttenmoser.   Zürich: Büchergilde Gutenberg,
     160 pp.

1949

FICTION

Shorter Writings

1   "Bright and Morning Star."   In American Literature Since 1900.
    Edited by J. H. Nelson and Oscar Cargill.   New York:
    Macmillan, pp. 581-602.
        Reprint of 1938.2.

2   "Bright and Morning Star."   In U.S. Stories: Regional Stories
    from the 48 States ("Tennessee").   Edited by Martha Foley
    and Abraham Rothberg.   New York: Hendricks House,
    pp. 214-46.
        Reprint of 1938.2.

3   ["The Man Who Killed a Shadow"] "L'homme qui tua une ombre."
    Zero (Paris) 1 (Spring):45-53.   [1945-1946]
        First published in French in Les Lettres Françaises,
    4 October 1946, pp. 1-10.   See 1960.3.

    Typescript (carbon): 17 numb. leaves.
    Early draft of story.
    JWJ Wright 131.

71

1949

Carbon of above.
JWJ Wright 132.

Another typescript (original):   19 numb. leaves.
Revised draft.
JWJ Wright 133.

Carbon of above, signed.
JWJ Wright 134.

Another typescript (carbon):   17 numb. leaves.
JWJ Wright 135.

Another typescript (carbon):   21 numb. leaves.
Final draft, with a few typed revisions.
JWJ Wright 136.

Carbon of above.
JWJ Wright 137.

Another typescript (original):   1 leaf.
First leaf only.
JWJ Wright 138.

Related Material:
["The Man Who Killed a Shadow," background essay.]
Autograph MS: 8 numb. leaves.
An account of a conversation with Charles Houston, attorney
for the NAACP, that becomes the basis for the story.
JWJ Wright 139.

Typescript (carbon):   79 numb. leaves.
Final copy, with a few typed corrections and a deleted leaf
laid in.
JWJ Wright 140.

Carbon of above.
JWJ Wright 141.

[Blurb for Eight Men.]
Typescript (carbon):   1 leaf.
Published, revised, on dust jacket of book (1961).
JWJ Wright Misc. 328.

"Roots and Branches."
Typescript (original):   5 numb. leaves.
With extensive MS revisions. On his creative process in
the development of stories, in particular those in Eight
Men.   Intended as an introduction to Eight Men, but never
published.
JWJ Wright Misc. 751.

1949

Books

4   [Native Son] "Un Enfant du Pays." Translated by Hélène
     Bokanowski and Marcel Duhamel. La Nouvelle République de
     Bordeaux et du Sud-Ouest (Summer-Fall).
     Serial publication of Native Son.

5   [Native Son] Filho Nativo. Translated by Monteiro Lobato.
     Lisbon: Arcadia.

6   [Native Son] Paura. Milan: Bompiani, 427 pp.

7   [Uncle Tom's Children] I figli dello zio Tom. Translated by
     Fernanda Pivano. Turin: Einaudi, 318 pp.

8   [Uncle Tom's Children] Onkel Toms Kinder. Translated by
     H. Rosbaud. Zürich: Steinberg Verlag, 261 pp.

NONFICTION

Shorter Writings

Essays

9   ["I Tried to be a Communist"] "J'ai essayé d'être un commu-
     niste." Translated by René Guyonnet. Les Temps Modernes
     65, no. 45 (July):1-45.
         Later a part of The God That Failed. See 1949.10.

10   "I Tried to be a Communist." In The God That Failed. Edited
     by Richard Crossman. London: Hamish Hamilton, 272 pp.
         Reprint of 1944.7.

11   "Introducing Some American Negro Folk Songs." Présence
     Africaine (Paris), no. 6 (January-March):70.

Blurb

12   On Annie Allen, by Gwendolyn Brooks. New York: Harper.
         Dust jacket comment.

Introduction

13   Preface to "Human, All Too Human," by E. Franklin Frazier.
     Présence Africaine (Paris), no. 6 (January-March):47.

1949

Letter

14 "Comrade Strong, Don't You Remember?" New York Herald Tribune
(European ed.), 4 April, p. 3.
Letter to Anna Louise Strong in response to her article
in the New York Herald Tribune.

Autograph MS: 11 leaves.
First draft of a letter to Anna Louise Strong. With a few
MS corrections.
JWJ Wright Misc. 353.

Typescript (original): 5 leaves.
Working draft, with extensive MS corrections and revisions.
JWJ Wright Misc. 354.

Another typescript (original): 5 leaves.
Later working draft, with extensive MS corrections.
JWJ Wright Misc. 355.

Another typescript (carbon): 5 numb. leaves.
Final draft.
JWJ Wright Misc. 356.

Liner Notes

15 ["Note on Jim Crow Blues"] "Note sur les Blues." Translated
by Madeleine Gauthier. La Revue du Jazz (Paris), no. 4
(April):113. [1941]
From a note on a record album cover, Josh White's
"Southern Exposure." See 1941.23

Books

16 [Black Boy] Feketék es Fehérek. Translated by Imre Koszegi.
Budapest: Dante, 228 pp.

17 Black Boy excerpt. In American Literature. Edited by J. L.
Davis et al. Vol. 2. Chicago: Scribner, pp. 913-16.
"Discovery of Reading" passage.

POETRY

18 "Between the World and Me." In Poetry of the Negro. Edited
by Langston Hughes and Arna Bontemps. New York: Doubleday,
pp. 202-3.
Reprint of 1935.3.

19   "The F B Eye Blues."   Mimeographed sheet folded in four.
      Pirated ed.   New York.
         Song lyrics.   Reprinted: 1971.35; 1978.24; (1979.3).

      Autograph MS: 9 leaves.
      Written on verso of stationery of the Exiled Writers
      Committee.   With MS notes, laid in, 3 leaves.
      JWJ Wright Misc. 573.

      Typescript (original):   1 leaf.
      Version used for pirated edition, dated 1949.
      JWJ Wright Misc. 574.

      Another typescript (original):   1 leaf.
      With additional verse and with author's MS notes, signed.
      JWJ Wright Misc. 575.

      Autograph MS: 1 leaf.
      Score of song for solo voice and piano accompaniment, by
      James Moody.   Lyrics by Richard Wright.
      JWJ Wright Misc. 576.

20   "I Have Seen Black Hands."   In The Poetry of the Negro.   Ed-
      ited by Langston Hughes and Arna Bontemps.   New York:
      Doubleday, pp. 156-57.
         Reprint of 1934.3.

                              1950

FICTION

Shorter Writings

1   "Early Days in Chicago."   Negro Digest 8 (July):52-68.
         Reprint of 1946.9.

2   ["The Man Who Lived Underground"] "L'homme qui vivait sous
     terre."   Translated by Claude-Edmonde Magny.   Les Temps
     Modernes 6, no. 69 (July):1-43; no. 70 (August):244-60.

Books

3   Native Son.   New York: New American Library (Signet), 413 pp.
         Reprint of 1940.8.

4   [Native Son] Un Enfant du Pays.   With an introduction by
        Maurice Nadeau.   Paris: Le Club Français du Livre, 448 pp.

5   [Uncle Tom's Children] Los hijos del Tio Tom.   Buenos Aires:
        Sudamericana, 345 pp.

1950

NONFICTION

Shorter Writings

Essays

6   "I Tried to be a Communist." In The God That Failed. Edited
    by Richard Crossman. New York: Harper, pp. 115-63.
    Reprint of 1944.7.

7   ["I Tried to be a Communist."] In Le Dieu des Ténèbres [The
    God That Failed]. Paris: Calmann-Lévy, pp. 135-88.

8   ["I Tried to be a Communist."] In De God die faalde [The God
    That Failed]. Translated by Koos Schuur. Amsterdam: De
    Bezige Bij, 296 pp.

9   ["I Tried to be a Communist."] In Ein Gott, der keiner war
    [The God That Failed]. Constance, West Germany: Europa
    Verlag, 302 pp.

10 ["I Tried to be a Communist."] In Ein Gott, der keiner war
    [The God That Failed]. Zürich: Diana Verlag, 302 pp.

11 ["I Tried to be a Communist."] In Testimonianze sul Comunismo
    (Il dio che è fallito) [The God That Failed]. Translated
    by M. V. Malvano, Giovanni Fei, Anita Rho, and Claudio
    Gorlier. Milan: Comunità, 382 pp.

12 ["I Tried to be a Communist."] In Vi trodde pa Kommunismen
    [The God That Failed]. Stockholm: Natur och Kultur,
    274 pp.

13 "I Tried to be a Communist" excerpt. "Ein Gott hat versagt."
    Der Monat (Berlin) 3, no. 25 (October):55-83.

14 "I Tried to be a Communist" excerpt. "Why I Quit Communism."
    New York Post, 13 July, p. 29.

15 "L'Homme du Sud" [The Man of the South]. France Etats-Unis
    (December):2.
        On the awarding of the Nobel Prize for Literature to
    William Faulkner. Unpublished in English.

    Typescript (carbon): 3 numb. leaves.
    Page 1 lacking.
    JWJ Wright Misc. 807.

1950

Blurb

16   On Our Lady of the Flowers, by Jean Genet. New York: Grove
     Press.
     Comments on back of dust jacket written at the request
     of Bernard Fretchman.

Introduction

17   Introduction to American Hunger. In One Hundred Five Greatest
     Living Authors Present the World's Best. Edited by Whit
     Burnett. New York: Dial Press, p. 303.
     First published as "Richard Wright nous présente Black
     Boy," L'Ordre (Paris), 14 January 1948, p. 3. See 1948.6;
     1977.1.

     [Comment on an excerpt.]
     Typescript (original): 1 leaf.
     With MS corrections. Excerpt is unidentified.
     JWJ Wright Misc. 282.

     Typescript (original): 1 leaf.
     With a few MS corrections. Published in One Hundred Five
     Greatest Living Authors Present the World's Best, edited by
     Whit Burnett (New York: The Dial Press, 1950), p. 303.
     JWJ Wright Misc. 283.

     Another typescript (original): 1 leaf.
     Partial draft, with MS corrections.
     JWJ Wright Misc. 283a.

Books

18   Black Boy. Illustrated by Ashley Bryan. New York: World
     Publishing Co. (Living Library), 289 pp.
     Reprint of 1945.22.

19   [Black Boy] El Negrito. Translated by Enrique Pascual.
     Madrid: Afrodisio Aguado, 345 pp.

20   Black Boy excerpt. In We Speak for Ourselves. Edited by
     Irving Stone. Garden City, N.Y.: Doubleday, pp. 238-46.
     Includes "Voodoo . . . " and graduation episodes.

1951

1951

FICTION

Books

1   Eight Men excerpt. Cinque Uomini. Translated by Fernanda
        Pivano. Milan: Mondadori, 180 pp.
        Includes first five stories of Eight Men.

2   Native Son excerpt. In Anthology of American Prose. Edited
        by Ebba Dalin. London: Zephyr Books, pp. 328-34.
        Includes the "Fate" section.

NONFICTION

Shorter Writings

Essays

3   ["American Negroes in France"] "Les Noirs américains et
        la France." France-Observateur (Paris) 2, no. 56 (3 May).
        Later published in the U.S. in English.

4   "American Negroes in France." The Crisis 58 (June-July):381-83.
        First published in French. See 1951.3.

        Typescript (original): 5 numb. leaves.
        With author's MS corrections. Dated Paris, France,
        24 April 1951.
        His title: "A Declaration of Solidarity from American
        Negroes in the French Community."
        JWJ Wright Misc. 234.

        Related Material:
        "Franco-American Fellowship Press Conference of 7 June
        1951, Relative to the American Hospital at Neuilly and the
        Case of Miss Margaret McCleveland."
        Reproduction from typewritten copy: 7 leaves.
        Statement by investigating committee of the Franco-American
        Fellowship concerning racial discrimination in employment
        at the American hospital.
        JWJ Wright Misc. 388.

5   "Derrière l'affaire McGee" [Behind the McGee Case]. Le Droit
        de Vivre (Paris), 15 May, p. 1.
        Unpublished in English.

1952

Typescript (carbon): 4 numb. leaves
On the execution of Willie McGee and its effect on world
opinion of American justice. Dated 4 June 1951.
JWJ Wright Misc. 273.

6 ["The Literature of the Negro in the United States"] "La Let-
teratura negra negli Stati Uniti." Translated by Romano
Rostan. Quaderni A.C.I. (Turin) 4 (19 June):41-72.

7 "Richard Wright Explains Ideas about Movie Making." Ebony 6
(January):84-85. [1950]
On the shooting of Native Son in Argentina.

8 "The Shame of Chicago." Ebony 7 (December):24-32. [1950]
On Wright's return to Chicago in 1949.

Typescript (carbon): 10 numb. leaves.
With a few MS additions and his title: "Chicago--Twelve
Years After." Essay describing his impressions of Chicago
after twelve years absence.
JWJ Wright Misc. 754.

Another typescript (carbon): 11 numb. leaves.
Final draft.
JWJ Wright Misc. 755.

Books

9 Black Boy. New York: New American Library, 201 pp.
Reprint of 1945.22.

10 [Black Boy] Crni Djecak. Translated by Stana Oblak. Zagreb:
Zora, 275 pp.

1952

FICTION

Books

1 Native Son excerpt. In This is Chicago. Edited by Albert
Harper. New York: Henry Holt, pp. 130-50.
Includes "Southside Boy," watching the plane, and
poolroom scenes.

1952

NONFICTION

Shorter Writings

Essays

2   ["I Tried to be a Communist."]   In O deus que falhou: uma
     confissao [The God That Failed].   Translated by Eneas
     Marzano.   Brazil: Pongetti.

3   ["I Tried to be a Communist."]   In Ein Gott, der keiner war
     [The God That Failed].   Cologne: Verlag Rote-Weissbücher,
     263 pp.

4   ["I Tried to be a Communist."]   In Ein Gott, der keiner war
     [The God That Failed].   Vienna: Europa Verlag, 263 pp.

Introduction

5   Preface to La Croisade de Lee Gordon [Lonely Crusade], by
     Chester Himes.   Paris: Correa, pp. 7-8.
        The English translation of the book was published in the
     U.S. without a preface.

     Typescript (carbon):   2 numb. leaves.
     English version of preface.
     Private collection.

Books

6   [Black Boy] Burakku Boi.   Translated by Masao Takahashi.
     Tokyo: Getsuyo Shobo, 287 pp.

7   Black Boy excerpt.   In The Literature of the South, ch. 7.
     Edited by Richmond Beat et al.   Glenview, Ill.:   Scott,
     Foresman & Co.

8   [Twelve Million Black Voices] Schwarz unter Weiss; Fern von
     Afrika.   Frankfurt: Europaische Verl. Anst., 147 pp.
        New title.   Old title was Wir Neger in Amerika.

1953

FICTION

<u>Books</u>

1   <u>The Outsider</u>. New York: Harper & Bros., 405 pp. [1947-1952]
        Reprinted: 1953.2; 1954.4; 1965.8; 1969.16.

    Typescript and autograph MS: 4 folders.
    First working drafts, with extensive MS and typed revisions
    and deletions.
    JWJ Wright +851[1-4].

    MS and typed notes and outlines: 34 leaves.
    Includes memo of critical suggestions by an outside reader.
    JWJ Wright 852.

    "Cross."
    Typescript (original): 4 leaves, 676 numb. leaves;
    30 leaves.
    Early working version, with typed corrections pasted in.
    JWJ Wright 853[1-3].

    Another typescript (original): 379 leaves, 55 leaves.
    Intermediate draft, with extensive MS corrections and with
    carbons of some leaves laid in.
    JWJ Wright 854[1-2].

    Carbon of above: 719 leaves.
    Some leaves removed and placed in preceding copy.
    JWJ Wright 855[1-3].

    "Man Upside Down."
    Typescript (original): 665 leaves.
    Late working draft, with extensive revisions and correc-
    tions, some pasted in. Includes some leaves (carbon) from
    intermediate draft (no. 854). Submitted to Paul Reynolds.
    JWJ Wright 856[1-3].

    Another typescript (original): 30 leaves.
    Opening episodes only. Includes revisions made in preced-
    ing copy.
    JWJ Wright 857.

    Setting typescript (original): 611 numb. leaves, 2 leaves.
    With MS corrections and deletions and MS editorial comments
    and markings. Preliminary material (leaves 1-24) lacking.
    JWJ Wright 858[1-3].

1953

"Cross Daemon, a Novel."
Setting typescript (original): 12 leaves, 326 [i.e., 324] numb. leaves.
Working draft of another version of The Outsider. With miscellaneous working notes, 3 leaves, and his MS corrections and typed revisions, some laid in.
JWJ Wright 859[1-2].

Autograph MS: 10 leaves.
Incomplete draft of an introductory chapter.
JWJ Wright 860.

Another typescript (original): 278 [i.e., 281] numb. leaves, 16 leaves.
Later complete draft, with some revised leaves laid in.
JWJ Wright 861.

Related Material:
[Autobiographical Sketch--Book Jacket of The Outsider]
Typescript (carbon): 2 leaves.
Concerning Wright's experiences since 1941 as background for his novel. Published on book jacket, Harper & Brothers (1953).
JWJ Wright Misc. 267.

[Medical data on multiple sclerosis.]
Typescript (original): 2 leaves.
With MS notes, 6 leaves. Data on symptoms and effects of multiple sclerosis. Related to development of Cross Daemon (a variant title of The Outsider).
JWJ Wright 472.

2   The Outsider. Toronto: Munson, 405 pp.
        Reprint of 1953.1.

3   The Outsider. London and Sydney: Angus (Panther Books),
        405 pp. Abridged ed., 283 pp.
        Reprint of 1953.1.

NONFICTION

Shorter Writings

Essays

4   ["I Tried to be a Communist."] In Ha-El she-hikhziv [The God
        That Failed]. Translated by Ephrayim Karlis. Tel-Aviv:
        Pales, 202 pp.

1954

5   "There is Always Another Café." The Kiosk (Paris), no. 10: 12-14.
    Reprinted: 1971.23; 1978.11.

    Typescript (original): 8 numb. leaves.
    JWJ Wright Misc. 772.

    Another typescript (carbon): 7 numb. leaves.
    Dated 18 May 1953.
    JWJ Wright Misc. 773.

6   ["What You Don't Know Won't Hurt You"] "Ce que tu ne sais pas ne peut pas te faire de mal." Les Lettres Nouvelles (Paris), no. 4 (January):385-93.

Introduction

7   Introduction to In the Castle of My Skin, by George Lamming. New York: McGraw-Hill, pp. ix-xii.

    Typescript (original): 4 numb. leaves.
    First draft, with author's MS corrections.
    JWJ Wright Misc. 431.

    Another typescript (original): 4 numb. leaves.
    Working draft, with MS corrections.
    JWJ Wright Misc. 432.

    Another typescript (original): 4 numb. leaves.
    Final version.
    JWJ Wright Misc. 433.

Letter

8   "From Richard Wright." In The Flowers of Friendship. Edited by Donald Gallup. New York: Knopf, pp. 379-80.
    Letter to Gertrude Stein, dated 27 May 1945.

1954

FICTION

Books

1   [Native Son] Domorodac. Translated by Bora Glisic. Subotica: Minerva, 441 pp.

2   [Native Son] Un Enfant du Pays. Brussels: Club du Livre Sélectionné.

1954

3   Native Son excerpt. "Une chasse à l'homme" [Manhunt]. In
     Panorama de la littérature contemporaine aux Etats-Unis.
     Edited by John Brown. Paris: Gallimard, pp. 401-5.
     Bigger's flight on the roofs.

4   The Outsider. New York: New American Library (Signet Giant).
     Reprint of 1953.1.

5   [The Outsider] De Buitenstaander. Translated by Margrit de
     Sablonière. Leiden: A. W. Sijthoff, 425 pp.

6   [The Outsider] El Extraño. Translated by León Mirlas.
     Buenos Aires: Sudamericana, 620 pp.

7   [The Outsider] Utanför. Translated by Torsten Blomkvist.
     Stockholm: Bonnier, 388 pp.

8   [The Outsider] Vidnet. Translated by Elsa Gress. Copenhagen:
     Gyldendal, 296 pp.

9   Savage Holiday. New York: Avon Publications, 220 pp.

     Autograph MS: 1 leaf, 165 [i.e., 166] numb. leaves.
     First draft, with some MS revisions laid in and a list of
     suggested titles.
     JWJ Wright 888.

     Another autograph MS: 37 leaves.
     Incomplete early working draft, beginning episodes only.
     With author's extensive revisions.
     JWJ Wright 889.

     Typescript (original): 264 leaves.
     Another working draft, with author's extensive MS correc-
     tions and revisions.
     JWJ Wright 890.

     Another typescript (original): 230 leaves.
     Another working draft, with author's extensive MS correc-
     tions and revisions.
     JWJ Wright 891.

     Typescript (original and carbon): 27 leaves.
     Miscellaneous drafts of alternate titles and suggestions
     for introductory quotations.
     JWJ Wright 892.

     Another typescript (original): 5 leaves, 220 numb. leaves.
     Later working draft, incorporating revisions of earlier
     drafts and with additional MS revisions, some pasted in.
     Leaf 219 lacking.
     JWJ Wright 893.

1954

"Monument to Memory."
Typescript.
N.Y. Public Library, Schomburg Coll. 134-136.
Setting typescript (original): 1 leaf, 268 [i.e., 238]
numb. leaves.
With numerous deletions and with MS editorial markings and
corrections. Some deleted leaves laid in, 7 leaves. His
title: "The Wish and the Deed."
JWJ Wright 894.

NONFICTION

Shorter Writing

Essay

10   "What is Africa to Me?" Encounter 3, no. 3 (September):22-31.
      [1953]
            Included in Black Power. See 1954.14.

Books

11   Black Boy excerpt. "Blancs et Noirs." In Panorama de la
      littérature contemporaine aux Etats-Unis. Edited by John
      Brown. Paris: Gallimard, pp. 348-401.

12   Black Boy excerpt. In Patterns for Living. Edited by
      M. Campbell, Van Grundy, and Shrodes. [Unverified]

13   Black Boy excerpt. In Symposium. Edited by G. W. Arms and
      L. D. Locke. New York: Rinehart, pp. 389-400.

14   Black Power: A Record of Reactions in a Land of Pathos. New
      York: Harper, 358 pp. [1953-1954]
            Includes "What is Africa to Me?" Reprinted: 1954.15.
      See also 1954.10.

      [Black Power: travel journal.]
      Typescript (original): 988 numb. leaves.
      Leaves 1-14, 253, 266, 707, 879, 909-48 lacking.
      Included in text is a typed letter (carbon) to Dorothy and
      George Padmore (leaves 434-35) and several mounted clip-
      pings. With typed and MS notes, an interview questionnaire,
      a statement "To the people of Ghana," and an itinerary for
      author's trip to the Gold Coast; 23 leaves.
      JWJ Wright 79.

1954

Typescript (original):   651 numb. leaves.
Early working draft, with MS corrections and revisions,
some pasted in.   Early title: "Africa is Moving.   An
Account of Reactions in a Land of Pathos."
JWJ Wright 59[1-3].

["Black Nation."]
Typescript (original):   317 leaves.
Long, uncut version, incomplete, with author's MS correc-
tions and some MS editorial comments.
JWJ Wright 60.

Carbon of above: 3 leaves, 664 numb. leaves.
Includes some carbons from setting typescript and some
readers suggestions, 3 leaves.
JWJ Wright 61[1-3].

Another carbon of above: 733 leaves.
Working draft with list of corrections laid in and with
extensive MS corrections, deletions, and revisions, some
laid in, others pasted in.
Tentative title: "The Trumpet Sounds in Africa."
JWJ Wright 62[1-4].

Setting typescript (original):   4 leaves, 549 numb. leaves.
Final version, with MS editorial markings.   With 2 revised
leaves laid in.   Without introduction.
JWJ Wright 63[1-3].

Carbon of above: 3 leaves, 55 numb. leaves.
Incomplete copy.   Leaves from this draft were used for
revisions of carbon working draft (no. 61).
JWJ Wright 64.

Typescript (original):   633 pp.
Stamped numbers on 592 original numbers, plus 41 pages of
handwritten MS and notes, the last 4 pages mimeographed.
Autograph revision and changes laid in.   Several pages un-
published.   MS by Okinko Zevu at end of last page.
Northwestern University Library.

[Conclusion.]
Typescript (original):   11 leaves.
Working draft of concluding chapter in the form of a letter
of advice to Kwame Nkrumah.   With typed and MS corrections
and MS notes laid in, 1 leaf.
JWJ Wright 65.

Another typescript (original):   4 leaves.
Working draft, incomplete, with MS corrections.
JWJ Wright 66.

1954

Another typescript (original): 1 leaf.
First leaf only of final version.
JWJ Wright 67.

Carbon of above: 1 leaf.
JWJ Wright 68.

Another typescript (original): 1 leaf, 6 numb. leaves.
Later copy prepared for publication in United Asia 7
(March 1955):54-58. His title: "An Open Letter to an
African Leader."
JWJ Wright 69.

"Black Power: A Propos Prepossessions. . . ."
Typescript (original): 5 numb. leaves.
Early working draft of the introduction, with MS correc-
tions and revisions.
JWJ Wright 70.

Another typescript (original): 6 numb. leaves.
Another working draft, with MS corrections.
JWJ Wright 71.

Another typescript (original): 4 numb. leaves.
Shorter version, incorporating earlier corrections.
JWJ Wright 72.

Another typescript (original): 6 numb. leaves.
Later draft, dated May 1954, Paris.
JWJ Wright 73.

Another typescript (original): 6 numb. leaves.
Another late draft.
JWJ Wright 74.

Carbon of above.
With a few MS corrections.
JWJ Wright 75.

Another typescript (original): 6 numb. leaves.
Later, revised copy with a typed (original) of leaf 3 and a
revised version laid in, 2 leaves.
JWJ Wright 76.

Another typescript (original): 4 numb. leaves.
Partial copy of final draft, with revised leaf laid in.
First leaf lacking.
JWJ Wright 77.

Carbon of above: 4 numb. leaves.
First leaf lacking.
JWJ Wright 78.

1954

15   Black Power. Toronto: Munson, 358 pp.
Reprint of 1954.14.

16   Black Power excerpt. "American [sic for African] Life Must Be
Militarized." United Asia 7, no. 2 (March):54-58.
Letter to Nkrumah. See 1954.14. See also JWJ Wright 69,
1954.

17   Black Power excerpt. "Deux portraits africains" [Two African
Portraits]. Preuves (Paris) 4, no. 45 (November):3-6.
[1953]
From the first unpublished chapter of Black Power.

18   Black Power excerpt. "Introducing Black Power." Book Find
News, no. 162:1.

1955

FICTION

Shorter Writings

1   "Almos' a Man." In Strange Barriers. Edited by J. Vernon
Shea. New York: Avon Publishers (Lion Library),
pp. 116-28.
Reprint of 1940.2.

2   "Long Black Song." Great Tales of the Deep South. New York:
Avon Publishers (Lion Library), pp. 104-27.
Reprint of 1938.8.

Books

3   [The Outsider] Ho bruciato la notte. Translated by Cesare
Salmaggi. Milan: Mondadori, 438 pp.

4   [The Outsider] Pikku jumalat. Translated by Kai Kaila.
Porvoo: Werner Söderström, 490 pp.

5   [The Outsider] Shitsuraku no Kodoku. Translated by Fukuo
Hashimoto. 2 vols. Tokyo: Shinchosha, 660 pp.

6   [The Outsider] Le Transfuge. Translated by Guy de Montlaur.
Paris: Gallimard, 493 pp.

7   [Savage Holiday] Le Dieu de Mascarade. Translated by Jane
Fillion. Paris: Editions Del Duca, 272 pp.

1955

8 [Uncle Tom's Children] Ankuru Tom no Kodomotachi. Translated
   by Sôichi Minagawa. Tokyo: Shinchosha, 266 pp.

NONFICTION

Shorter Writings

Essays

9 ["The Ethics of Living Jim Crow"] "Jim Crow Leveregler."
   København Dagbladet Pølitikens, 22 August, p. 6.

10 ["I Tried to be a Communist."] In Kegalan Tuhan Komunis [The
   God That Failed]. Translated by L. E. Hakim. Bandung:
   Front Antikomunis, 49 pp.

11 ["What is Africa to Me?"] "Que representa Africa para mi?"
   Cuadernos 5, no. 10 (January-February):26-34.

Books

12 [Black Power] Puissance Noire. Translated by Roger Giroux.
   Paris: Corréa, 400 pp.

13 Black Power excerpt. In Africa in the Modern World. Edited
   by George Padmore. Bombay: United Asia Publishers,
   pp. 12-16.
       Letter to Nkrumah.

14 Black Power excerpt. "Ein Neger zum ersten Male in Afrika."
   Die Woche (Berlin) (October):7-10.

15 No entry.

16 [The Color Curtain] Bandoeng, 1,500,000,000 d'hommes. Translated by Hélène Claireau. Paris: Calmann-Lévy, 207 pp.
       Includes "Vers Bandoeng via Seville," "Le congrès des
   hommes de couleur," "Indonesian Notebook," and "Le monde
   occidental à Bandoeng." See 1956.16.

17 The Color Curtain excerpt. "Le congrès des hommes de couleur"
   [The conference of colored people]. Preuves (Paris) 5,
   no. 54 (August):42-48.
       See 1956.16.

18 The Color Curtain excerpt. "De Sevilla a Bandung" [From
   Seville to Bandung]. Cuadernos 5, no. 15 (November-
   December):40-48.
       See 1956.16.

1955

19   The Color Curtain excerpt. "Indonesian Notebook." Encounter
     5 (August):24-31.
     See 1956.16.

20   The Color Curtain excerpt. "Indonesisches Tagesbuch" [Indo-
     nesian Notebook]. Der Monat (Berlin) 7, no. 83 (August):
     378-98; no. 84 (September):495-508.

21   The Color Curtain excerpt. "Le monde occidental à Bandoeng"
     [The western world at Bandung]. Preuves (Paris) 5, no. 55
     (September):45-55.
     See 1956.16.

22   The Color Curtain excerpt. "Vers Bandoeng via Seville" [To
     Bandung through Seville]. Preuves (Paris) 5, no. 53
     (July):6-15.
     See 1956.16.

1956

FICTION

Shorter Writings

1   "The Man Who Lived Underground." In Quintet. New York: Avon
     Publishers (Lion Library), pp. 7-58.
     Cross Section version. Reprint of 1944.5.

2   "The Man Who Lived Underground." Stag Magazine 7 (October):
     28-29, 84-87.
     Cross Section version. Reprint of 1942.3.

Books

3   [Native Son] Son av sitt land. Translated by Eric Palmqvist.
     Stockholm: Bonnier, 415 pp.
     New edition. Serial publication in Frihet (Stockholm)
     (July-September). Reprint of 1940.8.

4   [Savage Holiday] De la inocencia a la pesadilla. Translated
     by León Mirlas. Buenos Aires: Sudamericana, 200 pp.

5   [Savage Holiday] Ma nel settimo giorno. Translated by Cesare
     Salamaggi. Milan: Mondadori, 235 pp.

6   [Uncle Tom's Children] Otroci Strica Toma. Translated by
     Ciril Kosmac. Ljubljana: Mladinska Knjiga, 207 pp.

1956

NONFICTION

Shorter Writings

Essay

7   ["I Tried to be a Communist."] In <u>Kegagalan Tuhan Komunis</u>.
     Djakarta: Timun Mas, 128 pp.
        New edition.

Book Review

8   "Neurosis of Conquest." <u>The Nation</u> 183 (20 October):330-31.
     Review of <u>Prospero and Caliban</u>, by Octave Mannoni.

     Autograph MS: 8 leaves.
     First draft of review, with a few MS additions and correc-
     tions. Alternative title: "White Faces: Agents Provoca-
     teurs of Mankind."
     JWJ Wright Misc. 697.

     Typescript (original): 5 numb. leaves.
     Early working draft, with extensive MS corrections and
     revisions.
     JWJ Wright Misc. 698.

     Another typescript (original): 5 numb. leaves.
     Intermediate draft, with extensive MS corrections.
     JWJ Wright Misc. 699.

     Another typescript (carbon): 1 leaf.
     First leaf only.
     JWJ Wright Misc. 700.

     Another typescript (original), signed: 4 numb. leaves.
     Late draft, with a few MS corrections.
     JWJ Wright Misc. 701.

     "White Faces."
     Another typescript (carbon): 4 numb. leaves.
     Private collection.

Introduction

9   Introduction to <u>Pan-Africanism or Communism</u>, by George
     Padmore. London: Dobson, pp. 11-14.
        Translated and revised as a preface to "Panafricainisme
     ou Communisme?" <u>Présence Africaine</u> (Paris) (10 September
     1960):9-21. See 1960.19.

1956

Another typescript (original): 5 numb. leaves.
Late version, with a few typed corrections. Dated 2 March
1956, Paris.
JWJ Wright Misc. 444.

Another typescript (carbon): 5 numb. leaves.
JWJ Wright Misc. 445.

Typescript (original): 5 numb. leaves.
Final version, with a few typed corrections. Dated
2 March 1956, Paris.
JWJ Wright Misc. 439.

Two carbons of above.
JWJ Wright Misc. 440-441.

Another carbon.
N.Y. Public Library, Schomburg Collection.

Typescript (original): 4 leaves.
Working draft, with MS corrections.
JWJ Wright Misc. 442.

Another typescript (original): 5 numb. leaves.
Intermediate working draft, with MS corrections. Dated
2 March 1956.
JWJ Wright Misc. 443.

Another typescript (original): 5 numb. leaves.
Late version, with a few typed corrections. Dated
2 March 1956, Paris.
JWJ Wright Misc. 444.

Another typescript (carbon): 5 numb. leaves.
JWJ Wright Misc. 445.

Letters

10   "To Axel Lonnquist." New York Herald Tribune (European ed.),
        19 December, p. 8.
           Wright answers Lonnquist, whose complaint about Wright's
        lectures in Scandinavia appeared in New York Herald Tribune,
        17 December, p. 3.

11   "Letter to the Editor." Encounter (April):42.
           A reply to Mochtar Lubis's "Through Colored Glasses."

        Autograph MS: 2 leaves.
        Draft of the letter.
        JWJ Wright Misc. 459.

1956

Paper

12   "Tradition and Industrialization: The Plight of the Tragic
     Elite in Africa." Présence Africaine (Paris) 2, nos. 8-10
     (June-November):347-60.
          Paper given at the First Conference of Black Artists and
     Intellectuals in Paris, September 1956. Same issue also
     prints debates and questions by Wright. Reprinted:
     1957.13.

          Related Material:
     "On Leopold Senghor."
     Typescript (original): 1 leaf.
     Five questions raised at the Black Artists and Writers
     Conference, Paris, September 1956. Concerning statements
     by Senghor on the role of African culture in European
     imperialism.
     JWJ Wright Misc. 506.

Books

13   Black Power. London: Dobson, 358 pp. Illustrated.
          Text differs slightly from U.S. edition. See 1954.14.

14   [Black Power] Schwarze Macht. Translated by Christian Ernst
     Lewalter and Werner von Grünau. Hamburg: Claassen,
     342 pp.

15   [Black Power] Zwarte Kracht. Translated by Margrit de
     Sablonière. Illustrated. Leiden: Sijthoff, 312 pp.

16   The Color Curtain. With a foreword by Gunnar Myrdal. New
     York: World Publishing Co., 221 pp.
          First published in French as Bandoeng, 1,500,000
     d'hommes. Reprinted: 1956.17. See also 1955.16.

     [The Color Curtain: Travel Diary.]
     Typescript (original): 217 leaves.
     Diary written before departure and during trip to Bandung
     conference, Djakarta, Indonesia, 3 February-15 April 1955.
     With extensive MS corrections and revisions on recto and
     verso of leaves. Working title: "Jakarta--Asian and
     African Conference."
     JWJ Wright 80.

     Carbon of above.
     JWJ Wright 81.

[Questionnaire for Jakarta Afro-Asian Conference.]
Typescript (original):   6 leaves.
Working draft (untitled) with author's MS revisions and a
set of replies (2 leaves) marked "Asian Attitudes."
JWJ Wright 82.

Revised drafts: typescript (original and carbon).
Contents: typescript (original) and 4 typescript carbons,
30 leaves; typescript (original) and 5 typescript carbons,
36 leaves; typescript (original) and 4 typescript carbons,
30 leaves; and 5 typescript carbons, 30 leaves.
JWJ Wright 83.

[Notes.]
Typescript and autograph notes: 24 leaves.
Including results of interviews, a plan of organization for
the book and miscellaneous working material.
JWJ Wright 84.

[Gunnar Myrdal.   "Foreword."]
Typescript (carbon):   1 leaf.
Working draft, with MS corrections.
JWJ Wright 85.

Another typescript (original):   1 leaf.
JWJ Wright 86.

Typescript (original):   124 numb. leaves.
Developmental draft based on travel diary notes, with
extensive MS corrections and revisions. Working title:
"Bandung Left and Right."
JWJ Wright 87.

Another typescript (original):   176 numb. leaves.
Another working draft, with MS corrections and revisions.
With miscellaneous deleted material laid in, 12 leaves.
JWJ Wright 88.

Another typescript (carbon):   1 leaf, 186 [i.e., 185] numb.
leaves.
Later working draft, incorporating previous revisions.
JWJ Wright 89.

Carbon of above: 166 leaves.
Incomplete: leaves 147-67 lacking. With some MS notes and
corrections. Title leaf stamped by William Aspenwall
Bradley.
JWJ Wright 90.

Another typescript (original):   1 leaf, 187 numb. leaves.
Intermediate version submitted to Paul Reynolds. Includes
episode from Spanish travels, with quotations from Spanish
journal, deleted from book as published.
JWJ Wright 91.

1956

Setting typescript (original): 184 numb. leaves.
With MS editorial markings, directions, and corrections.
Includes foreword by Gunnar Myrdal.
JWJ Wright 92.

Galley proofs: 1 leaf, 69 numb. leaves.
With MS editorial markings and a few author's corrections.
Dated 21 November 1955.
JWJ Wright 93.

Page proofs: 223 numb. leaves.
JWJ Wright 94.

Another set of proofs: 209 numb. leaves.
Leaves 210-23 lacking. With MS editorial markings.
JWJ Wright 95.

Another set: 50 leaves.
Incomplete set of random leaves.
JWJ Wright 96.

Another set: 53 leaves.
Duplicates of above set, with 3 additional leaves.
JWJ Wright 97.

Advance uncorrected proofs: 137 leaves.
Signed by Margrit de Sablonière.
JWJ Wright 98.

[A summation of ideas in "Impressions of Asian and African
Nationalism."]
Typescript (original): 2 leaves.
First draft, with extensive MS corrections and additions.
JWJ Wright Misc. 768.

Another typescript (original): 2 leaves.
Second draft, with MS corrections.
JWJ Wright Misc. 765.

Another typescript (carbon): 7 numb. leaves.
Final draft.
JWJ Wright Misc. 770.

17   The Colour Curtain. London: Dobson, 188 pp.
          Reprint of 1956.16.

[Autobiographical sketch.]
Typescript (carbon): 1 leaf.
Published in condensed form on dust jacket. Written in
third person.
JWJ Wright Misc. 268.

1956

18   [The Color Curtain] De Kleurbarrière. Translated by Margrit
      de Sablonière. Illustrated. The Hague: Van Hoeve,
      204 pp.

19   Pagan Spain. New York: Harper, 201 pp. [1954-1956]
           Reprinted: 1957.16; 1960.24.

      Typescript (original and carbon) and autograph MS:
      1030 leaves.
      Developmental draft, with extensive MS and typed revisions
      and corrections. In approximate order of published epi-
      sodes.
      JWJ Wright 866[1-3].

      Another typescript (original): 197 leaves.
      Portions of sections 19-48 only. Mostly revised or deleted
      from later version.
      JWJ Wright 867.

      Another typescript (original): 540 leaves.
      Intermediate version, with author's MS corrections and
      revisions, some laid in, others pasted in, and with some
      duplicate leaves.
      JWJ Wright 868.

      Another typescript (original): 608 [i.e., 609] numb.
      leaves.
      Complete copy of revised intermediate version, including
      material deleted in final version. Submitted to John
      Farquharson, Ltd., London publishers.
      JWJ Wright 869.

      Carbon of above, signed: 608 [i.e., 607] numb. leaves.
      JWJ Wright 870.

      Another typescript (original): 557 leaves.
      Final version, with Wright's extensive deletions and revi-
      sions, prepared for publication.
      JWJ Wright 871.

      Related Material:
      "Las Fallas: A Pagan Celebration."
      Typescript (carbon): 12 numb. leaves.
      From his notes on the religious festival of Valencia,
      Spain, taken during 1954-1955 and originally intended for
      inclusion in his Pagan Spain. Early versions of this
      appear in working drafts of his book. With a revised
      introduction, 1 leaf laid in.
      JWJ Wright Misc. 374.

1957

"Spanish Snapshots: Granada and Seville."
Typescript (carbon): 125 numb. leaves.
MS originally intended for inclusion in Pagan Spain.
Chapter 1 was included in the French edition; chapters 7
and 8 were published separately in Two Cities (July 1959).
JWJ Wright Misc. 764.

Same typescript (carbon).
Files of Preuves Magazine, Paris.
Private collection.

1957

FICTION

Shorter Writing

1   "Big Black Good Man." Esquire 50 (November):76-80. [1956]
        Reprinted 1978.1. See also 1961.2.

        Typescript (original): 17 numb. leaves.
        Working draft, with MS corrections.
        JWJ Wright 111.

Books

2   Native Son. With an introduction by W. D. Owens. New York:
        Harper (Modern Classics), 359 pp.
        Reprint of 1940.8.

3   [Native Son] Un Enfant du Pays. Paris: Livre de Poche,
        493 pp.

4   [Uncle Tom's Children] Les Enfants de l'Oncle Tom. Paris:
        Albin Michel, 256 pp.
        Same as 1947 translation of these stories, followed by
        "Là-bas près de la rivière" ["Down by the Riverside"],
        translated by Boris Vian.

5   [Uncle Tom's Children] Onkel Toms Barn. Translated by Bertil
        Lagerström. Stockholm: Bonnier, 238 pp.

6   [Uncle Tom's Children] Onkel Toms Børn. Translated by Kurt
        Kreutzfeld. Copenhagen: Gyldendal, 246 pp.
        Reprinted 1971.16.

1957

NONFICTION

Shorter Writings

Essays

7   "The Ethics of Living Jim Crow." In The Literature of the
     United States. Edited by Walter Blair et al. Glenview,
     Ill.: Scott, Foresman. Rev. ed. in 1 vol.
     See 1937.226.

8   ["I Tried to be a Communist."] In Testimonianze sul Comu-
     nismo (Il dio che è fallito) [The God That Failed]. Trans-
     lated by M. V. Malvano, Giovanni Fei, Anita Rho, and Claudio
     Gorlier. Rev. ed. Milan: Comunità, 382 pp.

9   "The Literature of the Negro in the United States." In White
     Man, Listen! New York: Doubleday, pp. 105-50.
         Expanded and somewhat different version of "Littérature
     noire américaine." See 1948.5; 1957.17.

10   "What You Don't Know Won't Hurt You." In Doctor's Choice.
     Edited by Phyllis and Albert Blaustein. New York: Wilfred
     Funk, pp. 253-60.
         Chosen for inclusion by Drs. Carl and Gerty Cori.
     Reprint of 1942.11.

Book Review

11   "De la Côte de l'Or au Ghana" [From the Gold Coast to Ghana].
     Preuves (Paris) 7, no. 75 (May):11-14.
         Review of Kwame Nkrumah's Autobiography.

     Autograph MS: 5 leaves.
     Working draft of review. Published in French translation
     only. His title: "The Birth of a Man and the Birth of a
     Nation."
     JWJ Wright Misc. 359.

     Typescript (original): 5 leaves.
     Later draft, with author's MS corrections and revisions.
     In English.
     JWJ Wright Misc. 360.

1957

Interview

12   "Les Etats-Unis sont-ils une nation, une loi, une peuple?"
     [Is the United States One Nation, One Law, One People?].
     La Nef (Paris) 7, no. 11 (November):57-60.

     [Interview replies.]
     Typescript (original): 2 leaves.
     Replies to eleven questions concerning his writings.
     Questions lacking.
     JWJ Wright Misc. 422.

Paper

13   "Tradition and Industrialization."   In White Man, Listen!
     New York: Doubleday.
        Reprint of 1956.12.

Books

14   [Black Boy] Black Boy. Translated by Nils Holmberg.
     Stockholm: Bonnier, 256 pp.

15   [Black Power] Crna Snaga. Translated by Ivan Slamnig.
     Zagreb: Zora, 328 pp.

16   Pagan Spain. New York: Harper, 241 pp. [1954]
        Reprint of 1956.19.

17   White Man, Listen! New York: Doubleday, 190 pp.
        Includes slightly revised versions of "Littérature noire
     américaine" (1946), "Tradition and Industrialization, the
     Plight of the Tragic Elite in Africa" (1956), and the
     previously unpublished lectures "The Miracle of Nationalism
     in the African Gold Coast" and "The Psychological Reaction
     of Oppressed People." Reprinted: 1957.18; 1964.10.

     [On Negro literature in the United States.]
     Typescript (original): 6 numb. leaves, 3 leaves.
     Partial draft of a lecture, with MS corrections and addi-
     tions and with typed notes on black authors laid in. An
     expanded version of this appears in White Man, Listen!
     JWJ Wright Misc. 509.

     Typed and autograph MS: 5 numb. leaves, 2 leaves.
     Early partial draft. With miscellaneous background notes
     and outlines, 14 leaves.
     JWJ Wright 969.

99

1957

Typescript (original): 48 numb. leaves.
Working draft, with MS revisions.
JWJ Wright 970.

Another typescript (carbon): 47 numb. leaves.
Another draft, including revisions made above.
JWJ Wright 971.

Miscellaneous typescript leaves (originals and carbons):
14 leaves.
JWJ Wright 972.

Another typescript (original): 51 numb. leaves.
Another copy, with a few MS corrections.
JWJ Wright 973.

Carbon copy: 51 numb. leaves.
With title: "Negro Literature: A Conceptual Approach."
Hand stamped on first leaf by Paul Reynolds.
JWJ Wright 974.

Carbon of above: 6 leaves.
Incomplete copy, leaves 45-50 only.
JWJ Wright 975.

Another typescript (original): 59 numb. leaves.
Revised version, with MS corrections and deletions and with
an expanded conclusion describing literary trends after
1945.
JWJ Wright 976.

Carbon copy (signed): 56 numb. leaves.
Working draft, with additional MS revisions. Lacks new
conclusion.
JWJ Wright 977.

Another typescript (original): 64 numb. leaves.
Later working draft, with MS corrections and revisions.
Additional copy of leaf 44 laid in.
JWJ Wright 978.

Two carbon copies.
JWJ Wright 979-980.

Another typescript (original): 63 leaves.
Working draft of final version, with MS and typed revi-
sions, some pasted or laid in.
JWJ Wright 981.

Three carbon copies.
JWJ Wright 982-984.

1957

"Concepts of Oppressive Reactions."
Typescript (original): 7 leaves.
Definitions of concepts discussed in his lectures on "The
Psychological Reactions of Oppressed People."
JWJ Wright 966.

Typescript (original): 12 numb. leaves.
Incomplete early working draft, with MS additions and
corrections. With title: "White Man, Listen!: The
Miracle of Nationalism in the African Gold Coast."
JWJ Wright 985.

Another typescript (original): 45 numb. leaves.
With a few MS corrections and additions.
JWJ Wright 986.

Another typescript (original): 55 [i.e., 56] numb. leaves.
Intermediate draft, with extensive MS and typed revisions
and additions, many pasted in.
JWJ Wright +987.

Carbon copy: 52 numb. leaves.
Original text of this draft, with author's emendations.
JWJ Wright 988.

Another typescript (original): 65 numb. leaves.
Later draft, with a few MS corrections and revisions.
JWJ Wright 989.

Three carbon copies.
JWJ Wright 990-992.

Typescript (original) and autograph MS: 52 leaves.
Early working drafts of lecture, with extensive MS revisions. Including a draft of introductory remarks. With
title: "White Man, Listen! The Psychological Reactions
of Oppressed People."
JWJ Wright 993.

Another typescript (original): 61 leaves.
Intermediate version, with author's extensive MS revisions,
some pasted in.
JWJ Wright 994.

Carbon of above: 59 leaves.
With MS corrections.
JWJ Wright 995.

Another carbon copy.
JWJ Wright 996.

1957

Another typescript (original): 77 leaves.
Later working draft, incorporating previous revisions and
with additional textual changes. This version is closely
related to published text.
JWJ Wright 997.

Carbon copy: 68 numb. leaves.
Lacks additional textual changes made above.
JWJ Wright 998.

Another carbon copy.
JWJ Wright 999.

Another carbon copy (incomplete): 53 numb. leaves.
JWJ Wright 1000.

Typescript (original): 71 [i.e., 72] numb. leaves.
Expanded version, which combines parts of first and second
chapters, later published in revised form in White Man,
Listen!
JWJ Wright 1001.

Carbon copy.
JWJ Wright 1002.

Another carbon copy: 3 leaves.
Incomplete.
JWJ Wright 1003.

Typescript (original): 9 leaves.
One version of a lecture, with MS corrections and addi-
tions. Incomplete draft. With title: "White Man, Listen!
Tradition and Industrialization. The Plight of the Tragic
Elite in Africa."
JWJ Wright 1005.

Another typescript (original): 29 numb. leaves.
Another version of lecture. Working draft, with MS correc-
tions and additions.
JWJ Wright 1006.

Another typescript (mimeographed copy): 14 numb. leaves.
Same version as above, with author's additional corrections
and his emended title: "The Historic Meaning of the Plight
of the Tragic Elite in Asia and Africa."
JWJ Wright 1007.

Another typescript (carbon): 20 numb. leaves.
Another draft based on text of MS no. 1006. With MS addi-
tions and marginal notes, dated 14 August 1956. His title
inscribed on first leaf: "The Psychological Reactions of
Oppressed People, or White Faces, Agents Provocateurs of
Mankind."
JWJ Wright 1008.

Another typescript (carbon): 37 numb. leaves.
Intermediate version, incorporating above revisions.
JWJ Wright 1009.

Another typescript (original of above): 47 numb. leaves.
Working draft of intermediate version, with extensive
revisions, some pasted in.
JWJ Wright 1010.

Another typescript (original): 50 numb. leaves.
Later draft, with MS revisions, prepared for publication.
JWJ Wright 1011.

Three carbon copies.
JWJ Wright 1012-1014.

See also: "On Leopold Senghor" (unpublished), 1956.12.

Typescript (original): 2 leaves, 5 numb. leaves.
Draft of introduction, with title page and a table of
contents. With MS corrections.
With title: "White Man, Listen: Why and Wherefore. . . ."
JWJ Wright 1015.

Another typescript (original): 2 leaves, 5 numb. leaves.
Revised introduction, with title page and quotation.
JWJ Wright 1016.

Carbon copy: 2 leaves, 5 numb. leaves.
Lacks quotation page, but includes table of contents.
JWJ Wright 1017.

Two other carbons.
JWJ Wright 1018-1019.

[Complete copy.]
Typescript (carbon): 3 leaves, 199 numb. leaves.
Final draft prepared for publication by Doubleday
(c. 1957). Developed from a series of lectures given in
Europe, 1950-1956. With some MS revisions and corrected
leaves laid in, 11 leaves.
JWJ Wright 965.

Related Material:
[Promotional statement.]
Typescript (original): 6 numb. leaves.
Working draft, with MS revisions. Author's statement on
the background and development of his White Man, Listen!
JWJ Wright 967.

18 White Man, Listen! Toronto: Doubleday, 190. pp.
        Reprint of 1957.17.

1957

19 White Man, Listen! excerpt. "This I Believe." Commentary 24
    (November):iv.

20 White Man, Listen! excerpt. Dissent 4 (Fall):358-64.
    Excerpts from "Tradition and Industrialization."

1958

FICTION

Shorter Writing

1 "Big Black Good Man." Translated by Hélène Bokanowski. La
    Parisienne, (January-February):65-76.

Books

2 The Long Dream. New York: Doubleday, 384 pp. [1956-1957]
       Reprinted: 1960.6.

    Typescript (carbon): 7 leaves, 620 numb. leaves.
    Intermediate version incorporating revisions of earlier
    drafts. With miscellaneous revised material (some on typed
    originals of this draft) laid in, 55 leaves.
    JWJ Wright 188[1-2].

    Typescript of second draft.
    N.Y. Public Library, Schomburg Collection.

    Typescript (original) and autograph MS: 1051 leaves.
    First working draft of miscellaneous episodes to be in-
    cluded in the novel. With extensive MS corrections and
    additions and with developmental notes and outlines for
    structure and sequence, 20 leaves.
    JWJ Wright +185[1-2].

    Typescript (original): 23 leaves, 635 numb. leaves.
    With title: "Mississippi."
    Second working draft of The Long Dream, with extensive MS
    corrections and additions. Originally typed on short,
    individual leaves, numbered consecutively by hand stamp.
    With additional notes and revised episodes, 146 leaves.
    JWJ Wright 186[1-3].

    Carbon of above: 667 leaves.
    Incomplete draft, without corrections.
    JWJ Wright 187[1-2].

3 [Savage Holiday] Barbaarse Sabbat. Translated by Margrit de
    Sablonière. Leiden: Sijthoff, 221 pp.

1958

4 [Uncle Tom's Children] Os Filhos do Pai Tomas. Translated by
   Manuel de Seabra. Lisbon: Arcadia.

NONFICTION

Shorter Writings

Interview

5 "Le Noir est une création du Blanc" [The Black is a creation
   of the white man]. Preuves (Paris) 8, no. 87 (May):40-41.
   Answers to questions on black culture and art.

   Typescript (photostatic negative): 8 numb. leaves.
   English text of Wright's responses to questions, dated
   8 October 1957.
   JWJ Wright Misc. 421.

Introduction

6 "Une pièce qui aurait ravi Voltaire" [A play that would have
   delighted Voltaire]. L'Avant-Scène (Paris), no. 168
   (15 February):3-4.
       Introduction to Louis Sapin's Papa Bon Dieu, which
   Wright adapted the same year under the English title Daddy
   Goodness.

   Typescript (carbon): 4 numb. leaves.
   JWJ Wright Misc. 446.

Books

7 [Black Boy] Ich Negerjunge. Frankfurt: Büchergilde Gutenberg,
   330 pp.

8 [Black Boy] Ragazzo Negro. Milan: Mondadori, 272 pp.

9 [Black Boy] Svart Ungdom. Translated by Johan Borgen. Oslo:
   Gyldendal, 232 pp.

10 Black Boy excerpt. In The Book of Negro Folklore. Edited by
    Langston Hughes and Arna Bontemps. New York: Dodd & Mead,
    pp. 568-70.
        Sunday dinner passage.

11 Black Power excerpt. In Pageant of Ghana. Edited by
    Frederick Wolfson. London: Oxford University Press,
    pp. 252-53.
        Excerpts on Kumasi market and the spell of Africa.

1958

12   [Pagan Spain] Espagne Païenne. Translated by Roger Giroux.
     Paris: Buchet-Chastel-Corréa, 339 pp.

     Related Material:
     [Blurb for Pagan Spain.]
     Typescript (carbon): 1 leaf.
     For bookjacket.
     JWJ Wright Misc. 331.

     Another carbon.
     JWJ Wright Misc. 332.

13   [Pagan Spain] Det Hedniska Spanien. Translated by Staffan
     Andrae. Stockholm: Bonnier, 270 pp.

14   [Pagan Spain] Heidens Spanje. Translated by Margrit de
     Sablonière. Bussum: Kroonder, 233 pp.

15   [Pagan Spain] Heidens Spanje. Berchem-Antwerp: Internatio-
     nale Pres., 239 pp.

16   [Pagan Spain] Heidnisches Spanien. Translated by Werner von
     Grünau. Hamburg: Claassen-Verlag, 336 pp.

17   Pagan Spain excerpt. "Das grüne Büch der rebellischen
     Fraülein Carmen." Die Zeit, 3 November, pp. 21-24.

18   White Man, Listen! excerpt. "Homme Blanc, écoute!" Lettres
     Nouvelles (Paris) 6, no. 64 (October):338-53.

1959

FICTION

Books

1   [The Long Dream] Den långa Drömmen. Translated by Pelle
     Fritz-Crone. Stockholm: Bonnier, 441 pp.

2   [The Long Dream] Den lange drøm. Translated by Kurt
     Kreutzfeld. Copenhagen: Gyldendal, 340 pp.

3   [The Long Dream] De lange droom. Translated by Margrit de
     Sablonière. Leiden: Sijthoff, 380 pp.

4   Native Son. New York: New American Library (Signet), 400 pp.
     Reprint of 1940.8.

1959

5   [Native Son] Søn af de sorte. Translated by Tom Kristensen.
     Copenhagen: Gyldendal, 432 pp.

NONFICTION

Shorter Writings

Essays

6   "I Tried to be a Communist." In The God That Failed. Edited
     by Richard Crossman. New York: Bantam Books.
     Reprint of 1944.7.

7   ["Tradition and Industrialization"] In [White Man, Listen!]
     Razza: humana. Translated by Attilio Laudi. Milan:
     Il Saggiatore, 63 pp.

8   [Black Boy] Ragazzo Negro. Milan: Mondadori, 421 pp.

9   Pagan Spain excerpt. "Christ lebt im Untergrund" [On
     Protestantism in Spain]. Vorwärts (Bonn), 6 March,
     pp. 7-8.

10   Pagan Spain excerpt. "Fallas in Valencia." Illuspress
     (January):5 ff.
          From original MS of Pagan Spain; never published
     elsewhere.

11   Pagan Spain excerpt. "Spanish Snapshots: Granada, Seville."
     Two Cities (Paris), no. 2 (15 July):25-34. [1954-1955]
          Parts of unpublished section of Pagan Spain.

12   Pagan Spain excerpt. "Uralte Fastnachtsbrauche." Illuspress
     (May):5.
          Unpublished part of Pagan Spain, "Las Fallas."

13   [White Man, Listen!] Ecoute, homme blanc. Translated by
     Dominique Guillet. Paris: Calmann-Lévy, 229 pp.
          Includes a preface entitled "Avis au lecteur français"
     [Advice to the French reader], written by Wright in
     February 1959.

     Typescript (carbon): 8 numb. leaves.
     Concerning the rise of black nationalism in Africa. Dated
     February 1959.
     JWJ Wright 968.

     Private collection. Carbon copy.

1959

14   [White Man, Listen!] Escucha, hombre blanco! Translated by
      Floreal Mazía. Buenos Aires: Sudamericana, 177 pp.

1960

FICTION

Shorter Writings

1   "Almos' a Man." In Eight Men. New York: World Publishing
     Co., pp. 11-26.
     Slightly revised version of "The Man Who Was Almost a
     Man." See 1940.1.

2   ["Bright and Morning Star"; "Down by the Riverside"] Kagayaku
     ake no myojo; Dakuryu. Translated by Kenji Kobayashi and
     Katsuji Takamura. Tokyo: Nan'un-do, 134 pp.

3   "The Man Who Killed a Shadow." In Eight Men. New York:
     World Publishing Co., pp. 193-209.
     Reprinted: 1968.2. See also 1949.3.

4   "The Man Who Lived Underground." In Eight Men. New York:
     World Publishing Co., pp. 27-92.
     With slight changes in punctuation and phrasing Cross
     Section version. See 1944.5.

Books

5   Eight Men. New York: World Publishing Co., 250 pp.
         Reprinted: 1961.7-8; 1962.2; 1969.5.

6   The Long Dream. London: Angus & Robertson, 359 pp.
         Reprint of 1958.2.

7   [The Long Dream] Fishbelly. Translated by Hélène Bokanowski.
     Paris: Julliard, 436 pp.
         Includes portrait of Wright by Monique Métrôt and
     interview with Wright by Maurice Nadeau.

8   [The Long Dream] El largo sueno. Translated by Floreal Mazía.
     Buenos Aires: Sudamericana, 520 pp.

9   [The Long Dream] Pitkä Uni. Translated by Seppo Virtanen.
     Porvoo: Werner Söderström, 435 pp.

1960

10 [The Long Dream] Der schwarze Traum. Translated by Werner
   von Grünau. Hamburg: Claassen Verlag, 448 pp.

11 The Long Dream excerpt. "Fishbelly." Translated by Hélène
   Bokanowski. Pour l'art, no. 72 (May-June):20-25.
   Passage from chapter 8.

12 [Native Son] O Filho Nativo. Translated by Daniel Gonçalves.
   Lisbon: Ulisseia, 493 pp.

13 [Uncle Tom's Children] I figli dello zio Tom. Milan:
   Mondadori, 240 pp.

NONFICTION

Shorter Writings

Essays

14 "L'art est mis en question par l'âge atomique" [Art is called
   into question by the atomic age]. Arts, Lettres, Spec-
   tacles (Paris), 5 June, pp. 1, 4.

15 "The Ethics of Living Jim Crow." In The Experience of Prose.
   Edited by Walter B. Rideout. New York: Thomas Crowell,
   pp. 485-95.
       Reprint of 1937.226.

16 "Harlem." Les Parisiens, no. 1 (December):23.

   Autograph MS signed: 7 numb. leaves.
   Under title: "Harlem Is Human."
   JWJ Wright Misc. 402.

Book Review

17 "The Voiceless Ones." Saturday Review of Literature 43
   (16 April):53-54.
       Review of The Disinherited, by Michel Del Castillo.

   Typescript (carbon): 6 numb. leaves.
   Under title: "Locomotives of History."
   JWJ Wright Misc. 694.

1960

Introductions

18 Foreword to Blues Fell This Morning, by Paul Oliver. London:
   Horizon Press, pp. vii–xii.
      Reprinted: 1963.7.

   Typescript (original): 7 leaves.
   Working draft, with MS revisions and corrections. First
   leaf lacking.
   JWJ Wright Misc. 379.

   Another typescript (original): 7 numb. leaves.
   Intermediate draft, with MS corrections pasted in.
   JWJ Wright Misc. 380.

   Carbon copy.
   JWJ Wright Misc. 381.

   Another typescript (carbon): 7 numb. leaves.
   JWJ Wright Misc. 382.

   Another typescript (carbon): 7 numb. leaves.
   Published version, marked "uncorrected." Dated February
   1959, Paris.
   JWJ Wright Misc. 383.

   Carbon copy.
   JWJ Wright Misc. 384.

   Typescript (original): 5 numb. leaves.
   Final version, with a few typed corrections. Dated
   2 March 1956, Paris.
   JWJ Wright Misc. 439.

   Two carbons of above.
   JWJ Wright Misc. 440–441.

   Another carbon.
   N.Y. Public Library, Schomburg Collection.

19 Preface to "Panafricainisme ou Communisme?" by George Padmore.
   Présence Africaine (Paris) (10 September 1960):9–21.
      See 1956.9.

Liner Notes

20 "The Past Is Still With Us." Liner notes for recording of
   "Les Rois du Caf' Conc'" [Café Concert], by Luc Barney.
   Barclay Album 80128. [1960]

   Typescript (original): 3 numb. leaves.
   Published in French translation.
   JWJ Wright Misc. 308.

1961

Carbon copy.
JWJ Wright Misc. 309.

21   "So Long, Big Bill Broonzy." Liner notes for recording of
     "The Blues of Big Bill Broonzy." Mercury Album no. 7109.
     [1960, unsigned]

     Typescript (original):   5 numb. leaves.
     JWJ Wright Misc. 316.

     Carbon of above.
     JWJ Wright Misc. 317.

Books

22   [Black Boy] Heug'in Sonyeon. Translated by Jo Jeong-ho.
     Seoul: Bagyeongsa, 271 pp.

23   [Black Power] Crna Sila. Translated by Dusan Savnik.
     Ljubljana: Drzavna zalozba Slovenije, 342 pp.

24   Pagan Spain. London: The Bodley Head, 192 pp.
          Reprint of 1956.19.

25   Pagan Spain excerpt. "Espagne Payenne." Haute Société, no. 3
     (November):34-38. [1955]
          On Spanish festivals. Part of original MS.

26   Pagan Spain excerpt. "Die politische Katechismus" [The Polit-
     ical Catechism]. Die Deutsche Post, 5 January, pp. 18-19.

1961

FICTION

Shorter Writings

1   "Almos' a Man." In Strange Barriers. New York: Pyramid
     Books, pp. 116-28.
          Reprint of 1940.1.

2   "Big Black Good Man." In Eight Men. New York: World Pub-
     lishing Co., pp. 93-109.
          A revised version, with some important changes. See
     1957.1.

111

1961

3   ["Early Days in Chicago."] "The Man Who Went to Chicago."   In
    Eight Men. New York: World Publishing Co.
    See 1945.3; 1961.7.

4   "The Man Who Lived Underground." In Quintet.   New York:
    Pyramid Books.
    Reprint of 1944.5.

5   ["The Man Who Saw the Flood"] "Der Mann, der das Hochwasser
    sah."   Die Deutsche Zeitung, 23-24 September, p. 22.

6   ["Silt."]   "The Man Who Saw the Flood." In Eight Men.   New
    York: World Publishing Co., pp. 110-17.
    Appeared here for the first time under the title by
    which the story is now known.   See 1937.1.

Books

7   Eight Men.   New York: World Publishing Co., 250 pp.
    Includes: "The Man Who Went to Chicago" (see "Early
    Days in Chicago," 1945.3); "The Man Who Saw the Flood"
    (see "Silt," 1937.1); "The Man Who Was Almost a Man" (see
    "Almos' a Man," 1941.3); "Big Black Good Man" (see 1957.1);
    "Man, God Ain't Like That" [1958]; "Man of All Work" [1957];
    "The Man Who Lived Underground" (see 1945.5); "The Man Who
    Killed a Shadow" (see 1946.4).   The collection was prepared
    by Wright in 1960.   Reprint of 1960.5.

    Page proofs: 83 leaves.
    With title leaf from a typescript submitted to John
    Farquharson, Ltd., and Wright's notes for titles: 2 leaves.
    JWJ Wright 110.

    "Big Black Good Man."
    Typescript (original):   21 numb. leaves.
    Later working draft, with MS corrections and typed
    revisions.
    JWJ Wright 112.

    Another typescript (carbon):   20 numb. leaves.
    Incorporating above corrections.
    JWJ Wright 113.

    Carbon of above.
    JWJ Wright 114.

    Another typescript (carbon):   21 numb. leaves.
    Final copy.
    JWJ Wright 115.

Carbon of above.
JWJ Wright 116.

"Man, God Ain't Like That."
Typescript (original): 66 numb. leaves.
Early working draft, with extensive MS revisions. And an
epilogue, 2 leaves.
JWJ Wright 117.

Another typescript (original): 42 numb. leaves.
Working draft, with MS revisions; on blue paper.
JWJ Wright 118.

Carbon of above.
With some MS corrections.
JWJ Wright 119.

Another typescript (original): 1 leaf, 32 numb. leaves.
Intermediate working draft, with extensive MS revisions.
JWJ Wright 120.

Carbon of above.
JWJ Wright 121.

Another typescript (carbon): 1 leaf, 33 numb. leaves.
Revised version.
JWJ Wright 122.

Another typescript (carbon): 1 leaf, 33 numb. leaves.
With 4 miscellaneous leaves deleted from other drafts.
JWJ Wright 123.

Another typescript (carbon): 1 leaf, 37 numb. leaves.
Final copy prepared for publication.
JWJ Wright 124.

Carbon of above: 3 leaves.
Leaves 18, 21, and 32 only.
JWJ Wright 125.

"Man of All Work."
Typescript (original): 51 numb. leaves.
Working draft, with extensive MS revisions and corrections.
JWJ Wright 126.

Carbon of above.
Unrevised copy.
JWJ Wright 127.

Another typescript (carbon): 1 leaf, 51 numb. leaves.
Another copy, with his subtitle "Bonne à toute faire, [Maid
of all work] a radio play." Submitted to his agent, Paul
Reynolds.
JWJ Wright 128.

1961

Two additional carbon copies of above.
JWJ Wright 129.[1-2]

"The Man Who Saw the Flood."
Another typescript (carbon): 7 numb. leaves.
With revised title and introductory haiku.
JWJ Wright 145.

Another typescript (carbon): 1 leaf, 9 numb. leaves.
Final copy, with title leaf.
JWJ Wright 146.

Carbon of above.
See "Silt," 1937.1.
JWJ Wright 147.

"The Man Who Was Almost a Man."
Typescript (original): 18 numb. leaves.
Later version.
JWJ Wright 150.

Carbon of above.
JWJ Wright 151.

Another typescript (carbon): 17 numb. leaves.
JWJ Wright 152.

Another typescript (carbon): 19 numb. leaves.
With a few typed corrections.
JWJ Wright 153.

Carbon of above.
See "Almos' a Man," 1941.3
JWJ Wright 154.

"The Man Who Went to Chicago."
Typescript (carbon): 1 leaf, 54 numb. leaves.
Final copy prepared for publication in Eight Men.
JWJ Wright 158.

Carbon of above.
With revised leaves laid in, 2 leaves.
JWJ Wright 159.

See "Early Days in Chicago," 1945.3.
JWJ Wright 155-157.

8   Eight Men. Toronto: Nelson, 250 pp.
        Reprint of 1960.5.

9   [Eight Men] Nuancer i Sort. Translated by Jorgen Årup Hansen.
        Copenhagen: Spektrum, 253 pp.

10   [The Long Dream] Den langa Drommen. Translated by Pelle
        Fritz-Crone. Stockholm: Bonnier, 476 pp.

11   Native Son. With an afterword by R. Sullivan. New York: New
        American Library (Signet Classic), 399 pp.
            Reprint of 1940.8.

NONFICTION

Shorter Writings

Essay

12   ["The Literature of the Negro in the United States"] "La
        letteratura negra negli Stati Uniti." Translated by
        A. Laudi. Milan: Il Saggiatore, 87 pp.

Introduction

13   Introduction to Tant qu'il y aura la peur, by Françoise
        Gourdon. Paris: Flammarion, pp. 1-3. [1960]
            Published in French.

        Typescript (original): 5 numb. leaves.
        Dated Paris, 1960.
        JWJ Wright Misc. 429.

        Another typescript (carbon): 4 numb. leaves.
        Another version, with revised duplicate of leaf 4 and
        another draft of it laid in, 2 leaves.
        JWJ Wright Misc. 430.

Liner Notes

14   "Hommage à Quincy Jones." Les Cahiers du Jazz, no. 4 (Spring):
        53-54.
            Translation of a piece written as liner notes for a
        record by Quincy Jones, preceded by a two-page interview
        with Wright entitled "Le jazz et le désir."

        "Another Heroic Beginning."
        Typescript (carbon): 4 numb. leaves.
        JWJ Wright 245.

Books

15   Black Boy. New York: New American Library, 201 pp.
            Reprint of 1945.22.

1961

16   [Black Boy] Ben Ha-Kushim. Translated by Noah Stern.
     Tel-Aviv: Am 'Oved, 240 pp.

17   [Black Boy] Sort Ungdom. Translated by Tom Kristensen.
     Copenhagen: Gyldendal, 247 pp.

18   [White Man, Listen!] Blanke, luister toch! Translated and
     with an introduction by Margrit de Sablonière. Bussum:
     Kroonder, 194 pp.

19   White Man, Listen! excerpt. In Die psychologische Lage unter-
     drückter Völker [The Psychological Reactions of Oppressed
     People]. Munich: Ner-Tamid Verlag, 45 pp.

POETRY

20   [Haiku poems.]   In "The Last Days of Richard Wright," by
     Ollie Harrington. Ebony, (16 February):93-94.
          Includes: (1) "I am Nobody." (2) "Make up Your Mind,
     Snail," (3) "In the Falling Snow," (4) "Keep Straight Down
     this Block," (5) "With a Twitching Nose," (6) "The Spring
     Lingers On," (7) "Whose Town Did You Leave," (8) "The Crow
     Flew so Fast." Reprinted 1963.10.

1962

FICTION

Shorter Writing

1   ["The Man Who Saw the Flood"] "Der Mann, der das Hochwasser
    sah." Die Westphalische Rundschau, 12-13 May, pp. 4-5.
    [Unverified]

Books

2   Eight Men. New York: Avon Publications, 191 pp.
         Reprint of 1960.5.

3   [Eight Men] Acht mannen. Translated and with an introduction
        by Margrit de Sablonière. Bussum: F. G. Kroonder, 209 pp.

4   [Eight Men] Ocho Hombres. Translated by León Mirlas. Buenos
        Aires: Sudamericana, 299 pp.

1963

5   [Eight Men] Der Mann, der nach Chicago ging. Translated by
    Enzio von Cramon and Erich Fried. Hamburg: Claassen
    Verlag, 265 pp.

6   [The Long Dream] Il lungo sogno. Translated by Maria Luisa
    Cipriani Fagiola. Milan: Mondadori, 412 pp.

7   [The Long Dream] Sanje Nekega. Translated by Mira Mihelic.
    Ljubljana: Cankarjeva zalozba, 463 pp.   [Unverified]

8   Native Son excerpt.   In The Angry Black.   Edited by John A.
    Williams.   New York: Lancer Books, pp. 142-60.
    "The Plea."

9   [Savage Holiday] Våldsam Weekend. Translated by Staffan
    Andrae. Stockholm: Bonnier, 217 pp.

NONFICTION

Books

10 [Black Boy] Burakku Boi. Translated by Takashi Nozaki.
    2 vols. Tokyo: Iwanami Shoten.

11 Black Boy. Paris: Livre de Poche, 437 pp.

12 [Black Boy] Mi Vida en Negro. Translated by Clara Diament.
    Buenos Aires: Sudamericana, 229 pp.

13 [Pagan Spain] Spagna pagana. Translated by Guiliana De Carlo.
    Milan: Mondadori, 444 pp.

                            1963

FICTION

Shorter Writings

1   "Five Episodes."   In Soon, One Morning.   Edited by Herbert
    Hill.   New York: Knopf, pp. 149-64.
        Excerpts from "Island of Hallucinations," an unpublished
    novel completed in 1959. Reprinted 1964.2.

    ["Island of Hallucinations"]:   Five Episodes From an Un-
    published Novel.
    Typescript (carbon):   34 leaves.
    Episodes from chapters 15, 16, 35, 37, and 38. Typescript

1963

prepared for publication by Ellen Wright. With an
addressed envelope.
JWJ Wright Misc. 453.

Typescript (carbon): 9 numb. leaves.
Working draft of concluding chapter. With miscellaneous
deleted leaves laid in, 9 leaves.
JWJ Wright 189.

Another carbon of concluding chapter: 12 numb. leaves.
JWJ Wright 190.

Another typescript (original and carbon): 2 leaves,
767 numb. leaves.
Late draft submitted to Paul Reynolds.
JWJ Wright 191[1-2].

Typescript (original and carbon) of above: 3 leaves,
767 numb. leaves.
With author's extensive MS revisions and corrections
incorporating suggestions by Edward Aswell, his editor in
his typed letter, signed, to Wright, 23 December 1957.
JWJ Wright 192[1-2].

Another typescript (original): 76 numb. leaves.
Incomplete copy, incorporating corrections in preceding
draft and with additional corrections.
JWJ Wright 193.

Two carbons of above.
JWJ Wright 194[1-2].

Books

2   [Eight Men] Huit Hommes. Translated by J. Bernard. Paris:
    Julliard, 254 pp.

3   Lawd Today. New York: Walker, 189 pp.

Typescript (original): 252 leaves.
Working draft, with author's MS corrections and revisions,
some pasted in and with leaves from earlier version, entitled "3344," laid in. With miscellaneous typed and
autograph working notes, 26 leaves.
JWJ Wright 179.

Another typescript (original): 274 numb. leaves.
Final version.
JWJ Wright 180.

Carbon of above.
JWJ Wright 181.

Setting typescript (original): 2 leaves, 288 numb. leaves.
With MS editorial markings. Published in 1963.
JWJ Wright 182.
See "3344, A Play in 3 Acts," U.29.
Unpublished MS.
JWJ Wright +184.

Typescript (carbon): 4 leaves.
Leaves 116-19 of the early version of Lawd Today, developed
in 1936. Under title, "Cesspool." With author's MS marginal notes.
JWJ Wright 183.

4   [The Long Dream] Der schwarze Traum. Zürich: Buchclub Ex
    Libris, 487 pp.

5   [Native Son] Domorodac. 2 vols. Sarajevo: Svjetlost.

6   [Native Son] Søn af de sorte. Translated by Tom Kristensen.
    Copenhagen: Gyldendal, 410 pp.

NONFICTION

Shorter Writing

Introduction

7   Foreword to Blues Fell This Morning: The Making of the Blues,
    by Paul Oliver. New York: Collier, pp. 7-12.
    Reprint of 1960.18.

Book

8   Black Boy. New York: New American Library, 285 pp.
    Reprint of 1945.22.

POETRY

9   "Between the World and Me." In American Negro Poetry.
    Edited by Arna Bontemps. New York: Hill & Wang, p. 103.
    Reprint of 1935.3.

10 Haiku poems. In American Negro Poetry. Edited by Arna
    Bontemps. New York: Hill & Wang, p. 104.
    Haiku nos. 1, 2, 3, 4, 5, 6, 7, and 8. Reprint of
    1961.20.

1964

1964

FICTION

Shorter Writings

1   "Big Black Good Man." In Big Black Good Man. Edited by
    Tomoshichi Konishi. Osaka: Daigkusha, 114 pp.
    Also includes "Man of all Work."

2   "Five Episodes." In Black Voices. Edited by Herbert Hill.
    London: Elek Books, pp. 139-64. [1959]
    From the unpublished novel "Island of Hallucinations."
    Reprint of 1963.1.

Books

3   Eight Men excerpt. In Man of All Work. Edited by I. Sekiguchi
    and T. Hamamoto. Kyoto: Appolon-Sha, 86 pp.

4   [Lawd Today] ¡Que dia Señor! Translated by León Mirlas.
    Buenos Aires: Sudamericana, 288 pp.

5   [The Long Dream] Der schwarze Traum. Frankfurt on the Main:
    Büchergilde Gutenberg, 464 pp.

6   Native Son. With an afterword by Theodore Solotaroff. New
    York: New World Library, 394 pp.
    Reprint of 1940.8.

7   [Native Son] Son av sitt land. Translated by Gösta Olson.
    Stockholm: Aldus/Bonnier, 378 pp.

8   [Uncle Tom's Children] Abna' al 'Amm Tom. Translated by
    Munir Ba'abaki. Beirut: Al-Maktabah al-Ahliyah, 221 pp.

NONFICTION

Books

9   [Pagan Spain] Spagna pagana. Translated by Giuliana DeCarlo.
    Milan: Mondadori, 372 pp.

10 White Man, Listen! With an introduction by John A. Williams.
    Garden City, N.J.: Anchor Books, 137 pp.
    Reprint of 1957.17.

1965

POETRY

11   "I Have Seen Black Hands." Labor's Independent Weekly Tribune
      28 (1 May):1.
      Reprint of 1934.3.

                              1965

FICTION

Shorter Writings

1   "Almos' a Man." In Come Out of the Wilderness. Edited by
     M. L. Schuman. n.p., pp. 107-19. [Unverified]
     Reprint of 1940.1.

2   "Bright and Morning Star." In Fifty Best American Short
     Stories, 1915-1965. Edited by Martha Foley. Boston:
     Houghton Mifflin, pp. 214-46.
     Reprint of 1938.2.

Books

3   [Lawd Today] Bon Sang de Bonsoir. Translated and with a
     preface by Hélène Bokanowski. Paris: Mercure de France,
     267 pp.

4   [Lawd Today] Glad Dag i Chicago. Copenhagen: Gyldendal,
     244 pp.

5   [Lawd Today] Heer, wat een dag! Translated by Margrit de
     Sablonière. Bussum: Kroonder, 229 pp.

6   [Lawd Today] I Dag, Herre! Translated and with an introduc-
     tion by Maj and Paul Frisch. Stockholm: Rabén and
     Sjögren, 276 pp.

7   [Native Son] Ragazzo Negro. Milan: Mondadori, 336 pp.

8   The Outsider. New York: Harper & Row (Perennial Library),
     440 pp.
     Reprint of 1953.1.

                              121

1965

NONFICTION

Shorter Writings

Essays

9   "I Tried to Be a Communist." In The God that Failed. Edited
    by Richard Crossman. New York: Bantam Books, pp. 115-62.
    Reprint of 1944.7.

10 "I Tried to Be a Communist." In The God that Failed. Edited
    by Hiroshi Edinzuka. Yamagushi: Shoten, 77 pp.

11 ["I Tried to Be a Communist."] In Le Dieu des Ténèbres [The
    God that Failed]. Abridged ed. Paris: Seghers, Nouveaux
    Horizons, pp. 162-218.

Book

12 Black Boy excerpt. In Introduction to Non-Fiction. Edited by
    John R. Ascott. Wichita: McCormick-Mathers, pp. 10-17.
    "Hunger."

                              1966

FICTION

Shorter Writing

1   "Bright and Morning Star." In American Negro Short Stories.
    Edited by John H. Clarke. New York: Hill & Wang,
    pp. 75-107.
    Reprint of 1938.2.

Books

2   Eight Men excerpt. In Der Mann, der nach Chicago ging.
    Frankfurt on the Main: Fischer Bücherei, 235 pp.

3   [The Long Dream] Dlugi Sen. Translated by Zophia Klinger and
    Krzysztof Klinger. Warsaw: Czytelnik, 665 pp.

4   Native Son. With an afterword by John M. Reilly. New York:
    Harper & Row (Perennial Classics), 398 pp.
    Reprint of 1940.8.

                              122

1966

5   [Native Son] Filho Nativo. Translated by Monteiro Lobato.
     Sao Paolo: Cia. Edit. Nacional, 376 pp.

6   [Native Son] Søn af de sorte. Translated by Tom Kristensen.
     Copenhagen: Gyldendal, 416 pp.

7   Native Son excerpt. In Beyond the Angry Black. Edited by
     John A. Williams. New York: Cooper Square Publishing,
     pp. 174-91.
     "The Plea."

8   [The Outsider] Der Mörder und die Schuldigen. Translated by
     Ruth Malchow-Huth. Hamburg: Claassen Verlag, 486 pp.

9   [Uncle Tom's Children] De kinderen van Oom Tom. Translated by
     Margrit de Sablonière. Hilversum: Kroonder, 282 pp.

NONFICTION

Shorter Writing

Essay

10 "What You Don't Know Won't Hurt You." In The Book of Negro
     Humor. Edited by Langston Hughes. New York: Dodd, Mead,
     pp. 242-51.
     Reprint of 1942.11.

Books

11 Black Boy. With an afterword by John M. Reilly. New York:
     Harper & Row (Perennial Classic), 285 pp.
     Reprint of 1945.22.

12 Black Boy. Edited by Taiyosha Editorial Dept. Abridged ed.
     Tokyo: Taiyosha Press, 106 pp.

13 [Black Boy] Sort Ungdom. Translated by Tom Kristensen.
     Copenhagen: Gyldendal, 256 pp.

14 [Black Boy]. Musta Poika. Porvoo: Werner Söderström,
     268 pp.

15 Black Boy excerpt. In Gateway English. Edited by Robert F.
     Beauchamps et al. New York: Macmillan, p. 13.
     "Valedictorian."

1967

1967

FICTION

Shorter Writing

1   "Almos' a Man." The Best Short Stories by Negro Writers.
     Edited by Langston Hughes. Little, Brown, pp. 91-104.
     Reprint of 1940.1.

Books

2   The Long Dream excerpt. In Les Noirs Américains. Edited by
     Michel Fabre. Paris: A. Colin, pp. 237-42.
     Dancing fire funeral.

3   Native Son excerpt. In Les Noirs Américains. Edited by
     Michel Fabre. Paris: A. Colin, pp. 187-93, 221-24.
     Killing the rat; Bigger fights Gus.

4   Native Son excerpt. In The Outnumbered. Edited by Charlotte
     Brooks. New York: Delacorte Press, pp. 145-56.
     "Fate," first pages.

5   [Uncle Tom's Children] Onkel Toms Kinder. East Berlin:
     Verlag Volk und Welt, 274 pp.

NONFICTION

Shorter Writing

Essay

6   "The Ethics of Living Jim Crow." In In Their Own Words.
     Edited by Milton Meltzer. New York: Thomas Y. Crowell,
     pp. 6-14.
     "My First Lesson." Reprint of 1937.226.

Books

7   Black Boy excerpt. In Education in the Metropolis. Edited
     by Harry L. Miller and Marjorie Smiley. New York:
     Macmillan (The Free Press), pp. 27-32.
     "Hunger."

8   Twelve Million Black Voices excerpt. In In Their Own Words.
     Edited by Milton Meltzer. New York: Thomas Y. Crowell,
     pp. 16-22.
     "The One Room Kitchenette."

1968

POETRY

9   ["Between the World and Me."]   In <u>Les Noirs Américains</u>.
     Edited by Michel Fabre. Paris: A. Colin, pp. 208-10.

10   Haiku poems excerpt. In <u>Poems to Enjoy</u>. Edited by Dorothy
     Pettit. New York: Macmillan, p. 93.
     Haiku no. 3.

                              1968

FICTION

<u>Shorter Writings</u>

1   "Bright and Morning Star." <u>Negro Digest</u> 18 (December):53-77.
     Reprint of 1938.2.

2   "The Man Who Killed a Shadow." In <u>Dark Symphony</u>. Edited by
     James A. Emanuel and Theodore L. Gross. New York:
     Macmillan (The Free Press), pp. 227-37.
     Reprint of 1960.3.

3   "The Man Who Lived Underground." In <u>Black Voices</u>. Edited by
     Abraham Chapman. New York: New American Library (Mentor
     Books), pp. 114-60.
     Reprint of 1944.5.

<u>Books</u>

4   <u>Native Son</u> excerpt. In <u>Illinois Prose Writers</u>. Edited by
     Howard Webb, Jr. Carbondale: Southern Illinois University
     Press, pp. 3-12.
     Beginning of novel.

5   <u>Native Son</u> excerpt. In <u>Point of View</u>. Edited by Nancy
     Lighthall. Vol. 3. Chicago: Follett Publishing Co.,
     pp. 63-92.
     "Flight."

1968

NONFICTION

Shorter Writings

Essays

6   "The Ethics of Living Jim Crow." In Dark Symphony. Edited by
    James A. Emanuel and Theodore L. Gross. New York:
    Macmillan (The Free Press), pp. 238-48.
    Reprint of 1937.226.

7   "How 'Bigger' was Born." In Black Voices. Edited by Abraham
    Chapman. New York: New American Library, pp. 538-63.
    Reprint of 1942.7.

Letters

8   "Letters to Joe C. Brown." Edited by Thomas Knipp. Kent,
    Ohio: Kent State University Libraries, 16 pp.
        An unauthorized edition whose circulation has been pro-
    hibited by Mrs. Ellen Wright. Includes eight letters from
    1938 to 1941. Another MS in Kent State University Library
    contains ten letters.

Books

9   Black Boy. Abridged ed. Edited by Kenishi Sato. N.p.:
    Hoyamma, 98 pp. [Unverified]

10 [Black Boy] Al-Walad Al-'Aswād. Translated by Tumādir Tawfiq.
    Cairo: Dār-al m'arif, 356 pp.

11 [Black Boy] Kara Coçuk. Translated by Hasan Aslan.
    Istanbul: Yaylacik Mataasi, 274 pp.

12 [Black Boy] Um Negro que quis viver. Translated by Luisa
    Sampaio. Lisbon: Ulisseia, 417 pp.

13 Black Boy excerpt. In At Your Own Risk. Edited by Charlotte
    Brooks and Lawana Trout. New York: Holt, Rinehart &
    Winston, pp. 1-3.
    "At School."

14 Black Boy excerpt. In Biography. Edited by Paul R. Craven.
    Belmont, Calif.: Dickenson Publishing Corp., pp. 37-43,
    214-21.

Richard Wright's Published Works

1969

15 <u>Black Boy</u> excerpt. In <u>Growing Up Black</u>. Edited by Jay David.
   New York: William Morrow, pp. 235-40.
   Uncle Hoskins episode.

16 <u>Black Boy</u> excerpt. In <u>The Negro in the City</u>. Edited by
   Gerard Leinward. New York: Washington Square Press,
   pp. 77-81.
   Last pages.

POETRY

17 "Between the World and Me." In <u>Black Voices</u>. Edited by
   Abraham Chapman. New York: New American Library,
   pp. 436-37.
   Reprint of 1935.3.

18 Haiku poem excerpt. In <u>Poetry USA</u>. Edited by Paul Molloy.
   New York: Scholastic Book Services, p. 91.
   Haiku no. 3.

19 Haiku poem. In <u>Way Out--A Thematic Reader</u>. Edited by Lois
   Mitchell. New York: Holt, Rinehart & Winston, p. 163.
   Includes haiku nos. 2, 3, 5, and 7.

20 Haiku poem. In <u>Intergroup Relations in the Classroom</u>.
   Edited by Charlotte Epstein. Boston: Houghton Mifflin,
   p. 194.
   Haiku no. 1.

1969

FICTION

Shorter Writings

1 "Almos' a Man." In <u>Black American Literature: Fiction</u>.
   Edited by Darwin T. Turner. Columbus, Ohio: Charles E.
   Merrill, pp. 72-85.
   Reprint of 1940.1.

2 "Big Boy Leaves Home." In <u>Modern American Classics</u>. Edited
   by David R. Winer. New York: Random House, pp. 216-51.
   Reprint of 1936.1.

3 "Bright and Morning Star." In <u>Readings Towards Composition</u>.
   Belmont, Calif.: Wadsworth Publishing Co., pp. 260-90.
   Reprint of 1938.2.

1969

4   "Silt." In <u>Speaking for Ourselves</u>. Edited by Lilian Federman
    and Barbara Bradshaw. Glenview, Ill.: Scott, Foresman,
    pp. 12-17.
    Reprint of 1937.1.

<u>Books</u>

5   <u>Eight Men</u>. New York: Pyramid Books, 204 pp.
    Reprint of 1960.5.

6   [<u>Eight Men</u>] <u>8 Nin no Okoto</u>. Translated by Akamatsu Mitsuo and
    Tajima Tsuneo. Tokyo: Shobunsha, 341 pp.

7   [<u>The Long Dream</u>] <u>Dugi San</u>. Translated by Vladimir Ristic.
    Subotica: n.p., 404 pp. [Unverified]

8   <u>The Man Who Lived Underground</u>. Edited by Hiromi Furukawa.
    Osaku: Aoyama, 90 pp.

9   <u>Native Son</u>. New York: Harper & Row, 329 pp.
    Reprint of 1940.8.

10 [<u>Native Son</u>] <u>Søn af de sorte</u>. Translated by Tom Kristensen.
    Copenhagen: Gyldendal, 416 pp.

11 [<u>Native Son</u>] <u>Syn Swego Kraju</u>. Translated by Zofia Kierszys.
    Warsaw: Panstw. Instytut Wydawn, 461 pp.

12 <u>Native Son</u> excerpt. In <u>The Political Imagination in Litera-
    ture</u>. Edited by Philip Green and Michael Waltzer. New
    York: Macmillan (The Free Press), pp. 14-25, 482-94.

13 <u>Native Son</u> excerpt. In <u>Types of Literature</u>. Edited by
    Edward J. Gordon. Lexington, Mass.: Ginn & Co.,
    pp. 126-36.
    Preacher's visit to Bigger.

14 <u>Native Son</u> excerpt. In <u>Faith on Monday</u>. Edited by Rev.
    Joseph Petulla. New York: William E. Sadler, pp. 17-19.
    Watching the plane.

15 <u>Native Son</u> excerpt. <u>The Bitter Years, The Thirties in Liter-
    ature</u>. Edited by Max Bogart. New York: Scribner's,
    pp. 53-64.
    Watching the plane.

16 <u>The Outsider</u>. New York: Harper & Row, 440 pp.
    Reprint of 1953.1.

1969

17 [The Outsider] Der Mörder und die Schuldigen. Zürich: Neue
    Schweizer Bibliothek, 468 pp.

NONFICTION

Shorter Writings

Essays

18 "How Bigger was Born." In Native Son. New York: Harper &
    Row, pp. vii-xxxiv.
    Reprint of 1942.7.

19 "Joe Louis Uncovers Dynamite." In New Masses Anthology.
    Edited by Joseph North. New York: International
    Publishers, pp. 160-83.
    Reprint of 1935.1.

20 "The Literature of the Negro in the United States." In Black
    Expression. Edited by Addison Gayle. New York: Weybright
    & Talley, pp. 198-229.

Books

21 Black Boy. New York: Arno Press and the New York Times,
    258 pp.
    Facsimile reprint of 1945.22.

22 [Black Boy] Ragazzo Negro. Translated by Bruno Fonzi. Turin:
    Einaudi, 378 pp.

23 [Black Boy] Sort Ungdom. Translated by Tom Kristensen.
    Copenhagen: Gyldendal, 248 pp.

24 Black Boy excerpt. In The Negro in American History. Edited
    by Mortimer Adler et al. 3 vols. Chicago: Encyclopaedia
    Britannica Educational Corp., pp. 364-85.
    Memphis Public Library episode.

25 Black Boy excerpt. In New Worlds Ahead. Edited by Irene and
    Richard Willis. Chicago: Harcourt, Brace, pp. 19-23,
    54-59.
    "Stray kitten."

26 Black Boy excerpt. In Success in Language and Literature.
    Vol. 2, Getting There. Edited by Ethel Fincke et al.
    Chicago: Follett Publishing Co., pp. 150-58.
    Leaving Greenwood; valedictorian.

1969

27 Black Boy excerpt. In Thrust. Edited by Robert Pooley et al.
    Glenview, Ill.: Scott, Foresman, pp. 403-8.
    "Hunger."

28 Black Boy excerpt. In Voices of Man: Let Us Be Men. Edited
    by Bethel Bodine et al. Menlo Park, Calif.: Addison-
    Wesley, pp. 9-13, 77-83.

29 Black Boy excerpt. In The World of Language. Edited by
    Louie T. Camp et al. Chicago: Follett Publishing Co.,
    pp. 127-33.
    Scene in which Wright's mother prevents him from making
    too much noise.

30 Black Boy excerpt. In The World of Language. Edited by Ruth
    Ellen Crews. Vol. 3. Chicago: Follett Publishing Co.,
    pp. 8-9, 147.

31 Black Power excerpts. In Africa: Selected Readings. Edited
    by Fred Burke. Boston: Houghton Mifflin, pp. 84-90,
    201-6.

32 Black Power excerpt. In Apropos of Africa. Edited by
    Adelaide Hill and Martin Kilson. London: Frank Cass,
    pp. 263-71.
    "Open letter to Kwame Nkrumah."

33 Twelve Million Black Voices excerpt. In The Art of Writing.
    Edited by Bessie Rehder and Wallace Kaufman. New York:
    Scholastic Book Services, pp. 48-53.
    "We are Leaving . . . On Black Migration."

34 [White Man, Listen!] Hakuyin yo Kike. Translated by Kaiko
    Masao and Suzuki Chikara. Tokyo: Ogawa shuppan, 250 pp.

POETRY

35 "I Have Seen Black Hands." In The New Masses Anthology.
    Edited by Joseph North. New York: International
    Publishers, pp. 49-51.
    Reprint of 1934.3.

36 "I Have Seen Black Hands." In Keys to Understanding the Poem.
    Edited by Paul C. Holmes and Anita J. Lehman. New York:
    Harper & Row, pp. 58-60.
    Reprint of 1934.3.

1970

37   [Haiku poems excerpt.]   In Black Heritage Series.   Edited by
     Alice J. Hugh.   Dayton, Ohio: George A. Pflaum, p. 23.
     Haiku no. 3.

38   [Haiku poems excerpt.]   Scholastic Teacher's Practical
     English 46 (11 April):11-12.
     Haiku nos. 1, 3, and 8.

1970

DRAMA

1   Native Son.   In Black Drama, An Anthology.   Edited by William
    Brasmer and Dominick Consolo.   Columbus, Ohio: Charles
    Merrill, pp. 70-178.
    This version, revised by Paul Green, is largely differ-
    ent from the one written in collaboration with Wright.   See
    1941.1.

FICTION

Shorter Writings

2   "Almos' a Man."   In About Language.   Edited by Marden J.
    Clark.   New York: Scribner, pp. 412-23.
    Reprint of 1940.1.

3   "Almos' a Man."   In The American Disinherited: A Profile in
    Fiction.   Edited by Abe Ravitz.   Belmont, Calif.:
    Dickinson Publishing Corp., pp. 120-32.
    Reprint of 1940.1.

4   "Almos' a Man."   In Black Literature in America.   Edited by
    Raman K. Singh and Peter Fellowes.   New York: Thomas
    Crowell, pp. 61-72.   [Unverified]
    Reprint of 1940.1.

5   "Big Boy Leaves Home."   In A Native Son's Reader.   Edited by
    Edward Margolies.   Philadelphia: Lippincott, pp. 101-43.
    Reprint of 1936.1.

6   "Big Boy Leaves Home."   In Right On.   Edited by Bradford
    Chambers and Rebecca Moon.   New York: New American
    Library, pp. 52-88.
    Reprint of 1936.1.

1970

7   "Early Days in Chicago." In A Native Son's Reader. Edited by
     Edward Margolies. Philadelphia: Lippincott, pp. 143-77.
     Reprint of 1945.3.

8   "Early Days in Chicago." In Afro-American Literature: Non-
     Fiction. Edited by Will Adams et al. Boston: Houghton
     Mifflin, pp. 65-78.
     Reprint of 1945.3.

9   "Early Days in Chicago." In The Black Experience. Edited by
     Francis E. Kearns. New York: Viking Press, pp. 451-85.
     Reprint of 1945.3.

10   "Fire and Cloud." In Afro-American Voices. Edited by
     Kendricks Levitt. N.p.: Oxford Book Co., pp. 243-71.
     [Unverified]
     Reprint of 1938.5.

11   "Fire and Cloud." In Fifty Years of the American Short Story.
     Edited by William Abrahams. Vol. 2. New York: Doubleday,
     pp. 449-96.
     Reprint of 1938.5.

12   "Long Black Song." In Forgotten Pages in American Literature.
     Edited by Gerald W. Hasham. Boston: Houghton Mifflin,
     pp. 289-312.
     Reprint of 1938.8.

13   "The Man Who Lived Underground." In Afro-American Literature:
     An Introduction. Edited by Robert Hayden et al. New York:
     Harcourt, Brace, pp. 19-61.
     Cross Section version. Reprint of 1944.5.

Books

14   [Native Son] Sohn dieses Landes. Zürich: Diana Verlag,
     461 pp.

15   Native Son excerpt. In The Eye of the Beholder. Edited by
     Bruce Vance. [?], Canada: Thomas Nelson & Sons, pp. 6-19.
     "Fear," killing the rat.

16   Native Son excerpt. In On Being Black. Edited by Charles T.
     Davis and Daniel Walden. Greenwich, Conn.: Fawcett Books,
     pp. 187-213.
     "Fear."

1970

NONFICTION

Shorter Writings

Essays

17   "The Ethics of Living Jim Crow." In Black Identity. Edited
     by Francis E. Kearns. New York: Holt, Rinehart & Winston,
     pp. 247-58.
     Reprint of 1937.226.

18   "The Ethics of Living Jim Crow." In The Black Man and the
     Promise of America. Edited by Lettie Austin et al.
     Glenview, Ill.: Scott, Foresman, pp. 321-31.
     Reprint of 1937.226.

19   "The Ethics of Living Jim Crow." In Grooving the Symbol.
     Edited by Richard W. Lid. New York: Macmillan (The Free
     Press), pp. 55-68.
     Reprint of 1937.226.

20   "The Ethics of Living Jim Crow." In Hard Rains. Edited by
     Robert Disch and Barry Schwartz. Englewood Cliffs, N.J.:
     Prentice-Hall, pp. 233-37.
     Reprint of 1937.226.

21   "The Ethics of Living Jim Crow." In Junior English Teaching.
     Edited by Inge Barglund. Malmö, Sweden. Jet-Hemods,
     pp. 123-39.
     Reprint of 1937.226.

22   "The Ethics of Living Jim Crow." In The Literature of the
     United States. Edited by Walter Blair et al. 3d ed.
     Glenview, Ill.: Scott, Foresman (Heritage Printing),
     pp. 1394-1403.
     Reprint of 1937.226.

23   "The Ethics of Living Jim Crow." In Think Black. Edited by
     Franck McQuilkin. New York: Bruce Publishing Co.,
     pp. 142-43.
     Reprint of 1937.226.

24   "The Ethics of Living Jim Crow." In Toward the New America.
     Edited by James K. Bell and Adrian Cohn. Lexington, Mass.:
     D. C. Heath, pp. 122-29.
     Reprint of 1937.226.

1970

25 "The Ethics of Living Jim Crow." In <u>Richard Wright's Native
    Son</u>. Edited by Richard Abcarian. Belmont, Calif.:
    Wadsworth Publishing Co., pp. 4-13.
    Reprint of 1937.226.

26 "How Bigger Was Born." In <u>The Black Novelist</u>. Edited by
    Robert Hemenway. Columbus, Ohio: Charles Merrill,
    pp. 166-90.
    Reprint of 1942.7.

27 "How Bigger Was Born." In <u>Great Documents in Black American
    History</u>. Edited by George Ducas. New York: Praeger,
    pp. 230-53.
    Reprint of 1942.7.

28 "How Bigger Was Born." In <u>Richard Wright's Native Son</u>.
    Edited by Richard Abcarian. Belmont, Calif.: Wadsworth
    Publishing Co., pp. 14-35.
    Reprint of 1942.7.

29 "How Bigger Was Born." In <u>The Theory of the American Novel</u>.
    Edited by George Perkins. New York: Holt, Rinehart &
    Winston, pp. 425-36.
    Reprint of 1942.7.

30 "I Bite the Hand that Feeds Me." In <u>Black Dialogues</u>. Edited
    by George Ducas. Illustrated by Will Gallegher and Cynthia
    Peterson. Chicago: Encyclopaedia Britannica Educational
    Corp., pp. 443-45.
        Includes photo of Wright in Paris in 1954 by Inger
    Archausen. Reprint of 1940.17.

31 "I Bite the Hand that Feeds Me." In <u>Richard Wright's Native
    Son</u>. Edited by Richard Abcarian. Belmont, Calif.:
    Wadsworth Publishing Co., pp. 81-83.
    Reprint of 1940.17.

32 ["I Tried to be a Communist"] "The False Lure of Communism."
    In <u>The Negro in American Life</u>. Edited by Richard C. Wade.
    Boston: Houghton Mifflin, pp. 181-83.
    Reprint of 1944.7.

33 "Joe Louis Uncovers Dynamite." In <u>The Strenuous Decade</u>.
    Edited by Daniel Aaron and Robert Bendiner. New York:
    Doubleday (Anchor Books), pp. 392-97.
    Reprint of 1935.1.

1970

34   "Rascoe Baiting." In Richard Wright's Native Son. Edited by
      Richard Abcarian. Belmont, Calif.: Wadsworth Publishing
      Co., pp. 89-90.
      Reprint of 1940.25.

Books

35   Black Boy. With an introduction and notes by Geoffrey
      Summerfield. With photographs by Joel Laughlin. London:
      Longman, 254 pp.
      Reprint of 1945.22.

36   [Black Boy] Sort Ungdom. Translated by Tom Kristensen.
      Copenhagen: Gyldendal, 248 pp.

37   Black Boy excerpt. In Afro-American Literature: An Introduc-
      tion. Edited by Robert Hayden et al. New York: Harcourt,
      Brace, pp. 189-97.
      From chapter 13: the beating.

38   Black Boy excerpt. In American Literature. Vol. 2. Edited
      by Richard Poirier and William Vance. Boston: Little,
      Brown, pp. 870-83.
      Chapter 12.

39   Black Boy excerpt. In About Language. Marden J. Clark et al.
      New York: Scribner, pp. 46-54.
      "I hungered for books. . . ."

40   Black Boy excerpt. In Backlash. Edited by Stewart H.
      Benedict. New York: Popular Library, pp. 99-113.
      Chapter 13.

41   Black Boy excerpt. In Conflict. Edited by Lawana Trout et
      al. New York: Holt, Rinehart & Winston, pp. 62-71.
      The streets of Memphis.

42   Black Boy excerpt. In English as a Second Language. Edited
      by Edward T. Erazmus and Harry T. Cargas. Dubuque, Iowa:
      William Brown Publishers, pp. 343-45.
      Learning to read and count.

43   Black Boy excerpt. In Family and School. Edited by David
      Jackson. Baltimore: Penguin Books, pp. 64-65.
      First day at school.

1970

44　Black Boy excerpt.　In Forward in Reading.　Edited by H. E.
　　Hughes and Hazel Hart.　New York:　Bobbs, Merrill,
　　pp. 30-34.
　　Wright fights for acceptance at school.

45　Black Boy excerpt.　In The History of America:　20th Century.
　　Edited by Mark Shorer.　New York:　McGraw-Hill, pp. 883-914.

46　Black Boy excerpt.　In Ideas and Patterns in Literature.
　　Vol. 2.　Edited by Allan Glasshorn et al.　New York:
　　Harcourt, Brace, pp. 79-80, 481-83.
　　The fight.

47　Black Boy excerpt.　In Introduction to Literature.　Edited by
　　Edward J. Gordon.　Rev. ed.　New York:　Ginn & Co., p. 46.
　　Chapters 13-14.

48　Black Boy excerpt.　In Oral and Written Composition.　Bk. 1.
　　Edited by May K. Ely et al.　New York:　Ginn & Co.,
　　pp. 68-69.
　　Addie and the whip.

49　Black Boy excerpt.　In New Worlds of Literature.　2d ed.
　　Edited by Warren J. Halliburton et al.　New York:
　　Harcourt, Brace, pp. 21-26, 86-90.
　　Valedictorian speech.

50　Black Boy excerpt.　In The Reader's Digest Family Treasury of
　　Great Biographies.　Illustrated by Thomas Beecham.
　　Pleasantville, N.Y.:　Reader's Digest Association,
　　pp. 327-458.

51　Black Boy excerpt.　In Readings to Enjoy.　Edited by Norman H.
　　Naas and Morton H. Lewittes.　New York:　Macmillan, p. 189.
　　Valedictorian speech.

52　Black Boy excerpt.　In The Study of Literature.　Edited by
　　Edward J. Gordon.　Boston:　Ginn & Co., pp. 446-49.
　　Valedictorian speech.

53　Black Boy excerpt.　In Think Black.　Edited by Nathan Hare.
　　New York:　Bruce Publishing Co., pp. 141-43, 161-63.

54　Black Boy excerpt.　In Voices of Man:　Like It Is.　Edited by
　　Bethel Bodine et al.　Menlo Park, Calif.:　Addison-Wesley,
　　pp. 29-37.
　　Errand for Mother and fight.

1970

55 Twelve Million Black Voices excerpt. In Black Americans.
       Edited by John Hope Franklin. New York: Time/Life Books,
       pp. 114-16.
          Going North.

56 Twelve Million Black Voices excerpt. In Black Identity.
       Edited by Francis E. Kearns. New York: Holt, Rinehart &
       Winston, pp. 5-15.
          "Our Strange Birth" section.

POETRY

57 "Between the World and Me." In Afro-American Literature:
       Poetry. Edited by Will Adams et al. Boston: Houghton
       Mifflin, pp. 63-64.
          Reprint of 1935.3.

58 "Between the World and Me." In I Am the Darker Brother.
       Edited by Arnold Adoff. New York: Collier Books,
       pp. 63-64.
          Reprint of 1935.3.

59 "Between the World and Me." In A Little Treasury of Modern
       Poetry. 3d ed. Edited by Oscar Williams. New York:
       Scribner, pp. 657-58.
          Reprint of 1935.3.

60 "Between the World and Me." In Types of Literature. Edited
       by Edward J. Gordon. Lexington, Mass.: Ginn & Co.,
       pp. 482-83.
          Reprint of 1935.3.

61 "Fourteen Haikus." Studies in Black Literature 1, no. 3
       (Summer):1-27.
          A new selection. Followed by a study of Richard
       Wright's poetry by Michel Fabre.

62 "I Have Seen Black Hands." In Black Images, by Wilfred
       Cartey. New York: Teachers College Press (Columbia
       University), p. 44.
          Six lines of the poem. Reprint of 1934.3.

63 "I Have Seen Black Hands." In Soulscript. Edited by June
       Jordan. New York: Doubleday, pp. 112-14.
          Reprint of 1934.3.

1971

1971

FICTION

Shorter Writings

1 "Almos' a Man." In Cavalcade. Edited by Arthur P. Davis and
  J. Saunders Redding. Boston: Houghton Mifflin,
  pp. 470-80.
       Reprint of 1940.1.

2 "Almos' a Man." In The World of the Short Story. Edited by
  Oliver Evans and Harry Fine Stone. New York: Knopf,
  pp. 449-58.
       Reprint of 1940.1.

3 "Big Boy Leaves Home." In Modern Short Stories. Edited by
  Arthur Mizener. New York: Norton, pp. 554-90.
       Reprint of 1936.1.

4 "Big Boy Leaves Home." In Synthesis. Edited by Charles
  Sanders et al. New York: Knopf, pp. 186-206.
       Reprint of 1936.1.

5 "Bright and Morning Star." In The Southern Experience in
  Short Fiction. Edited by Allen F. Stein and Thomas N.
  Walters. Glenview, Ill.: Scott, Foresman, pp. 59-69.
       Reprint of 1938.2.

6 "Down by the Riverside." In Blackamerican Literature. Edited
  by Ruth Miller. With a foreword by John Hope Franklin.
  Beverly Hills, Calif.: Glencoe Press, pp. 426-72.
       Reprint of 1938.4.

7 "Early Days in Chicago." In Big City Stories. Edited by Tom
  and Susan Cahill. New York: Bantam Books, pp. 214-44.
       Reprint of 1945.3.

8 "Long Black Song." In The Southern Experience in Short
  Fiction. Edited by Allen F. Stein and Thomas N. Walters.
  Glenview, Ill.: Scott, Foresman, pp. 39-59.
       Reprint of 1938.8.

9 "Silt." In Major Black Writers. Edited by Alan Murray and
  Robert Thomas. New York: Scholastic Book Services,
  pp. 72-80.
       Reprint of 1937.1.

1971

10   "Silt."   In Black and White.   Edited by Carol Anselmet and
     Donald Gibson.   New York: Washington Square Press,
     pp. 60-66.
     Reprint of 1937.1.

11   "Silt."   In Promise of America.   Bk. 3.   Edited by Larry Cuban
     and Philip Roden.   Glenview, Ill.:   Scott, Foresman
     (Spectra Program), pp. 86-91.
     Reprint of 1937.1.

Books

12   [The Long Dream] Der schwarze Traum.   With an afterword by
     Karl-Heinz Schönfelder.   East Berlin: Volk und Welt,
     485 pp.

13   The Man Who Lived Underground: L'homme qui vivait sous terre.
     Translated by Claude-Edmonde Magny.   Edited and with an
     introduction and notes by Michel Fabre.   Paris: Aubier-
     Flammarion, 192 pp.
     Reprint of 1944.5.

14   [Native Son] Syn Ameriki.   Translated by N. Samukasvili and
     G. Cikovani.   Illustrated.   Tbilisi: Nakaduli, 630 pp.

15   [Uncle Tom's Children] Abna' al 'amm Tom.   Damascus:
     Ministère de l'Information.

16   [Uncle Tom's Children] Onkel Toms Børn.   Translated by Kurt
     Kreutsfeld.   Copenhagen: Gyldendal, 260 pp.

NONFICTION

Shorter Writings

Essays

17   "The American Problem."   New Letters 38 (Winter):9-16.
     [Early 1950s]

     "The American Problem: Its Negro Phase."
     Autograph MS: 11 leaves.
     Incomplete working draft of a series of essays for French
     audiences.   With MS corrections.
     JWJ Wright Misc. 240.

     Typescript (original):   8 leaves.
     Another working draft, with extensive MS revisions.
     JWJ Wright Misc. 241.

1971

Typescript (original): 8 leaves.
Later draft, incomplete, with a few MS corrections.
JWJ Wright Misc. 242.

Related Material:
"Notes--Changing Aspects of the Negro Problem."
Typescript (original): 2 numb. leaves.
JWJ Wright Misc. 495.

Another typescript (carbon): 7 numb. leaves.
Typescript made by Michel Fabre.
JWJ Wright Misc. 496.

18 "Blueprint for Negro Writing." In The Black Aesthetic.
    Edited by Addison Gayle, Jr. Garden City, N.Y.:
    Doubleday, pp. 333-47.
        Reprint of 1937.225.

19 ["Blueprint for Negro Writing"] "Blueprint for Negro Litera-
    ture." In Amistad 2. Edited by John A. Williams and
    Charles F. Harris. New York: Random House (Vintage
    Books), pp. 3-20.
        This is the third, but not the definitive version of
    Wright's essay. Reprint of 1937.225.

20 "The Ethics of Living Jim Crow." In Black Literature in
    America. Edited by Houston A. Baker. New York: McGraw-
    Hill, pp. 297-302.
        Reprint of 1937.226.

21 "How Bigger was Born." In Black Hands on a White Face.
    Edited by Whit Burnett. New York: Dodd, Mead, pp. 216-28.
        Reprint of 1942.7.

22 "How Jim Crow Feels." In Bondage, Freedom and Beyond. Edited
    by Addison Gayle, Jr. New York: Doubleday (Zenith Books),
    pp. 82-89.
        Reprint of 1946.9.

23 "There is Always Another Café." Teacher Travel 1 (April):1.
        Reprint of 1953.5.

Liner Notes

24 "King Joe." New Letters 38 (Winter):42-45.
        Reprint of 1941.22.

1971

Letter

25   To Owen Dodson. New Letters 38 (Winter):125-27. [9 June 1946]

Books

26   [Black Boy] Cerno Momce. Translated by Vera Stoimenova. Sofia: Nar. mladez, 271 pp.

27   [Black Boy] Kara Cokuk. Istanbul: Ahmet Sari Matbaasi, 248 pp.

28   Black Boy excerpt. In Cavalcade. Edited by Arthur P. Davis and J. Saunders Redding. Boston: Houghton Mifflin, pp. 460-70.
      Chapter 9.

29   Black Boy excerpt. In Challenge and Promise. Edited by David Cox et al. New York: John Wiley & Sons, pp. 214-37.
      Learning to read.

30   Black Boy excerpts. In A Mirror of Society. Edited by Van Huizen et al. Culemborg, Holland: Stam-Robbijus, pp. 122-30.
      Bicycle episode; work at Crane's office.

31   Black Boy excerpt. In The Oxford Reader. Edited by Frank Kermode and Richard Poirier. New York: Oxford University Press, pp. 104-12.
      Boxing match.

32   Black Boy excerpt. In Ventures. Edited by Harvey R. Granite Granite et al. Boston: Houghton Mifflin, pp. 80-86.

33   Black Boy excerpts. In Ventures. Edited by Harvey R. Granite et al. Boston: Houghton Mifflin, pp. 82-88.
      The Streets of Memphis.

POETRY

34   ["Between the World and Me"] "Entre le monde et moi." Translated by Michel Fabre. In "Ensemble Afro-Américain," Change 9:27-28.

35   "F B Eye Blues." Intrepid, no. 20; Floating Bear, no. 38 (Summer):93.
      (These two magazines combined for this issue.) Reprint of 1949.19.

1971

36   "I Have Seen Black Hands." In <u>Prosperity Panic and Poverty</u>.
Edited by Richard E. Gross. San Francisco: Field Educa-
tion Corp. (Profile of America Series), pp. 96-97.
Reprint of 1934.3.

1972

FICTION

Shorter Writing

1   "Big Boy Leaves Home." In <u>Black Writers in America</u>. Edited
by Richard Barksdale and Keneth Kinnamon. New York:
Macmillan, pp. 548-63.
Reprint of 1936.1.

Books

2   [Native Son] <u>Amerika no Musuko</u>. Translated by Hashimoto Fukuo.
2 vols. Tokyo: Shinchosha.

3   [Native Son] <u>Amerikan Poika</u>. Translated by Antero Tiusanen
and Eva Siikarla. Porvoo: Werner Söderström, 508 pp.

4   [Native Son] <u>Søn af de Sorte</u>. Translated by Tom Kristensen.
Copenhagen: Gyldendal, 410 pp.

NONFICTION

Shorter Writings

Essays

5   "The Ethics of Living Jim Crow." In <u>Black Writers in America</u>.
Edited by Richard Barksdale and Keneth Kinnamon. New York:
Macmillan, pp. 542-47.
Reprint of 1937.226.

6   "Ethnological Aspects of Chicago's Black Belt." <u>New Letters</u>
39 (Fall):61-67. [1935]
With Wright's 1935 "Bibliography on the Negro in
Chicago," pp. 68-76.

"Some Ethnological Aspects of Chicago's Black Belt."
Typescript (original): 3 numb. leaves.
With MS corrections. Typed by L. Washovsky. 11 December
1935.
Chicago Public Library.

1974

"Bibliography on the Negro in Chicago."
Carbon (uncorrected).
Chicago Public Library.

Typescript (original): 14 numb. leaves and 3 numb. leaves
of added items.
Chicago Public Library.

7   No entry.

Books

8   [Black Boy] Musta Poika. Porvoo: Werner Söderström, 268 pp.

9   [Black Boy] Ragazzo Negro. Milan: Mondadori, 339 pp.

1973

FICTION

Books

1   [The Long Dream] Der schwarze Traum. East Berlin: Volk und
Velt, 485 pp.

2   [Native Son] Syn Ameriki. Tbilisi: Merani, 702 pp.

POETRY

3   "Between the World and Me." In You Better Believe It. Edited
by Paul Breman. Baltimore: Penguin Books, pp. 109-10.
Reprint of 1935.3.

4   Haiku poems excerpt. In You Better Believe It. Edited by
Paul Breman. Baltimore: Penguin Books, p. 11.
Haiku no. 3.

1974

NONFICTION

Book

1   [Black Boy] Sort Ungdom. Translated by Tom Kristensen.
Copenhagen: Gyldendal, 248 pp.

143

1975

1975

NONFICTION

Book

1   [Black Boy] Musta Poika. Porvoo: Werner Söderström, 268 pp.

1976

NONFICTION

Shorter Writing

Essay

1   "Blueprint for Negro Writing." In Voices from the Harlem
     Renaissance. Edited by Nathan Huggins. New York: Oxford
     University Press, pp. 394-402.
     Reprint of 1937.225.

Books

2   [Black Boy] Jeunesse Noire. Paris: Folio, 448 pp.

3   [Black Boy] Sort Ungdom. Translated by Tom Kristensen.
     Copenhagen: Gyldendal, 247 pp.

1977

NONFICTION

Book

1   American Hunger. With an afterword by Michel Fabre. New
     York: Harper & Row, 146 pp.
        Includes already published extracts "American Hunger,"
     "Early Days in Chicago," and "I Tried to be a Communist."
     Reprinted 1978.12. See also Black Boy, 1945.22.

     Setting copy (Xerox): 3 leaves, 121 numb. leaves.
     Author's proofs originally prepared for publication in 1944
     by Harper as part of his Black Boy.
     JWJ Wright 27.

     "A hitherto unpublished manuscript by Richard Wright being
     a continuation of Black Boy." A photo-offset reprint of

144

1978

these galleys was edited by Constance Webb for private cir-
culation in July 1946; 125 pp. and notes by C. Webb. One
hundred numbered copies (one at Yale University Library,
one at Princeton University Library, one at Bibliothèque
Nationale, Paris).

1978

FICTION

Shorter Writings

1   "Big Black Good Man." In Richard Wright Reader. Edited by
    Ellen Wright and Michel Fabre. New York: Harper & Row,
    pp. 721-36.
       Reprint of 1957.1.

2   "Fire and Cloud." In Richard Wright Reader. Edited by Ellen
    Wright and Michel Fabre. New York: Harper & Row,
    pp. 288-345.
       Reprint of 1938.5.

3   "Long Black Song." In Richard Wright Reader. Edited by Ellen
    Wright and Michel Fabre. New York: Harper & Row,
    pp. 258-86.
       Reprint of 1938.8.

4   "The Man Who Lived Underground." In Richard Wright Reader.
    Edited by Ellen Wright and Michel Fabre. New York: Harper
    & Row, pp. 518-76.
       Reprint of 1944.5.

Books

5   The Long Dream excerpts. In Richard Wright Reader. Edited by
    Ellen Wright and Michel Fabre. New York: Harper & Row,
    pp. 738-871.
       Dance hall fire; Tyree's confrontation with the police.

6   Native Son excerpts. In Richard Wright Reader. Edited by
    Ellen Wright and Michel Fabre. New York: Harper & Row,
    pp. 418-516.

7   The Outsider excerpts. In Richard Wright Reader. Edited by
    Ellen Wright and Michel Fabre. New York: Harper & Row,
    pp. 579-705.
       From "Dread," "Descent," "Despair," and "Decision"
    chapters.

1978

NONFICTION

Shorter Writings

Essays

   8   "Blueprint for Negro Writing." In Richard Wright Reader.
       Edited by Ellen Wright and Michel Fabre. New York:
       Harper & Row, pp. 36-50.
       Reprint of 1937.225.

   9   "I Bite the Hand that Feeds Me." In Richard Wright Reader.
       Edited by Ellen Wright and Michel Fabre. New York: Harper
       & Row, pp. 52-67.
       Reprint of 1940.17.

  10   "Joe Louis Uncovers Dynamite." In Richard Wright Reader.
       Edited by Ellen Wright and Michel Fabre. New York:
       Harper & Row, pp. 32-35.
       Reprint of 1935.1.

  11   "There is Always Another Cafe." In Richard Wright Reader.
       Edited by Ellen Wright and Michel Fabre. New York:
       Harper & Row, pp. 80-85.
       Reprint of 1953.5.

Book Review

  12   "Gertrude Stein's Story Is Drenched in Hitler's Horrors."
       In Richard Wright Reader. Edited by Ellen Wright and
       Michel Fabre. New York: Harper & Row, pp. 75-78.
       Reprint of 1945.12.

Letters

  13   "Rascoe Baiting." In Richard Wright Reader. Edited by Ellen
       Wright and Michel Fabre. New York: Harper & Row,
       pp. 55-57.
       Reprint of 1940.25.

  14   "Richard Wright and Antonio Frasconi: An Exchange of Let-
       ters." In Richard Wright Reader. Edited by Ellen Wright
       and Michel Fabre. New York: Harper & Row, pp. 67-73.
       Reprint of 1945.19.

1978

Books

15   American Hunger. London: Gollancz, 146 pp.
     Reprint of 1977.1.

16   [American Hunger] Amerika no ue.   Translated by Maseo
     Takahashi, n.p.   222 pp.
     Includes "Postface."

17   [American Hunger] Sort Sult.   Translated by Kurt Kreutzfeld.
     With an afterword by Michel Fabre.   Stockholm: Gyldendal,
     188 pp.

18   Black Boy excerpt.   In Richard Wright Reader.   Edited by Ellen
     Wright and Michel Fabre.   New York: Harper & Row, pp. 3-30.

19   Black Boy; American Hunger.   Japanese omnibus ed.   World's
     Famous Classics no. 92.   Kodan sha, 428 pp.

20   Black Power excerpts.   In Richard Wright Reader.   Edited by
     Ellen Wright and Michel Fabre.   New York: Harper & Row,
     pp. 87-109.
     Effects of colonization on Africa; letter to Nkrumah.

21   Pagan Spain excerpts.   In Richard Wright Reader.   Edited by
     Ellen Wright and Michel Fabre.   New York: Harper & Row,
     pp. 110-43.
     Chapters 16-22, 25, and 26.

22   Twelve Million Black Voices.   In Richard Wright Reader.
     Edited by Ellen Wright and Michel Fabre.   New York:
     Harper & Row, pp. 145-241.
     Complete text, with most of the original pictures.
     Reprint of 1941.26.

POETRY

23   "Between the World and Me."   In Richard Wright Reader.
     Edited by Ellen Wright and Michel Fabre.   New York:
     Harper & Row, pp. 246-47.
     Reprint of 1935.3.

24   "F B Eye Blues."   In Richard Wright Reader.   Edited by Ellen
     Wright and Michel Fabre.   New York: Harper & Row, p. 246.
     First authorized printing.   Reprint of 1949.19.

1978

25 "I Have Seen Black Hands." In <u>Richard Wright Reader</u>. Edited
    by Ellen Wright and Michel Fabre. New York: Harper & Row,
    p. 248.
    Reprint of 1934.3.

26 "Red Clay Blues." In <u>Richard Wright Reader</u>. Edited by Ellen
    Wright and Michel Fabre. New York: Harper & Row, p. 248.
    Reprint of 1939.6.

1979

FICTION

<u>Book</u>

1 [<u>Savage Holiday</u>] <u>Le Barbare du Septième Jour</u>. Paris:
   Editions des Autres.

NONFICTION

<u>Book</u>

2 [<u>American Hunger</u>] <u>Une Faim d'Egalité</u>. Translated by Andrée
   Picard. With a postface by Michel Fabre. Paris:
   Gallimard, 173 pp.

POETRY

3 "King Joe"; ["F B Eye Blues"] "Blues du F.B.I."; ["Red Clay
   Blues"] "Blues de la terre rouge." In "Les blues de
   Richard Wright." Translated by Michel Fabre. <u>Jazz
   Magazine</u>, no. 275 (May):42.

Richard Wright's Unpublished Works

DRAMA, FILM, AND TV SCRIPTS

1   "The Battle of the Books."
        Typescript (original): 1 leaf.
        Idea for play about authors.
        JWJ Wright Misc. 272.

2   [The Burkes.]
        Typescript (original): 1 leaf, 17 numb. leaves.
        Incomplete draft of a play concerning a Negro family on
        the South Side of Chicago.
        JWJ Wright Misc. 339.

3   "Daddy Goodness."
        Typescript (original): 125 numb. leaves.
        Early draft of Wright's translation and adaptation of Louis
        Sapin's Papa bon Dieu. With extensive MS corrections and
        revisions, including typed and MS notes and revised por-
        tions of Acts II and III; 67 leaves.
        JWJ Wright 99[1-2].

        Carbon of above.
        Without revised material for Acts II and III.
        JWJ Wright 100.

        Another carbon copy.
        JWJ Wright 101.

        Another typescript (original): 2 leaves, 128 numb. leaves.
        Another early working draft, including revisions made in
        prior draft and with additional MS revisions.
        JWJ Wright 102.

        Carbon of above: 3 leaves, 128 numb. leaves.
        JWJ Wright 103.

        Typescript (original): 4 leaves, 161 [i.e., 166] numb.
        leaves.
        Later working draft, with extensive corrections and textual
        revisions, including major additions of new material for

Act III and miscellaneous leaves deleted from text (9
leaves).
JWJ Wright 104.

Carbon of above: 4 leaves, 161 [i.e., 164] numb. leaves.
Without corrections.
JWJ Wright 105.

Another typescript (carbon): 151 numb. leaves.
Another working draft of later version, with MS corrections
and typed revisions (some pasted in).
JWJ Wright 106.

Another typescript (original): 3 leaves, 145 numb. leaves.
Retyped copy of above draft, incorporating revisions.
JWJ Wright 107.

Mimeographed typescript, signed: 6 leaves, 138 numb.
leaves.
With extensive MS revisions and deletions. Play performed
by American Theatre Association of Paris, 19 February 1959.
JWJ Wright 108.

Another mimeographed typescript: 123 leaves.

Another version, with a few MS notes and corrections.
Signed by Derry Hall, composer of musical accompaniment.
JWJ Wright 109.

4   [Dramatic Sketch.]
        Typescript (original): 2 leaves.
        Concerning white attitudes toward blacks during World
        War II.
        JWJ Wright 369.

5   [The Farmer in the Dell.]
        Typescript (original): 2 numb. leaves.
        A short play about celebrating Thanksgiving in Paris.
        JWJ Wright Misc. 375.

6   "Freedom Train or the World Between."
        Typescript (carbon) signed: 4 numb. leaves.
        Scenario for a film concerning the stories of passengers
        on a train hijacked in Czechoslovakia; written with Audrey
        Davenport. With receipt from Association des Auteurs de
        Films dated 12 May 1951.
        JWJ Wright Misc. 389.

        Carbon of above.
        JWJ Wright Misc. 390.

        Another typescript (original): 12 numb. leaves.
        Another version, opening scenes and some dialogue only.
        With additional title: "No Man's Land or Public Enemies."
        JWJ Wright Misc. 391.

7   "Last Flight."
    Typescript (carbon):   5 numb. leaves, 2 leaves.
    Developmental draft, with MS corrections and additions, of
    a motion picture story.   Includes a scene outline.
    JWJ Wright 176.

    Another typescript (carbon):   7 numb. leaves.
    Later draft, with MS corrections and additions.   With can-
    celed title "Indicted for Treason."
    JWJ Wright 177.

    Typescript (carbon):   1 leaf, 8 numb. leaves.
    Final version of an original motion picture story, written
    with Crosby George, concerning the flight and capture of an
    American Nazi.   With typescript (original) copy of title
    leaf.
    JWJ Wright 178.

    Original typescript of preceding item.
    Private collection.

    "The Voice of Death."
    Typescript (original):   1 leaf, 4 numb. leaves.
    Early working draft of "Last Flight."
    JWJ Wright 174.

    "Anna Crane."
    Typescript (original):   1 leaf, 4 numb. leaves.
    Early working draft of "Last Flight."
    JWJ Wright 175.

8   "Lucy Comes Marching Home."
    Autograph MS: 1 leaf, 6 numb. leaves.
    Scene outline for script of a motion picture.
    JWJ Wright Misc. 465.

    Another typescript (original):   1 leaf, 11 numb. leaves.
    An original motion picture story, written with Crosby
    George, submitted to Columbia Pictures, 1945.   With a few
    MS corrections.
    JWJ Wright Misc. 467.

    Typescript (original) signed: 9 numb. leaves.
    Working draft of script, with extensive MS corrections and
    additions by Wright and Crosby George.
    JWJ Wright Misc. 466.

    Two carbons of above.
    JWJ Wright Misc. 468-469.

9   ["Melody Limited."]
    "Freedom's Song."
    Typescript (original):   78 numb. leaves.
    Early working draft of the screenplay based on efforts of
    Fisk University Jubilee Singers and similar singing groups

to raise funds for education of blacks after the Civil
War. With author's MS revisions. With his MS notes for
screenplay scenes and other miscellaneous material deleted
from working draft, 16 leaves.
JWJ Wright 220.

"Melody Limited."
Typescript (original): 88 numb. leaves.
First rough running narrative draft. With a few MS correc-
tions.
JWJ Wright 221.

Carbon of above, signed: 88 numb. leaves.
Uncorrected copy.
JWJ Wright 222.

Same as above. 88 numb. leaves.
Princeton University Library, Story Magazine Files.

Another carbon.
JWJ Wright 223.

Another typescript (carbon): 3 leaves, 88 numb. leaves.
Includes Wright's background synopsis, "The Idea," and a
list of characters. With 2 typescripts (carbons) of a
reader's comment by Emily Brown, 19 April 1944.
JWJ Wright 224.

"Jubilee."
Typescript (original): 25 leaves.
With author's MS corrections. Early version of the screen-
play.
JWJ Wright 219.

10   Native Son [film].
Typescript (original and carbon) autograph MS: 241 leaves.
Early, developmental draft, with author's extensive MS
revisions, some printed sections pasted in, and with work-
ing drafts of early scenes, 39 leaves.
JWJ Wright 819[1-2].

Another typescript (original): 98 leaves.
Another early draft, incomplete, with author's MS correc-
tions and deletions, scenes 1-143 only.
JWJ Wright 820.

Another typescript (original): 99 leaves.
Later draft, incomplete, scenes 162-85 only. With author's
MS corrections and revisions.
JWJ Wright 824.

Native Son [costume directions].
Typescript (original): 4 numb. leaves.
Dress requirements, listed by scene.
JWJ Wright 825.

Another typescript (carbon):   4 numb. leaves.
JWJ Wright 826.

Carbon copy.
JWJ Wright 827.

Another typescript (original):   4 leaves.
With MS corrections.
JWJ Wright 828.

Native Son [notes].
Typed and autograph MS: 53 leaves.
Includes directions for camera and stage action for scenes
252-314, lighting directions, with dialogue and miscel-
laneous notes for script and scene development.
JWJ Wright +829.

Native Son [notes on film contract].
Autograph MS: 5 leaves.
With draft (photocopy) of a cable and a typed letter
(carbon) concerning film rights and payments.
JWJ Wright 830.

Native Son [scene synopsis].
Typescript (carbon):   35 numb. leaves.
Working draft, with MS corrections.
JWJ Wright 831.

Another typescript (original):   46 leaves.
Final draft, with a folder.
JWJ Wright 832.

Native Son [synopsis for film treatment].
Typescript (original):   5 numb. leaves.
With MS corrections by the author.
N.Y. Public Library, Schomburg Collection.

Screenplay typescript: 11 leaves.
JWJ Wright 833.

Related material:
"The Problem of the Hero."
Typescript (original):   8 leaves.
Working draft, with extensive MS notes and revisions.   Un-
published play based on conversations with Paul Green con-
cerning their efforts to dramatize Native Son.
JWJ Wright Misc. 631.

Another typescript (carbon) signed: 7 numb. leaves.
With a few MS corrections and handstamped by Paul R.
Reynolds.
JWJ Wright Misc. 632.

"Classic Pictures, Inc., in the Supreme Court of Ohio:
Classic Pictures Inc., Plaintiff vs. the Department of

Education of the State of Ohio, Defendant No. 33283;
Plaintiff's Brief."
Mimeograph typescript: 4 leaves, 18 numb. leaves [5
leaves].
Concerning the denial by the State of Ohio to exhibit the
film of Richard Wright's Native Son.
JWJ Wright, MSS about Wright 6.

"A Boy I Know Is Dead."
Typescript (carbon): 1 leaf.
Blues lyrics with author's signed note: "This is to be
used at the end of the movie [i.e., Native Son]."
JWJ Wright Misc. 549.

Another typescript (carbon): 1 leaf.
Another version.
Title: "Another Boy's Dead."
JWJ Wright Misc. 550.

"The Dreaming Kind."
Typescript (carbon): 1 leaf.
JWJ Wright Misc. 568.

Carbon copy, signed.
With author's MS note concerning the use of the poem as
"the song Bessie sings in the movie [Native Son]."
JWJ Wright Misc. 569.

Another carbon copy.
JWJ Wright Misc. 570.

Another typescript (original): 1 leaf.
JWJ Wright Misc. 571.

Another typescript (carbon): 1 leaf.
Verses appear in a different sequence from above.
JWJ Wright Misc. 572.

11   [Play.]
Typescript (original): 4 leaves.
Short play concerning the suicide of a black domestic
worker.
JWJ Wright Misc. 518.

12   [Play Synopsis.]
Autograph MS: 1 leaf.
Restricted.
JWJ Wright Misc. 519.

13   [The Return of a Black War Hero.]
Typescript (original): 3 numb. leaves.
Short play, with author's MS corrections.
JWJ Wright Misc. 648.

Another typescript (original): 8 numb. leaves.
JWJ Wright Misc. 649.

Another typescript (original): 2 leaves.
JWJ Wright Misc. 650.

14   "Sacrifice" [Notes for a play].
Autograph and typed MSS: 42 leaves, 4 numb. leaves.
Miscellaneous developmental notes and ideas for a play.
JWJ Wright 883.

"Sacrifice"
Typescript (original): 35 numb. leaves [26 leaves].
Developmental draft of a play, with extensive MS revisions
and corrections. With the author's working notes and cor-
rected leaves laid in.
JWJ Wright 884.

Another typescript (original): 106 leaves.
Working draft of Acts I and II only. With MS and typed
corrections and revisions (some pasted in) and author's
notes, 12 leaves.
JWJ Wright 885.

Another typescript (original): 80 leaves.
Another draft of Acts I-III, with MS and typed corrections
and revisions (some laid in).
JWJ Wright 887.

15   "The Sunny Side of the Street."
Typescript (original): 51 leaves.
Early draft story outline and partial reading script for a
radio series concerning a black family. Based on a story
idea supplied by Leston Huntley.
JWJ Wright 900.

Autograph MS: 2 leaves.
Author's working notes for characters in the radio series.
JWJ Wright 901.

Typescript (original) of above: 2 leaves.
Revised and expanded descriptions of characters.
JWJ Wright 902.

Another typescript (carbon): 60 leaves.
Later working draft of story synopsis, a daily outline, and
a partial reading script. With MS corrections.
JWJ Wright 903.

Another typescript (carbon): 99 leaves.
Final script and plans for a radio series submitted to
Leston Huntley for production (but not used). Included is
story plan, a description of the characters, a "day by
day" outline for ten days, and a script for episodes 1-3,
8, 10.
JWJ Wright 904.

16   "United We Stand: Divided We Fall" [Lenin Memorial Pageant].
      Typescript (original) signed: 11 leaves.
      Working draft of a synopsis and verses for the prologue to
      a Lenin memorial pageant. With MS corrections and revi-
      sions and with Wright's typed and MS notes, 12 leaves, laid
      in. Written for the New York State Committee of the Com-
      munist party.
      JWJ Wright Misc. 785.

FICTION

Shorter Writings

17   [Claire Spence.]
      Autograph MS and typescript (original): 7 leaves.
      Working notes for the development of the character of Clair
      Spence (also called Claire Hudson) for a story.
      JWJ Wright Misc. 349.

18   "The Colored Angel."
      Typescript (original): 24 leaves.
      With MS notes on verso of final leaf. Alternate leaves
      numbered.
      JWJ Wright Misc. 350.

      Another typescript (original): 5 leaves.
      Shorter version, with MS corrections.
      JWJ Wright Misc. 351.

      [The Angel That Could Not Fly Straight.]
      Autograph MS: 15 leaves.
      Notes for scenes and dialogue related to the theme of "The
      Colored Angel."
      JWJ Wright Misc. 244.

      [On Airplanes.]
      Typescript (carbon): 13 numb. leaves.
      Draft of an untitled story about airplanes and flying, with
      MS corrections and revisions. A portion of this work
      relates to his theme in "The Colored Angel." On verso of
      announcement flyers for the Third Annual Cavalcade of
      American Folk Music, sponsored by Earl Robinson and Wright.
      JWJ Wright Misc. 504.

19   [Curtis at the Barber's.]
      Autograph MS: 26 leaves.
      A short story.
      JWJ Wright Misc. 358.

20   "Doodley-Funn."
      Typescript (original):   3 leaves.
      Working draft of a fantasy, with author's MS corrections.
      JWJ Wright Misc. 367.

      Another typescript (original):   9 numb. leaves.
      JWJ Wright Misc. 368.

21   "Graven Image."
      Typescript (original):   11 numb. leaves.
      A short story.
      JWJ Wright Misc. 398.

22   [He Was Dying and He Knew It.]
      Typescript (original):   1 leaf.
      With MS corrections and additions (some laid in).   [Title
      is first sentence.]
      JWJ Wright Misc. 403.

      Another typescript (original):   1 leaf.
      Incomplete draft, with MS corrections.
      JWJ Wright Misc. 404.

23   "The Man Who Built a House."
      Typescript (original):   3 numb. leaves.
      Draft of a story (incomplete).
      JWJ Wright Misc. 470.

24   "The Man Who Led the Sheep."
      Typescript (original):   20 leaves.
      Draft of a story.   Alternate leaves numbered.
      With a MS note laid in, 1 leaf.
      JWJ Wright Misc. 471.

25   [Notes for Stories, Titles, etc.]
      Typescript (original):   78 index cards.
      Miscellaneous notes and ideas for development into stories,
      titles, and characters, including a series of philosophical
      "concepts."
      JWJ Wright Misc. 498.

      [Notes: fragments of miscellaneous fiction.]
      Typed and autograph MSS: 30 leaves.
      Includes ideas for stories, incomplete episodes, etc.
      JWJ Wright Misc. +499.

      Typed and autograph MSS: 33 leaves.
      Ideas for essays and incomplete drafts, etc.
      JWJ Wright Misc. +500.

26 "Pimp Situation."
    Typescript (original): 22 leaves, alternate leaves num-
    bered.
    The first person narrative may be an account of an episode
    related to "How Jim Crow Feels."
    JWJ Wright Misc. 516.

27 "Sleeping and Waking."
    Autograph MS: 4 leaves.
    JWJ Wright Misc. 757.

    Typescript (original): 5 numb. leaves.
    Working draft, with MS corrections and additions. First
    person narrative of impressions at sea.
    JWJ Wright Misc. 758.

    Another typescript (original): 2 numb. leaves.
    Final draft, incomplete, leaves 1 and 2 only.
    JWJ Wright Misc. 759.

28 "Song of the Bleeding Throat."
    Autograph MS: 150 numb. leaves.
    Early draft of a story. Leaf 15 lacking.
    JWJ Wright Misc. 761.

    Another autograph MS and typescript (original): 84 leaves.
    Working draft, with extensive MS corrections and additions.
    JWJ Wright Misc. 762.

    Another typescript (original): 90 numb. leaves.
    With extensive MS corrections.
    JWJ Wright Misc. 763.

29 "3344, A Play in 3 Acts."
    Typescript (original): 14 leaves.
    Act I only. Written prior to 1937 and related to opening
    chapter of his novel Lawd Today. See 1963.3.
    JWJ Wright +184.

30 "Trees and Rope."
    Typescript (original): 1 leaf.
    Draft of a short dramatic episode, with a few MS correc-
    tions.
    JWJ Wright Misc. 783.

FICTION

Books

31 "Black Hope" [excerpt].
    Typescript (carbon): 7 numb. leaves.
    An episode derived from developmental draft of Wright's

late version, leaves 47-54 (folders 33[1-4]).
JWJ Wright 38.

"Black Hope" [excerpt].
Typescript (original): 10 numb. leaves.
With typed MS corrections. Episode derived from develop-
mental draft of Wright's late version, leaves 96-106
(folders 33[1-4]).
JWJ Wright 39.

Another typescript (carbon): 8 numb. leaves.
Another draft, with MS corrections.
JWJ Wright 40.

[Interviews and notes.]
Typescript (original): 78 numb. leaves, 69 leaves.
Interviews with domestic workers. Extensive working notes.
Outline describing plot and character development, a typed
letter (photocopy) to Paul Reynolds concerning the plot and
a confidential New York State report on corner markets,
etc.
JWJ Wright 41.

Carbon copy of interviews: 78 numb. leaves.
JWJ Wright 42.

Additional notes: 140 leaves.
Typed and MS notes and reports on the use of arsenic,
domestic labor laws, and other miscellaneous working notes,
including suggestions for titles, brief draft of an opening
episode, etc.
JWJ Wright 43.

[Description of novel.]
Typescript (original): 4 numb. leaves.
Early draft summary of purpose and action in the novel.
With extensive MS revisions.
JWJ Wright 44.

Another typescript (original): 2 leaves.
Partial draft.
JWJ Wright 45.

Another typescript (original): 5 numb. leaves.
Later draft, with MS corrections.
JWJ Wright 46.

Another typescript (carbon): 5 numb. leaves.
Final draft.
JWJ Wright 47.

[Introduction to a reading from a work in progress.]
Typescript (original): 3 leaves.
On his interviews with black domestic workers.
JWJ Wright Misc. 284.

32   [Book Unspecified.]
     Autograph MS: 4 leaves, 221 numb. leaves.
     Incomplete draft of various episodes placed in approximate
     order, with some typed leaves laid in and some MS additions
     on versos of leaves.
     His working title: "Little Sister."
     JWJ Wright 28.

     Typescript (original): 961 numb. leaves, 12 leaves.
     Early draft, with MS corrections and revisions.
     JWJ Wright 29[1-4].

     Another typescript (original): 961 numb. leaves, 65 leaves.
     Intermediate working draft, with extensive MS revisions and
     additions.
     JWJ Wright 30[1-5].

     Carbon of above: 961 numb. leaves.
     Complete and unrevised, with duplicates of leaves 847-69
     laid in.
     JWJ Wright 31[1-5].

     Typescript (original): 142 leaves, 35 leaves, 73 leaves.
     Developmental draft of a late version, with extensive MS
     revisions, additions, and notes. With miscellaneous ma-
     terials deleted from a still later version.
     JWJ Wright 32.

     Typescript (original): 737 [i.e., 738] numb. leaves.
     Late version, with extensive typed revisions, many pasted
     in. Numbering omits leaves 56-119.
     JWJ Wright 33[1-4].

     [Newest version.]
     Typescript (original): 137 leaves, 6 leaves.
     Characters and plot vary from long drafts.
     JWJ Wright 34.

     Carbon of above: 137 leaves.
     JWJ Wright 35.

     Another typescript (original): 66 leaves.
     With MS corrections. Incomplete copy, numbered in
     sections.
     JWJ Wright 36.

     Carbon of above: 55 leaves.
     Lacks first section.
     JWJ Wright 37.

33   [Escapee.]
     Autograph MS: 5 numb. leaves.
     Outline of action for a novel about an army escapee during
     World War II in France.
     JWJ Wright Misc. 371.

34   "Fancy Man."
      Typescript notes for a novel.
      N.Y. Public Library, Schomburg Collection.

35   "A Father's Law." [1960]
      Typescript (original): 1 leaf, 306 numb. leaves.
      Unfinished novel. Restricted.
      JWJ Wright 160.

36   "Island of Hallucinations."
      This material was sealed by Mrs. Ellen Wright and is not
      available to readers. See "Five Episodes," published
      excerpts, 1963.1.
      JWJ Wright 173[1-2].

37   "Life in the Streets of Harlem."
      Typescript (original): 151 numb. leaves.
      Intermediate version, with a work outline for the story,
      1 leaf laid in.
      JWJ Wright 874.

      Carbon copy.
      With author's extensive MS revisions.
      JWJ Wright 875.

      Another typescript (original): 2 leaves.
      Another version of first page of above. With a few MS
      corrections and title: "Johnny Gibbs or The Jackal."
      JWJ Wright 876.

      Carbon copy.
      JWJ Wright 877.

      ["Rite of Passage."] [1944]
      Typescript (carbon): 49 leaves.
      Early chapters of a work on juvenile crime in Harlem.
      Originally called "The Jackal."
      First leaf lacking. With typed and autograph notes and
      background material on juvenile crime, 16 leaves.
      JWJ Wright 873[1-2].

      "Rite of Passage."
      Typescript (original): 1 leaf, 79 numb. leaves.
      Late version with a few typed corrections. With new title
      pasted on first leaf.
      JWJ Wright 878.

      Carbon of above.
      With earlier title: "Leader Man."
      JWJ Wright 879.

      Another typescript (original): 94 numb. leaves.
      Final version submitted to Wright's agent, Paul R.
      Reynolds, and with Reynolds's stamp.
      JWJ Wright 880.

161

Carbon of above.
With new title on title leaf and earlier title ("Leader
Man") on first page.
JWJ Wright 881.

Another carbon.
With earlier title ("Leader Man").
JWJ Wright 882.

38   "A Strange Girl."
     Typescript (original): 5 leaves.
     Outline of story with MS corrections. A copy of this ver-
     sion is included in Wright's Celebration, submitted to
     Edward Aswell for comments in Wright's typed letter
     (carbon) of 21 August 1955.
     JWJ Wright Misc. 766.

     Another typescript (original): 56 leaves.
     Complete draft, including dialogue, with MS corrections.
     JWJ Wright Misc. 767.

39   "Tarbaby's Dawn."
     Typescript (original): 2 leaves, 322 [i.e., 320] numb.
     leaves.
     Working draft of a first version, related to "Almos' a
     Man," with extensive MS revisions. His canceled title:
     "Tarbaby's Sunrise."
     JWJ Wright 906.

     Another typescript (original): 4 leaves, 285 numb. leaves.
     Another draft, incorporating above revisions. With criti-
     cal comments by an unidentified reader laid in, 7 leaves.
     JWJ Wright 907.

     Carbon of above: 2 leaves, 285 numb. leaves.
     JWJ Wright 908.

     Another typescript (original): 3 leaves.
     Early incomplete draft of opening episode. With MS
     corrections.
     JWJ Wright 909.

     Typescript (original): 11 leaves.
     Miscellaneous notes for above version, including outline
     of scenes used in his "Almos' a Man."
     JWJ Wright 910.

     Typescript (original) and autograph MS: 1 leaf, 4 numb.
     leaves; 9 leaves.
     Early draft of episodes marked "a" and "b," concerning
     events occurring after Tarbaby's arrival in Memphis.
     His title: "Tarbaby's Sunrise."
     JWJ Wright 911.

Another typescript (original): 11 leaves.
Outline and notes for a story on Tarbaby as a prize-
fighter.
JWJ Wright 912.

See "Almos' a Man," 1940.1.

Related Material:
[Pikowsky, Theodora.]
"'Tarbaby's Dawn,' a Critique."
Typescript (original): 2 leaves.
On Richard Wright's novel.
JWJ Wright, MSS about Wright 8.

40 "When the World Was Red."
Typescript (original): 2 leaves, 23 numb. leaves.
Working draft for one story of a series based on his con-
cept of mood. With extensive MS corrections and revisions.
A final version is included in his <u>Celebration</u>, typed let-
ter (carbon) to Edward Aswell, 21 August 1955.
JWJ Wright Misc. 804.

Another typescript (original): 28 leaves.
Another working draft, with extensive MS notes and correc-
tions.
JWJ Wright Misc. 805.

NONFICTION

<u>Shorter Writings</u>

Essays

41 "Adventure and Discovery, a Personal Statement."
Typescript (original): 12 numb. leaves.
Working draft of speech accepting the Spingarn Medal,
1941. With MS corrections.
JWJ Wright Misc. 226.

42 "Alas, My Old Favorite Brooklyn Barbershop."
Typescript (original): 2 leaves.
First draft, with extensive MS corrections.
JWJ Wright Misc. +227.

Another typescript (original): 6 numb. leaves.
Second draft, with MS corrections.
JWJ Wright Misc. 228.

Another typescript (original): 6 numb. leaves.
Final draft.
JWJ Wright Misc. 229.

Carbon of above.
JWJ Wright Misc. 230.

43   [The American Negro.]
     Autograph and typed MS: 10 leaves.
     Early draft of outline and notes for an essay on problems
     of the American Negro.
     JWJ Wright Misc. 231.

     Typescript (original): 20 numb. leaves.
     Working draft of ". . . a report on the state of Negro
     feeling today. . . ."
     With MS deletions and corrections. Expanded version of his
     reading notes for a lecture on this topic (folder 233).
     JWJ Wright Misc. +232.

     [Lecture notes.]
     Typescript (original): 20 numb. leaves (index cards).
     On the "state of Negro feeling [and] about how Negroes feel
     about their feelings."
     JWJ Wright Misc. 233.

     Another typescript (original): 16 numb. leaves (index
     cards).
     Another set of notes, with briefer detail.
     JWJ Wright Misc. 233a.

44   "Avant Guard."
     Typescript (carbon): 3 leaves.
     On the role of avant-garde magazines.
     JWJ Wright Misc. +270.

45   "The Barometer Points to Storm."
     Typescript (original): 5 numb. leaves.
     Report on the American Writers' Congress of 1937 and its
     stand on fascism.
     JWJ Wright Misc. 271.

46   "Can the American Negro Survive?"
     Autograph MS: 7 leaves.
     Early draft. On the effect of southern industrialization.
     JWJ Wright Misc. 340.

     Typescript (original): 4 numb. leaves.
     Partial draft.
     JWJ Wright Misc. 341.

47   [Chicago.]
     Typescript (original): 2 leaves.
     Concerning a photographic essay commissioned by Life
     magazine on the Chicago environment of Bigger Thomas. With
     a few MS corrections. Not published by Life.
     JWJ Wright Misc. 345.

     Carbon copy.
     JWJ Wright Misc. 346.

48 "A European Appeal to America."
    Autograph MS: 1 leaf.
    Working draft. Voicing dismay over racial segregation of
    the American Army in Europe after World War II.
    JWJ Wright Misc. 372.

    Typescript (carbon): 1 leaf.
    JWJ Wright Misc. 373.

49 "France Must March!"
    Autograph MS: 4 leaves.
    JWJ Wright Misc. 386.

    Typescript (original): 2 numb. leaves.
    JWJ Wright Misc. 387.

50 [French Images of the American Negro.]
    Typescript (original): 1 leaf.
    Incomplete draft.
    JWJ Wright Misc. 392.

51 "French West Africa."
    Typescript (original): 72 numb. leaves.
    With author's typed corrections, dated 12 May 1959. His
    notes from interviews and research on culture and colonial-
    ism in French Africa. With carbons of leaves 70-72 laid
    in, 3 leaves, and his MS notes on ideas; altogether 5
    leaves.
    JWJ Wright Misc. 394.

    Original typescript: 69 leaves.
    N.Y. Public Library, Schomburg Collection.

52 "The Future of Literary Expression."
    Typescript (original): 2 leaves.
    With his MS notes on versos.
    JWJ Wright Misc. 395.

53 [Greetings from American Artists Who Live in France.]
    Typescript (original): 2 numb. leaves.
    With a few MS corrections. On his impressions of Paris.
    JWJ Wright Misc. 399.

    Another typescript (original): 3 numb. leaves.
    With a few MS corrections.
    JWJ Wright Misc. 400.

54 "The Heart, for Reasons That Reason Does Not Know, Is on Both
    Sides. . . ."
    Typescript (original): 12 numb. leaves.
    With author's extensive MS corrections and his MS notes on
    verso of leaves 1 and 2. Concerning Gunnar Myrdal.
    JWJ Wright Misc. 405.

55   "Hymn to the Sinking Sun."
      Typescript (carbon): 4 numb. leaves.
      Concerning censorship and closing of the Federal Negro
      Theatre's production of Paul Green's "Hymn to the Rising
      Sun."
      JWJ Wright Misc. 411.

56   "I Am an American, but--."
      Autograph MS: 32 leaves.
      Concerning his views on America.
      JWJ Wright Misc. 412.

57   "I Choose Exile." [1950]
      Typescript (original): 17 numb. leaves.
      With a few MS corrections. Restricted.
      JWJ Wright Misc. 419.

58   "Memories of My Grandmother."
      Typescript (original): 69 leaves.
      Working draft, with MS corrections and additions. An
      analysis of the background for "The Man Who Lived Under-
      ground."
      JWJ Wright Misc. 473.

      Another typescript (original): 26 numb. leaves.
      Later version, incomplete copy.
      JWJ Wright Misc. 474.

      See "The Man Who Lived Underground," 1942.3.

59   "Mobilization of Negro Opinion"
      Typescript (original): 11 numb. leaves.
      First draft of a plan for a propaganda project directed
      toward developing war arms during World War II. With
      extensive MS revisions and his working title: "Project
      for Mobilization of Negro Opinion."
      JWJ Wright Misc. 475.

      Carbon copy: 11 numb. leaves.
      With an additional leaf from another carbon copy laid in.
      Lacks corrections.
      JWJ Wright Misc. 476.

      Miscellaneous notes and general outline: typescript
      (original): 4 numb. leaves, 2 leaves.
      JWJ Wright Misc. 477.

      Another typescript (original): 9 numb. leaves.
      Final version.
      JWJ Wright Misc. 478.

      Carbon copy.
      JWJ Wright Misc. 479.

Another typescript (carbon):   8 numb. leaves.
Another copy.
JWJ Wright Misc. 480.

Carbon copy.
JWJ Wright Misc. 481.

Another typescript (carbon):   9 numb. leaves.
JWJ Wright Misc. 482.

Another typescript (original):   1 leaf, 7 numb. leaves.
Copy submitted to Paul Reynolds.   Partial draft consisting
of a plan of action only.   Preface lacking.
JWJ Wright Misc. 483.

[Democratic Testimony.]
Typescript (carbon):   8 numb. leaves.
Script for radio broadcast designed to mobilize Negro
opinion for support of the U.S. war effort during World
War II.   With a revised version of a message from Paul
Robeson speaking to Europe, 2 leaves.   Written with
Carleton Moss.
JWJ Wright Misc. 361.

See "Loyalty Pledge to the Constitution of the United
States," U.122, and "The Negro's Position in the Present
World Struggle," U.126.

60   [On Writing Autobiography.]
     Typescript (original):   1 leaf.
     With MS corrections and revisions.   Prepared for Christmas
     book section of the Chicago Tribune, 1944, but not
     published.
     JWJ Wright Misc. 512.

     Another typescript (original):   1 leaf.
     Partial draft.
     JWJ Wright Misc. 513.

61   "A Personal Report from Paris."
     Typescript (original):   6 leaves.
     With MS corrections.
     JWJ Wright Misc. 514.

62   "Personalism."   [1935-1937?]
     Typescript (original):   5 numb. leaves.
     Early essay on personal protest as a mode of artistic
     expression.   With MS corrections and MS notes, 1 leaf.
     JWJ Wright Misc. 515.

     Original MS: 4 leaves.
     N.Y. Public Library, Schomburg Coll. C13.

63   "The Position of the Negro Artist and Intellectual in American
      Society."
         Typescript (carbon and original): 4 leaves.
         With author's MS corrections and additions. Includes
         account of encounter with James Baldwin in a Paris cafe,
         his dispute with Time magazine over statements attributed
         to him, etc.
         JWJ Wright Misc. 622.

         Another typescript (original): 3 leaves.
         Incomplete copy, leaves 1-3 only.
         JWJ Wright Misc. 623.

         Two carbon copies.
         JWJ Wright Misc. 624-625.

64   "The Problem of Interference. . . ."
         Autograph MS: 14 leaves.
         His working title: "The Concept of Interference or the
         Extension of the European Enlightenment to the People of
         the Earth."
         JWJ Wright Misc. 633.

         Typescript (original): 14 leaves.
         With a few MS corrections.
         JWJ Wright Misc. 634.

65   "Repeating a Modest Proposal (With Apologies to Old Jonathan
      [Swift])."
         Typescript (original): 8 numb. leaves.
         Working draft, with extensive MS additions.
         JWJ Wright Misc. 632.

         Typescript (original): 1 leaf.
         Opening paragraphs only, with a few MS additions.
         JWJ Wright Misc. 644.

         Another typescript (carbon): 5 numb. leaves.
         Written while Wright was living in Chicago.
         JWJ Wright Misc. 645.

         Galley proof for Race magazine: 2 leaves.
         JWJ Wright Misc. 646.

66   [The Role of the Artist in America.]
         Typescript (original): 2 leaves.
         Drafts of an article on the role of the writer and artist
         in the United States after 1929. On verso of second leaf
         are MS notes for an article on the Joe Louis-Max Schmeling
         prize fight, 1938, published in the Daily Worker, 22 June
         1938.
         JWJ Wright Misc. 750.

67   "Roots and Branches."
      Typescript (original):   5 numb. leaves.
      With extensive MS revisions. On his creative process in
      the development of stories, in particular those in Eight
      Men.
      JWJ Wright Misc. 751.

68   "There Are Still Men Left." [1941?]
      Typescript (original):   6 numb. leaves.
      On why Wright joined the Communist Party. With MS addi-
      tions and corrections.
      JWJ Wright Misc. 771.

69   "Things I Never Knew about Negroes Before."
      Typescript (original):   2 leaves.
      Early working draft, with extensive MS revisions and dele-
      tions. With his MS typed notes and lists of facts (16
      leaves).
      JWJ Wright Misc. 774.

      Another typescript (original):   2 numb. leaves.
      Working draft, with MS corrections and deletions.
      JWJ Wright Misc. 775.

      Another typescript (original):   5 numb. leaves.
      Final draft.
      JWJ Wright Misc. 776.

      Carbon of above: 5 leaves.
      With typed copy, original of leaf 4 laid in.
      JWJ Wright Misc. 777.

70   "Towards the Conquest of Ourselves."
      Typescript (original):   28 leaves.
      Working draft, with extensive MS corrections and revisions.
      A plea to Negroes to fight for recognition of their rights
      and humanity. Includes excerpts of events from American
      Hunger.
      JWJ Wright Misc. 781.

      Another typescript (original):   3 leaves (leaves 5-7 only).
      Partial draft of closing section of MS. Other parts of
      this draft are inserted and revised in preceding copy.
      JWJ Wright Misc. 782.

71   "What We Think of Their War."
      Typescript (original):   13 leaves.
      Early working draft of a speech delivered at the Fourth
      American Writers Conference, 6-8 June 1941, New York. With
      MS corrections and additions.
      JWJ Wright Misc. 794.

Another typescript (original): 12 numb. leaves.
Intermediate draft, with MS corrections.
JWJ Wright Misc. 795.

Another typescript (carbon): 12 numb. leaves.
Final draft on Wright's stationery. With revised and
deleted material laid in, 3 leaves.
JWJ Wright Misc. 796.

Another typescript (mimeographed): 9 numb. leaves.
JWJ Wright Misc. +797.

Another mimeographed copy.
JWJ Wright Misc. +798.

72 "Where Do We Go from Here?"
Typescript (original): 6 numb. leaves.
Relates in style and tone to Twelve Million Black Voices.
JWJ Wright Misc. +806.

See Twelve Million Black Voices, 1941.26.

73 "The World Needs a Conscience."
Typescript (original): 3 numb. leaves.
With a few MS corrections. On the need for world govern-
ment.
JWJ Wright Misc. 808.

Another typescript (original): 3 numb. leaves.
JWJ Wright Misc. 809.

74 "Writing from the Left."
Typescript (original): 9 numb. leaves.
With MS corrections.
JWJ Wright Misc. 812.

Blurbs

75 [On Lonely Crusade, by Chester Himes.]
Typescript (original): 1 leaf.
Eight-line blurb based on introduction.
Private collection.

76 [On Poems, by Naomi Replansky.]
Typescript (original): 1 leaf.
Working draft of comment for dust jacket. With MS
corrections.
JWJ Wright Misc. 311.

Typescript (carbon): 1 leaf.
Final draft.
JWJ Wright Misc. 312.

Another typescript (original): 1 leaf
JWJ Wright Misc. 313.

77   [On Dark Symphony, by Melvin Tolson.]
      Typescript (original): 1 leaf.
      Early working draft for a comment on dust jacket. With
      Wright's MS corrections.
      JWJ Wright Misc. 322.

      Another typescript (original): 1 leaf.
      Working draft, with MS corrections.
      JWJ Wright Misc. 323.

      Another typescript (original): 1 leaf.
      Another draft, with MS corrections.
      JWJ Wright Misc. 324.

      Another typescript (carbon): 1 leaf.
      Final draft.
      JWJ Wright Misc. 325.

Book Reviews and Reports

78   [On Black Moon, by Clark McMeekin.]
      Typescript (original): 1 leaf.
      Working draft of a first reader's report. With author's
      MS corrections and additions.
      JWJ Wright Misc. 695.

      Another typescript (original): 1 leaf.
      With author's MS corrections.
      JWJ Wright Misc. 696.

79   [On Dragon Harvest, by Upton Sinclair.]
      Typescript (original): 1 leaf.
      Working draft of a first reader's report for the Book-of-
      the-Month Club (1945). With MS corrections and MS notes
      laid in, 8 leaves.
      JWJ Wright Misc. 721.

      Another typescript (original): 2 leaves.
      Another working draft, with MS revisions and with a
      synopsis of the plot.
      JWJ Wright Misc. 722.

      Another typescript (original): 1 leaf.
      Final draft.
      JWJ Wright Misc. 723.

80   [On Heritage of the River, by Muriel Elwood.]
      Autograph MS: 2 leaves.
      First draft of a reader's report for the Book-of-the-Month
      Club. With Wright's MS notes laid in, 3 leaves.
      JWJ Wright Misc. 666.

      Typescript (original): 1 leaf.
      Working draft, with MS corrections.
      JWJ Wright Misc. 667.

Another typescript (original): 1 leaf.
On printed form, with MS corrections.
JWJ Wright Misc. 668.

81 [On Hunky Johnny, by E. J. Nichols.]
Typescript (original): 1 leaf.
First draft, with author's MS corrections. Reader's report
for the Book-of-the-Month Club.
JWJ Wright Misc. 702.

Another typescript (original): 1 leaf.
Working draft, with author's MS corrections.
JWJ Wright Misc. 703.

Another typescript (original): 1 leaf.
JWJ Wright Misc. 704.

82 [On Ploughman of the Moon, by Robert Service.]
Typescript (original): 2 leaves.
Working draft of a first reader's report for the Book-of-
the-Month Club (1945-1946).
JWJ Wright Misc. 717.

Another typescript (original): 1 leaf.
Final draft on printed form from the Book-of-the-Month
Club, with recommendations for acceptance.
JWJ Wright Misc. +718.

Two carbons of above.
Incomplete copies.
JWJ Wright Misc. +719-720.

83 [On Sixty Million Jobs, by Henry Wallace.]
Autograph MS: 2 numb. leaves.
Draft of a reader's report (1945). With typed working
materials on verso of leaf 2.
JWJ Wright Misc. 731.

Typescript (original): 1 leaf.
Working draft, with MS corrections.
JWJ Wright Misc. 732.

Another typescript (original): 1 leaf.
Later draft, with a few MS corrections.
JWJ Wright Misc. 733.

84 [Review of The Age of Defeat, by Colin Wilson.]
Points of criticism. Typescript: 1 leaf.
N.Y. Public Library, Schomburg Coll. C40.

85 [Review of American Negro Music, by Ernest Borneman.]
Typescript (original): 3 numb. leaves.
Working draft, with MS corrections and a MS addition, 1
leaf, laid in.
JWJ Wright Misc. 660.

86 [Review of <u>Deep Are the Roots</u>, by Armand D'Usseau and James
     Gow.]
     Typescript (original): 3 leaves.
     Early developmental draft of a play review for <u>Life</u> maga-
     zine. With MS corrections.
     JWJ Wright Misc. +661.

     Another typescript (original): 17 leaves.
     Working draft, with extensive MS revisions, additions, and
     MS notes laid in.
     JWJ Wright Misc. 662.

     Another typescript (original): 4 leaves.
     Intermediate working draft, with extensive MS corrections
     and revisions.
     JWJ Wright Misc. 663.

     Another typescript (original): 7 numb. leaves.
     Later working draft, with MS corrections.
     JWJ Wright Misc. 664.

     Another typescript (original): 7 numb. leaves.
     Final draft, dated 29 September 1945.
     JWJ Wright Misc. 665.

     Carbon copy.
     Private collection.

87 [Review of <u>Inside U. S. A.</u>, by John Gunther.]
     Typescript (original): 1 leaf.
     With MS revisions.
     JWJ Wright Misc. 686.

     Another typescript (original): 1 leaf.
     Incomplete copy.
     JWJ Wright Misc. 687.

88 [Review of <u>Mr. Allenby Loses the Way</u>, by Frank Baker.] [1945]
     Autograph MS: 1 leaf.
     First draft. On Baker's novel (New York: Coward-McCann,
     1945).
     JWJ Wright Misc. 658.

     Typescript (original): 1 leaf.
     With a few MS corrections.
     JWJ Wright Misc. 659.

89 [Review of <u>The Silver Darlings</u>, by Neil Gunn.]
     Autograph MS: 1 leaf.
     First draft of a short version, with MS corrections and
     with MS notes laid in, 6 leaves. Gunn's book published in
     1941.
     JWJ Wright Misc. 677.

Typescript (original): 1 leaf.
Early working draft, with MS corrections.
JWJ Wright Misc. +678.

Another typescript (original): 1 leaf.
Another working draft, with MS corrections and revisions.
JWJ Wright Misc. +679.

Another typescript (original): 1 leaf.
With a few MS corrections.
JWJ Wright Misc. 680.

Another typescript (original): 1 leaf.
With a few MS corrections.
JWJ Wright Misc. 681.

Another typescript (original): 1 leaf.
Revised intermediate draft.
JWJ Wright Misc. 682.

Another typescript (original): 2 leaves.
Expanded version, with extensive MS corrections and additions.
JWJ Wright Misc. 683.

Another typescript (original): 1 leaf.
Working draft of expanded version, with extensive MS corrections.
JWJ Wright Misc. 684.

Another typescript (original): 1 leaf.
Working draft of expanded version, with a few MS corrections.
JWJ Wright Misc. 685.

Interviews

90   [Interview (1953).]
     Typescript (original): 7 numb. leaves.
     Incomplete copy, first leaf lacking. Concerning Wright's
     opinions on racial issues, etc.
     JWJ Wright Misc. 420.

91   [Interview with Edwin Seaver.]
     Typescript (original): 8 numb. leaves.
     Script no. 12, for Readers and Writers Series, dated
     23 December 1941.
     JWJ Wright Misc. 423.

92   [Interview with Raymond Barthe.]
     Typescript (original): 5 numb. leaves.
     Working draft, with typed and MS corrections. Mostly con-
     cerning his Savage Holiday. In French, for French Radio
     Broadcast.
     JWJ Wright Misc. 424.

Another typescript (original): 5 numb. leaves.
Later draft, with some MS corrections.
JWJ Wright Misc. 425.

Introductions

93   [Introduction to The Negro American, by Russell Warren Howe.]
      Typescript (original): 5 numb. leaves.
      Early draft, with extensive MS corrections. Concerning
      other nations' views of American attitudes toward the
      Negro.
      JWJ Wright Misc. 627.

      Another typescript (original): 6 leaves.
      Working draft, with MS corrections.
      JWJ Wright Misc. 628.

      Another typescript (carbon): 8 numb. leaves.
      With a few MS corrections and a MS note on verso of final
      leaf. Dated 9 March 1956, Paris.
      JWJ Wright Misc. 629.

      Another typescript (original): 8 numb. leaves.
      Final draft, with a few MS corrections.
      JWJ Wright Misc. 630.

94   "Lest We Forget . . ." [introduction to The Violent Conflict,
      by Whit Burnett].
      Typescript (original), signed: 5 numb. leaves.
      Dated 28 July 1955. Working draft of introduction to
      Burnett's compilation of short stories on Negro life.
      With his discussion of the selected stories, 1 leaf, and
      with MS corrections. A collection by Burnett appeared in
      1971, titled Black Hands on a White Face, but its contents
      only partly duplicated the earlier collection.
      JWJ Wright Misc. 456.

      Another typescript (original): 5 numb. leaves.
      Intermediate draft, with MS corrections.
      JWJ Wright Misc. 457.

      Another typescript (original): 5 numb. leaves.
      Final draft. With letter to Whit Burnett, 28 July 1955.
      Princeton University Library, Story Magazine files.

      Another typescript (carbon): 5 numb. leaves.
      JWJ Wright Misc. 458.

      Another typescript (carbon): 4 numb. leaves.
      With "A Note by the Editor" (Whit Burnett).
      Private collection.

95   [Preface to Black Metropolis, by St. Clair Drake and Horace R.
     Cayton.] [1960]
     Typescript (original): 20 numb. leaves.
     Draft for an introduction to the paperback reprint of the
     book, never published.
     JWJ Wright 58.

Letters

96   [Letter to Mike Gold.]
     Typescript (original): 9 numb. leaves.
     Draft of a reply to comments and articles about Native Son
     in the New Masses.
     JWJ Wright Misc. 460.

97   [Letter to John Strachey.]
     Autograph MS: 36 leaves.
     Draft describes Wright's experiences with the British immi-
     gration service and the Aliens division of the British Home
     Office, September 1959.
     JWJ Wright Misc. 460a.

Liner Notes

98   "It's Louis Jordan All the Way . . ."
     Typescript (original): 2 numb. leaves.
     Liner notes for record album (Barclay records).
     JWJ Wright Misc. 297.

     Carbon of above.
     JWJ Wright Misc. 298.

     Another typescript (carbon): 2 numb. leaves.
     Another version.
     JWJ Wright Misc. 299.

     Carbon of above.
     JWJ Wright Misc. 300.

99   [Precious Memories, etc.]
     Autograph MS: 5 leaves.
     Liner notes for Barclay records.
     JWJ Wright Misc. 310.

Miscellaneous

100 "American Pages: Suggestions for the Launching of a
     Magazine. . . ."
     Autograph MS: 8 leaves.
     Early draft of a proposal for "A magazine reflecting the
     minority mood and point of view." With MS notes laid in,
     2 leaves.
     JWJ Wright Misc. 235.

Typescript (original): 4 numb. leaves.
Working draft, with MS corrections. With typed working
notes laid in, 6 leaves. With his complete subtitle:
"Suggestions for launching of a magazine whose popular
contents would appeal to the white middle class in an
effort to clarify the personality and cultural problems of
minority groups, using the Negro question as an abstract
and concrete frame of reference to reflect a constructive
criticism upon the culture of the nation as a whole."
JWJ Wright Misc. 236.

Another typescript (original): 1 leaf, 15 numb. leaves.
Later draft, with MS corrections.
JWJ Wright Misc. 237.

Another typescript.(carbon), signed: 17 numb. leaves.
Final draft of proposal submitted to Edwin Seaver, with
Seaver's reply of 26 November 1943. Duplicates of p. 11
and its carbons (3 leaves) deleted for retyping are laid
in.
JWJ Wright Misc. 238.

101 [Authors' League of America: Invitation to a Speaker.]
     Autograph MS: 4 leaves.
     Draft of an invitation to an unidentified recipient to
     speak before the Authors' Guild of the Authors' League of
     America, 8 May 1947, at Town Hall, New York.
     JWJ Wright Misc. 257.

     Typescript (original): 2 leaves.
     Another draft.
     JWJ Wright Misc. 258.

102 [Authors' League of America: Introductory Remarks.]
     Typescript (original): 2 leaves.
     Wright's remarks on why he chose to become an officer of
     the League, and introduction of an unidentified speaker.
     JWJ Wright Misc. 259.

103 [Autobiographical Sketch.] [1938-1940]
     Typescript (original): 3 leaves.
     Working draft, with MS revisions. Written [1938-1940] for
     promotion of Uncle Tom's Children.
     JWJ Wright Misc. +262.

     Another typescript: 3 leaves.
     With typescript of Story announcement of prize award to
     Uncle Tom's Children.
     Princeton University Library, Story Magazine files.

     Another typescript (carbon): 1 leaf.
     Later draft.
     JWJ Wright Misc. +263.

Another typescript (carbon): 3 numb. leaves.
Another draft, with some MS revisions; revised for Harper
(1940).
JWJ Wright Misc. +264.

Another typescript (carbon and original): 2 leaves,
3 numb. leaves.
Another version, expanded and revised for Harper, sum-
marizing his life up to the publication of Native Son
(1940).
JWJ Wright Misc. +265.

104   [Autobiographical Sketch.]   [1945]
       Typescript (carbon): 2 numb. leaves.
       Brief summary of his life through the publication of Black
       Boy (1945). Written in the third person.
       JWJ Wright Misc. 266.

105   [Autobiographical Statement (1959).]
       Typescript (carbon): 4 numb. leaves.
       Wright's curriculum vitae, dated 6 October 1959.
       JWJ Wright Misc. 269.

106   [Autobiographical Notes.]
       Typescript (original): 5 numb. leaves.
       With MS additions and corrections and his MS note on verso.
       Description of his early life through his arrival in
       Memphis.
       JWJ Wright Misc. +261.

107   [Celebration.]
       Typescript (original): 10 leaves.
       Working draft of plan for two new approaches to writing,
       based on his concept of "mood." With MS outline of titles
       for parts of series.
       JWJ Wright Misc. 342.

       Another typescript (original): 7 leaves.
       Later draft, with MS corrections and some revisions pasted
       in.
       JWJ Wright Misc. 343.

       Typed letter (carbon) to Edward Aswell, 21 August 1955
       (Paris, France).
       Includes statement on his departure from the Communist
       party, his emigration to France, and his proposal for a
       series of novels called "Celebration" based on "mood."
       With a MS note from draft of letter. Two leaves bear
       no. 31.
       JWJ Wright Misc. 344.

108 [The Communist Party and the Negro.] [after 1941]
Typescript (original): 1 leaf.
Statement on the lack of support by the Communist party
for the Negro. With typed notes laid in, 1 leaf.
JWJ Wright Misc. 352.

109 [Contemporary Negro Life in the United States.]
Typescript (original): 9 leaves.
Incomplete copy of a lecture to an unidentified group of
writers, prepared for a broadcast (?) in Quebec, Canada.
Material closely related to his introduction to Black
Metropolis, by St. Clair Drake and Horace R. Cayton.
JWJ Wright Misc. 357.

110 [Diary (1945).]
Autograph MS: 366 pp.
Record of daily expenses, appointments, and literary
activities.
JWJ Wright Misc. 362.

111 [Engagement Calendars (1941-1945, 1948).]
Loose leaves of five desk appointment calendars, some
listing meetings with friends, publishers, lawyers, etc.,
but mostly unused. With his Hermes spiral pocket engage-
ment book for third trimester, 1948, listing appointments
with French colleagues.
JWJ Wright Misc. 370[1-6].

112 "The Folklore [of] Race Relations."
Autograph MS: 1 leaf.
Outline for a lecture. On verso of bill from The Hotel
Lowry, St. Paul, Minn., dated 16 November 1945.
JWJ Wright Misc. 376.

113 [French Lessons.]
Three folders.
Miscellaneous typed loose leaf pages of French grammar and
conversation lessons taken by Wright. With a bound note-
book, signed, of Wright's MS exercises.
JWJ Wright Misc. 393[1-3].

114 [George Gershwin.]
Autograph MS: 7 leaves.
Working notes for a discussion of the influence of Afro-
American music on the work of George Gershwin.
JWJ Wright Misc. 397.

115 "The Gamble for Freedom."
Autograph MS: 4 leaves.
Incomplete draft of a lecture.
JWJ Wright Misc. 396.

116   [Haitian Biographies.]
       Typed and autograph MS: 29 leaves.
       Notes for biographical sketches taken during a visit to
       Haiti. With MS corrections.
       JWJ Wright Misc. 401.

117   "High Blood Pressure."
       Typescript (original): 5 numb. leaves.
       Draft of a lecture on white attitudes toward blacks. With
       miscellaneous notes, 5 leaves.
       JWJ Wright Misc. 406.

       See [The American Negro], U.43.

118   [Introductory Remarks to an Address on the Negro in the United
       States.]
       Autograph MS: 2 leaves.
       Concerns the attitudes of whites toward the American Negro.
       JWJ Wright Misc. 452.

119   [Journal (1 January–19 April 1945).]
       Typescript (original): 188 leaves.
       Daily accounts of his activities, events relating to the
       publication of Black Boy, etc.
       JWJ Wright Misc. 454.

       See 1945.22.

120   [Journal (30 July–23 September 1947).]
       Typescript (original): 68 pp.
       Concerning his second voyage to France and his early days
       in Paris.
       JWJ Wright Misc. 455.

121   "Let's Give the World a Conscience." [1950]
       Typescript (original): 3 leaves.
       Draft, with MS corrections of statement in favor of world
       government and Greg Davis movement.
       Private collection.

       Typescript copy, 11 numb. leaves.
       Kent State University Library.

122   [Loyalty Pledge to the Constitution of the United States.]
       Typescript (original): 1 leaf.
       With MS corrections and notes.
       JWJ Wright Misc. 463.

       Another typescript (original): 2 leaves.
       Another draft, with MS corrections and additions.
       JWJ Wright Misc. 464.

123 "My Friends and Fellow Workers in the Cause of Freedom."
     Typescript (original): 3 numb. leaves.
     Dated 2 May 1949. Speech given in London. An expression
     of support for the African struggle against European
     colonialism.
     JWJ Wright Misc. 484.

124 [Negro Soldiers.]
     Typescript (carbon): 30 leaves. Leaves numbered 1-16,
     21-34.
     On the participation of Negro soldiers in the first World
     War and the effect of subsequent liberalizing trends on
     Negro expectations and attitudes toward a future war
     against fascism.
     JWJ Wright Misc. 489.

125 "The Negro Speaks."
     Typescript (original) and autograph MS: 21 leaves.
     Outline, notes, and general ideas for a collection of
     essays on the Negro experience in the United States.
     JWJ Wright Misc. 490.

126 [The Negro's Position in the Present World Struggle. . . .]
     Typescript (original): 1 leaf.
     With MS corrections. Statement endorsing black support of
     America in World War II.
     JWJ Wright Misc. 491.

     Another typescript (original): 2 leaves.
     With MS corrections.
     JWJ Wright Misc. 492.

127 [Notes: Financial Matters: Business and Personal Expenses,
     etc.]
     Typed and autograph MS: 106 leaves.
     Includes apartment floor plans and notes concerning houses,
     etc.
     JWJ Wright Misc. +497.

128 [Notes: Lists and Miscellaneous Papers.]
     Typescript and autograph MS: 238 leaves.
     Lists of books, ideas for titles and personal activities,
     etc.
     JWJ Wright Misc. +501[1-2].

129 [Notes on Jim Crowism in the United States Army.]
     Typescript (original): 4 leaves.
     Quotations from letters written by black soldiers during
     World War II on their feelings about fighting for
     democracy.
     JWJ Wright Misc. 505.

130 [Notes on Karl Jaspers.]
Typescript (original): 2 numb. leaves.
With MS notes (1 leaf). An analysis of the philosophy of
Karl Jaspers.
JWJ Wright Misc. 378.

131 [Notes on Reading.]
Typed and autograph MS: 28 leaves.
Notes on works by other authors, including Alexander
Pushkin's "The Shot."
JWJ Wright Misc. 502.

132 [On John O'Hara's Hell Box.]
Typescript (original): 4 leaves. On index cards.
Discussion of O'Hara's short stories for "Author Meets the
Critics" broadcast.
JWJ Wright Misc. 503.

Related Material:
Typescript (original): 1 leaf.
Advertising blurb for the radio broadcast.
JWJ Wright Misc. 289.

Another typescript (original): 1 leaf.
Another version, on leaf bearing personal notes.
JWJ Wright Misc. 290.

133 [On Literature.]
Typescript (original): 18 leaves.
An essay.
JWJ Wright Misc. 507.

134 [On Theodore Dreiser.]
Autograph MS: 1 leaf.
Notes praising Dreiser, written on invitation to a testi-
monial luncheon honoring Dreiser, 1 March 1941, New York,
given by the American Council on Soviet Relations.
JWJ Wright Misc. 510.

Related Material:
[American Writer's League: Agenda for a Meeting.]
Typescript (original): 2 leaves.
With MS notes by Wright for introducing Theodore Dreiser,
and a MS note by another.
JWJ Wright Misc. 243.

135 [On Writing.]
Typescript (original): 8 numb. leaves.
Notes for a lecture on "What I think writing is. . . ."
JWJ Wright Misc. 511.

136   [Personal Objects.]
        Assorted personal objects, including a Spingarn Medal
        (1941), on a red and black ribbon.
        JWJ Wright 1020.

137   [Personal Papers.]
        Miscellaneous personal documents, including driver's
        licenses, leases, library cards, passport, identification
        cards, etc.: 5 folders. For additional personal material,
        see U.127-28.
        JWJ Wright 1021[1-5].

138   [Politics and Personalities in the Gold Coast.]   [1957]
        Typescript (original): 2 leaves.
        Incomplete draft of a lecture.
        JWJ Wright Misc. +626.

139   [Proposing a World Congress of Intellectuals.]
        Typescript (original): 1 leaf.
        Fragment consists of one leaf of a MS. Four suggestions
        for the role of an international day and a world congress
        of intellectuals as a means of fighting Communism.
        JWJ Wright Misc. 635.

140   [Protest Statement on Serving in the United States Armed
        Forces.]
        Typescript (original): 1 leaf.
        Working draft, with MS corrections. Protesting service in
        the armed forces under segregated conditions.
        JWJ Wright Misc. 636.

        Another typescript (original): 1 leaf.
        JWJ Wright Misc. 637.

        Another typescript (carbon): 1 leaf.
        JWJ Wright Misc. 638.

        Carbon of above.
        JWJ Wright Misc. 639.

141   ["A Recommendation" on Helen Levitt's Photographs of
        Children.]
        Autograph MS: 1 leaf.
        Partial draft of a review of an exhibition of photographs
        by Helen Levitt at the Museum of Modern Art, New York,
        April 1943.
        JWJ Wright Misc. 692.

        Typescript (original): 1 leaf.
        With Wright's MS notes and corrections.
        JWJ Wright Misc. 693.

142   [Reply] "To Stakhanov Appeal."
       Typescript (original): 2 leaves.
       Working draft, with MS corrections and additions. With
       copy of Stakhanov's statement laid in, 1 leaf.
       JWJ Wright Misc. 747.

       Another typescript (original): 2 leaves.
       Final draft.
       JWJ Wright Misc. 748.

       Carbon of above.
       JWJ Wright Misc. 749.

143   [Reply] "To the Spingarn Award Committee."
       Typescript (original): 1 leaf.
       Working draft of his statement accepting the NAACP's
       Spingarn Medal for 1941.
       JWJ Wright Misc. 778.

       Another typescript (original): 1 leaf.
       Final draft dated 28 January 1940. [i.e., 1941]
       JWJ Wright Misc. 779.

       Carbon of above.
       JWJ Wright Misc. 780.

144   [The Results of European Oppression.]
       Typescript (original): 4 leaves.
       Introduction to a lecture on the effects of imperialism on
       Asia and Africa.
       JWJ Wright Misc. 647.

145   [Rural Sports.]
       Typescript (original): 2 leaves.
       On devising games out of one's environment.
       JWJ Wright Misc. 752.

146   [Translation of Introduction to L'Etre et le Néant (Being and
       Nothingness), by Jean Paul Sartre.]
       Typescript (original): 2 leaves.
       Incomplete draft of Wright's translation of Sartre's intro-
       duction, "The Pursuit of Being." With his working notes,
       laid in, 2 leaves.
       JWJ Wright Misc. 753.

147   [Solutions to World Race Problems.]
       Typescript (original): 19 numb. leaves.
       Draft of an essay on racial oppression and black national-
       ism in Africa. With author's MS corrections.
       JWJ Wright Misc. 760.

148 "Spiritual Illness."
      Typescript (original): 2 leaves.
      Draft of reply to a critic probably of his "What You Don't
      Know Won't Hurt You," Harper's Magazine 186 (December
      1942):58-61.
      JWJ Wright Misc. 765.

149 [Writers and Their Art.] [1955]
      Typescript (original): 4 leaves.
      Notes on eight issues.
      JWJ Wright Misc. 811.

150 "What Are Men to You?"
      Typescript (original): 1 leaf.
      Short draft, with MS corrections.
      JWJ Wright Misc. 790.

      Another typescript (original): 1 leaf.
      Longer working draft, with MS corrections.
      JWJ Wright Misc. 791.

POETRY

Shorter Writings

151 "After a Hard Day. . . ."
      Typescript (original): 2 leaves.
      With MS corrections. Title drawn from first line of poem.
      JWJ Wright Misc. 520.

152 "Alone in Town."
      Typescript (original): 1 leaf.
      JWJ Wright 521.

      "And he hath put a new song in my mouth."
      Typescript (original): leaf 27.
      Probably only part of a poem. First leaf or leaves
      missing?
      Private collection.

153 "As If."
      Autograph MS: 2 leaves.
      Early draft.
      JWJ Wright Misc. 522.

      Typescript (original): 2 leaves.
      Working draft, with typed notes.
      JWJ Wright Misc. 523.

      Another typescript (original): 1 leaf.
      Another draft, with MS corrections.
      JWJ Wright Misc. 524.

Carbon of above.
With extensive MS corrections.
JWJ Wright Misc. 525.

154   "Blue Black."
Autograph MS: 6 leaves.
Working draft, with MS corrections.
JWJ Wright Misc. 529.

Typescript (original): 3 leaves.
Working draft, with MS corrections.
JWJ Wright Misc. 530.

Another typescript (original): 1 leaf.
Short version.
JWJ Wright Misc. 531.

Carbon of above.
With MS corrections.
JWJ Wright Misc. 532.

Another typescript (original): 1 leaf.
Another short version.
JWJ Wright Misc. 533.

Another typescript (original): 1 leaf.
Longer version with his title, "Blue-black Blue."
JWJ Wright Misc. 534.

Carbon of above.
JWJ Wright Misc. 535.

155   "The Blues of the Hunted."
Typescript (original): 1 leaf.
Draft of early version, with some passages similar to his
"I Can't Remember: I Forgot. . . ." With MS corrections.
Title: "The Hunted Blues."
JWJ Wright Misc. 539.

Carbon copy.
With MS corrections.
JWJ Wright Misc. 540.

Another typescript (original): 1 leaf.
Working draft of early version, with MS corrections.
JWJ Wright Misc. 541.

Another typescript (original): 1 leaf.
Another working draft.
JWJ Wright Misc. 542.

Another typescript (original): 1 leaf.
Later draft, with MS additions.
JWJ Wright Misc. 543.

Carbon copy.
JWJ Wright Misc. 544.

Another typescript (original): 1 leaf.
Working draft of a later version, with extensive MS cor-
rections.
JWJ Wright Misc. 545.

Carbon copy.
JWJ Wright Misc. 546.

Another typescript (original): 1 leaf.
Another draft of later version, with a few MS corrections.
JWJ Wright Misc. 547.

Another typescript (original): 1 leaf.
Another draft of a still later version; sequence of verses
is altered.
JWJ Wright Misc. 548.

156   "Blue Snow Blues."
      Typescript (original): 3 numb. leaves.
      Dated 1960 [?].
      JWJ Wright Misc. 546.

      Two carbons of above.
      JWJ Wright Misc. 537-38.

157   "A Boy I Know Is Dead."
      Typescript (carbon): 1 leaf.
      Blues lyrics, with author's signed note: "This is to be
      used at the end of the movie" [i.e., Native Son].
      JWJ Wright Misc. 549.

      Another typescript (carbon): 1 leaf.
      Another version.
      Title: "Another Boy's Dead."
      See Native Son (film), U.10.
      JWJ Wright Misc. 550.

158   "Cat Blues."
      Autograph MS: 1 leaf.
      Working draft, with his title, "Black Cat Blues."
      JWJ Wright Misc. 551.

      Typescript (original): 1 leaf.
      Working draft, with MS corrections.
      JWJ Wright Misc. 552.

      Another typescript (original): 1 leaf.
      Another working draft, with extensive MS corrections.
      JWJ Wright Misc. 533.

      Another typescript (original): 1 leaf.
      Later version, with MS corrections.
      JWJ Wright Misc. 554.

Another typescript (original): 2 leaves.
Final draft on Wright's own stationery, with a few MS corrections and with his MS notes on verso of leaf 2.
JWJ Wright Misc. 555.

Carbon copy.
JWJ Wright Misc. 556.

Another carbon copy.
Private collection.

[Verse in] "Celebration."
See [Celebration], U.107.

159   "Dirty Talk."
Typescript (original): 1 leaf.
Early version.
JWJ Wright Misc. 557.

Carbon of above.
With MS and typed corrections and additions.
JWJ Wright Misc. 558.

Another typescript (original): 1 leaf.
Another version.
JWJ Wright Misc. 559.

Carbon of above.
With MS corrections.
JWJ Wright Misc. 560.

Another typescript (original): 1 leaf.
Final draft.
JWJ Wright Misc. 561.

Carbon of above.
JWJ Wright Misc. 562.

160   "Don't Misplace Me, Darling."
Autograph MS: 6 leaves.
With MS notes and corrections.
JWJ Wright Misc. 563.

Typescript (original): 1 leaf.
Working draft, with MS corrections.
JWJ Wright Misc. 564.

Another autograph MS: 1 leaf.
Later draft, with MS corrections.
JWJ Wright Misc. 565.

Another typescript (original): 1 leaf.
Same version as above.
JWJ Wright Misc. 566.

Carbon of above.
With extensive MS corrections and revisions.
JWJ Wright Misc. 567.

161   "The Dreaming Kind."
Typescript (carbon): 1 leaf.
JWJ Wright Misc. 568.

Carbon copy signed.
With author's MS note concerning the use of the poem as
"the song Bessie sings in the movie" [Native Son].
JWJ Wright Misc. 569.

Another carbon copy.
JWJ Wright Misc. 570.

Another typescript (original): 1 leaf.
JWJ Wright Misc. 571.

Another typescript (carbon): 1 leaf.
Verses appear in a different sequence from above.
JWJ Wright Misc. 572.

162   "The Fight That Wasn't Fixed."
Typescript (original): 2 leaves.
With his working title: "The Biggest Upset in History."
JWJ Wright Misc. 577.

Another typescript (original): 1 leaf.
Short version.
JWJ Wright Misc. 578.

163   "I Am So Tired Comrade. . . ."
Autograph MS: 5 leaves.
Title from first line.
Wright's commentary on meetings of the Communist party.
JWJ Wright Misc. 579.

164   "I Been North and East. . . ."
Typescript (original): 1 leaf.
Title from first line.
JWJ Wright Misc. 580.

165   "I Can't Remember: I Forgot. . . ."
Autograph MS: 2 leaves.
Early developmental draft, with passages similar to "The
Blues of the Hunted."
JWJ Wright Misc. 581.

Typescript (original): 2 leaves.
Working draft, with extensive MS and typed corrections.
JWJ Wright Misc. 582.

Another typescript (original): 1 leaf.
With MS corrections and deletions.
JWJ Wright Misc. 583.

Another typescript (original): 1 leaf.
Later draft.
JWJ Wright Misc. 584.

Carbon of above.
JWJ Wright Misc. 585.

Another typescript (original): 1 leaf.
JWJ Wright Misc. 586.

Carbon of above.
JWJ Wright Misc. 587.

Another typescript (original): 1 leaf.
Revised copy of above.
JWJ Wright Misc. 588.

Another typescript (original): 1 leaf.
Another revised draft, with MS corrections.
JWJ Wright Misc. 589.

Another typescript (original): 1 leaf.
Expanded version, with a second verse. With MS corrections.
JWJ Wright Misc. 590.

Another typescript (original): 1 leaf.
Working draft of second verse, with MS corrections.
JWJ Wright Misc. 591.

Another typescript (original): 1 leaf.
Second verse only.
JWJ Wright Misc. 592.

166   "I Got the Deadbeat Blues. . . ."
      Typescript (original): 1 leaf.
      Title from first line.
      JWJ Wright Misc. 593.

167   "In Music, in Writing, in Love. . . ."
      Typescript (original): 1 leaf.
      Title from first line.
      JWJ Wright Misc. 594.

168   "The Leaves Are Green Again. . . ."
      Typescript (original): 1 leaf.
      Title from first line.
      JWJ Wright Misc. 598.

169   "Let's Go Fishing."
      Typescript (original): 1 leaf.
      JWJ Wright Misc. 599.

170   "Machine Shop Blues."
      Typescript (original): 1 leaf.
      JWJ Wright Misc. 600.

171   "Midnight Rainbow."
      Typescript (original):   1 leaf.
      JWJ Wright Misc. 601.

      Carbon of above.
      With a few MS corrections.
      JWJ Wright Misc. 602.

      Another carbon.
      JWJ Wright Misc. 603.

172   "Nightmare Blues."
      Typescript (carbon):   3 numb. leaves.
      Dated 1960[?].
      JWJ Wright Misc. 604.

173   [Notes.]
      Autograph and typescript MS: 56 leaves.
      Includes copies of song lyrics by others.
      JWJ Wright Misc. 605.

174   "O Gathered Faces! O Sea of Sorrowful Faces."
      Typescript (original):   6 numb. leaves.
      With MS corrections and notes.   With additional MS verses,
      2 leaves.
      JWJ Wright Misc. 606.

175   "Oh, I'm Sorry. . . ."
      Typescript (original):   1 leaf.
      With a few MS additions.   Title from first line.
      JWJ Wright Misc. 607.

176   "A Psalm in Two Voices."
      Typescript (original):   1 leaf.
      JWJ Wright Misc. 608.

177   "Sand Slides from Lifeless Fingers. . . ."
      Autograph MS: 1 leaf.
      Title from first line.
      JWJ Wright Misc. 610.

178   "Son, You Are Young and Strong. . . ."
      Typescript (original):   1 leaf.
      Title from first line.
      JWJ Wright Misc. 610.

      Another typescript (original):   1 leaf.
      Another version.
      JWJ Wright Misc. 611.

179   "Sound All the Loud Horns Tonight. . . ."
      Typescript (original): 1 leaf.
      Working draft, with MS corrections. Title from first line.
      Inscribed on leaf is first line of "I Got the Deadbeat
      Blues."
      JWJ Wright Misc. 612.

      Another typescript (original): 1 leaf.
      First stanza only. Written on letterhead of Al Romans.
      JWJ Wright Misc. 613.

180   "Stars and Sands."
      Typescript (original): 1 leaf.
      His corrected title, "Sand and Stars."
      JWJ Wright Misc. 615.

      Carbon of above.
      JWJ Wright Misc. 616.

181   "Street Sweeper."
      Typescript (original): 4 leaves.
      With a few MS additions.
      JWJ Wright Misc. 617.

182   "To Love This World."
      Typescript (original): 1 leaf.
      On stationery bearing Ben Wright's address on Indiana
      Avenue, Chicago.
      Private collection.

183   "Today."
      Typescript (original): 1 leaf.
      JWJ Wright Misc. 618.

184   "Try and Catch Me!"
      Typescript (original): 1 leaf.
      JWJ Wright Misc. 620.

      Carbon of above.
      JWJ Wright Misc. 621.

Book

185 "This Other World: Projections in the Haiku Manner."
      Typescript (original): 58 numb. leaves.
      Working draft of sections "Spring" and "Autumn," with
      extensive MS deletions and comments and with some typed
      additions pasted in.
      JWJ Wright 161.

[Haiku.]
Typescript (original):   824 verses mounted on 20 cardboard
sheets.
With his MS canceled labels.
JWJ Wright 161a.

Another typescript (original):   [85] leaves.
Miscellaneous working drafts, with MS corrections and
deletions.
JWJ Wright 162.

Another typescript (carbon):   1 leaf, 82 numb. leaves.
Final draft of poems, with title leaf and with typed addi-
tions and corrections pasted in.
JWJ Wright 163.

Typescript (original):   33 leaves.
Selections from final draft, each with page numbers identi-
fying location in draft.
JWJ Wright 164.

Typescript (carbon):   302 leaves, 299 leaves.
Selected haiku on loose-leaf paper, in two sections; the
first with 1506 verses, the second with 1491.
JWJ Wright 165[1-2].

Another typescript (original):   4000 leaves.   On loose-leaf
paper and numbered 1-4000 in 20 packets.   Some poems have
MS corrections.
JWJ Wright 166[1-5].

Appendix I

Translations of Wright's Published Works

ARABIC

1 [Black Boy] Al-Walad Al-'Aswād. Translated by Tumādir Tawfiq. Cairo: Dār-Al m'arif, 1968, 356 pp.

2 [Uncle Tom's Children] Abna' al 'Amm Tom. Translated by Munir Ba'abaki. Beirut: Al-Maktabah al-Ahliyah, 1964, 221 pp.

[_____] _____. Damascus: Ministère de l'Information, 1971.

BENGALI

3 [Black Boy] Negro Chele. Translated by Nikhil Sen. Calcutta: Modern Publishers, 1948, 358 pp.

BULGARIAN

4 [Black Boy] Černo Momče. Translated by Vera Stoimenova. Sofia: Nar. mladež, 1971, 271 pp.

CZECH

5 [Native Son] Syn Černého Lidu. Translated and with a preface by Alois Humplik. Prague: Horizont, 1947, 361 pp.

DANISH

6 [American Hunger] Sort Sult. Translated by Kurt Kreutzfeld. Copenhagen: Gyldendal, 1978, 188 pp. With an afterword by Michel Fabre.

195

Appendix I

Danish

7   [Black Boy] Sort Ungdom. Translated by Tom Kristensen.
     Copenhagen: Gyldendal, 1961, 247 pp. Reprinted: 1966,
     256 pp.; 1969, 248 pp.; 1970, 248 pp.; 1974, 248 pp.;
     1976, 247 pp.

8   [Eight Men] Nuancer i Sort. Translated by Jørgen Årup Hansen.
     Copenhagen: Spektrum, 1961, 253 pp.

9   ["The Ethics of Living Jim Crow"] "Jim Crows Leveregler."
     København Dagbladet Pólitikens, 22 August 1955, p. 6.

10   [Lawd Today] Glad Dag i Chicago. Copenhagen: Gyldendal,
     1965, 244 pp. [Unverified]

11   [The Long Dream] Den lange drøm. Translated by Kurt
     Kreutzfeld. Copenhagen: Gyldendal, 1959, 340 pp.

12   [Native Son] Søn af de sorte. Translated by Tom Kristensen.
     Copenhagen: Gyldendal, 1959, 432 pp. Reprinted: 1963,
     410 pp.; 1966, 416 pp.; 1969, 416 pp.; 1972, 410 pp.

13   [The Outsider] Vidnet. Translated by Elsa Gress. Copenhagen:
     Gyldendal, 1954, 296 pp. Reprinted: 1966, 432 pp.

14   [Uncle Tom's Children] Onkel Toms Børn. Translated by Kurt
     Kreutzfeld. Copenhagen: Gyldendal, 1957, 246 pp. Re-
     printed: 1971, 260 pp.

                              DUTCH

15   [Black Boy] Negerjongen. Translated by J. van Dietsch.
     Leiden: Sijthoff, 1947, 236 pp. [Unverified]

16   [Black Power] Zwarte kracht. Translated by Margrit de
     Sablonière. Leiden: Sijthoff, 1956, 312 pp.

17   [The Color Curtain] De kleurbarrière. Translated by Margrit
     de Sablonière. The Hague: W. Van Hoeve, 1956, 204 pp.

18   [Eight Men] Acht mannen. Translated and with an introduction
     by Margrit de Sablonière. Bussum: Kroonder, 1962, 209 pp.

19   ["I Tried to Be a Communist."] In De God die faalde [The God
     That Failed]. Translated by Koos Schuur. Amsterdam: De
     Bezige Bij, 1950, 296 pp.

Appendix I

20 [Lawd Today] Heer, wat een Dag! Translated by Margrit de
    Sablonière. Bussum: Kroonder, 1965, 229 pp.

    [_____] _____. Bussum (Hilversum): Kroonder, 1966, 229 pp.

21 [The Long Dream] De lange droom. Translated by Margrit de
    Sablonière. Leiden: Sijthoff, 1959, 380 pp.

22 [Native Son] Zoon van Amerika. Translated by A. W. Ebbinge-
    van Nes. The Hague: U. M., 1947. Reprinted: 1961,
    440 pp.

23 [The Outsider] De buitenstaander. Translated by Margrit de
    Sablonière. Leiden: A. W. Sijthoff, 1954, 425 pp.

24 [Pagan Spain] Heidens Spanje. Translated by Margrit de
    Sablonière. Bussum: Kroonder, 1958, 233 pp.

    [_____] _____. Berchem-Antw.: Internationale Pers., 1958,
    239 pp.

25 [Savage Holiday] Barbaarse sabbat. Translated by Margrit de
    Sablonière. Leiden: Sijthoff, 1958, 221 pp.

26 [Uncle Tom's Children] De kinderen van Oom Tom. Translated
    by Margrit de Sablonière. Hilversum: Kroonder, 1966,
    282 pp.

27 [White Man, Listen!] Blanke, luister toch! Translated and
    with an introduction by Margrit de Sablonière. Bussum:
    Kroonder, 1961, 194 pp.

FINNISH

28 [Black Boy] Musta Poika. Translated by Eeva Kangasmaa.
    Turku: Aura, 1948, 374 pp.

    [_____] _____. Porvoo: Werner Söderström, 1966, 268 pp.
    Reprinted: 1970, 268 pp.; 1972, 268 pp.; 1975, 268 pp.

29 [Eight Men] Kahdeksan miestä. Translated by Seppo Loponen.
    Porvoo: Werner Söderström, 1974, 249 pp.

30 [The Long Dream] Pitkä Uni. Translated by Seppo Virtanen.
    Porvoo: Werner Söderström, 1960, 435 pp.

Appendix I

Finnish

31   [Native Son] Amerikan Poika. Translated by Antero Tiusanen
      and Eva Siikarla. Porvoo: Werner Söderström, 1972,
      508 pp.

32   [The Outsider] Pikku jumalat. Translated by Kai Kaila.
      Porvoo: Werner Söderström, 1955, 490 pp.

FRENCH

33   ["Almos' a Man"] "Presque un homme." Translated by Andrée
      Valette and Raymond Schwab. Samedi Soir, 19 April 1947,
      p. 6.

34   [American Hunger] Une faim d'égalité. Translated by Andrée
      Picard. With a postface by Michel Fabre. Paris:
      Gallimard, 1979, 173 pp.

35   [American Hunger excerpt.] "Un Américain affamé." Translated
      by René Lalou. Gavroche (Paris), 31 October 1946, pp. 1-2.

36   ["American Negroes in France"] "Les Noirs américains et la
      France." France-Observateur (Paris) 2, no. 56 (3 May
      1951).

37   ["Between the World and Me"] "Entre le monde et moi." Trans-
      lated by Michel Fabre. In "Ensemble Afro-Américain."
      Change, 9 (1971):27-28.

38   "Big Black Good Man." Translated by Hélène Bokanowski. La
      Parisienne, (January-February 1958):65-76.

39   ["Big Boy Leaves Home"] "Le départ de Big Boy." Translated by
      Marc Blanzat and Marcel Duhamel. L'Arbalète (Lyon), no. 9
      (August 1944):235-66.

40   "Black Boy." Translated by Marcel Duhamel and Andrée Picard.
      Les Temps Modernes 2, nos. 16-21 (January-June 1947):
      577-609, 806-45, 980 ff., 1430 ff., 1642 ff.
      Pre-publication of most of Black Boy.

41   "Black Boy." Gavroche (Paris), 12 September 1946, pp. 1, 6.
      Translation of excerpt published in Coronet.

42   Black Boy: Jeunesse noire. Translated by Marcel Duhamel and
      Andrée R. Picard. Paris: Gallimard, 1947, 264 pp. Re-
      printed: 1974, 438 pp.

French

    _____. Paris: Livre de Poche, 1962, 437 pp.

    _____. Paris: Folio, 1976, 448 pp.

43   [Black Boy excerpt.]   "Blancs et noirs."   In Panorama de la
     littérature contemporaine aux Etats-Unis.   Edited by John
     Brown.   Paris: Gallimard, 1954, pp. 348-401.

44   [Black Power] Puissance noire.   Translated by Roger Giroux.
     Paris: Corréa, 1955, 400 pp.

45   [Black Power excerpt.]   "Deux portraits africains" [Two Afri-
     can Portraits].   Preuves (Paris) 4, no. 45 (November 1954):
     3-6.   [1953]
     From the first chapter of Black Power.

46   ["Bright and Morning Star"] "Claire étoile du matin."   Trans-
     lated by Boris Vian.   Présence Africaine, no. 2 (January
     1948):299-316.

47   [The Color Curtain] Bandoeng (1.500.000.000 d'hommes).
     Translated by Hélène Claireau.   Paris: Calmann-Lévy, 1955,
     207 pp.

48   ["Down by the Riverside"] "Là-bas près de la rivière."
     Translated by Boris Vian.   L'Age Nouveau, no. 27 (April
     1948):6-40.

49   ["Early Days in Chicago"] "Débuts à Chicago."   Translated by
     J. B. Pontalis.   Les Temps Modernes 1, nos. 11-12 (August-
     September 1946):464-97.

50   [Eight Men] Huit hommes.   Translated by J. Bernard.   Paris:
     Juillard, 1963, 254 pp.

51   ["Fire and Cloud"] "Le feu dans la nuée."   Translated by
     Marcel Duhamel.   Les Temps Modernes 1, no. 1 (October
     1945):22-47; no. 2 (November 1945):291-312.

52   ["How Bigger Was Born"] "Naissance d'un roman nègre."   Trans-
     lated by Andrée Valette and Raymond Schwab.   La Nef 5,
     no. 44 (July 1948):43-64.

53   ["How Jim Crow Feels"] "Dans le monde entier, je sais recon-
     naître un nègre du Sud."   Paris-Matin, 27 June 1946, p. 2.
     First installment.

Appendix I

French

[   ] "Pas de nègre au wagon-restaurant." <u>Paris-Matin</u>, 30 June 1946, p. 2. Second installment.

[   ] "Dans le Sud, lorsqu'un Noir, parle à un Blanc, sa voix grimpe de deux octaves." <u>Paris-Matin</u>, 2 July 1946, p. 2. Third installment. Translated by Jacques de Montsalais.

54 ["I Tried to Be a Communist"] "J'ai essayé d'être un communiste." Translated by René Guyonnet. <u>Les Temps Modernes</u> 6, no. 45 (July 1949):1-45.
    Later a part of <u>The God That Failed</u>.

55 ["I Tried to Be a Communist."] In <u>Le Dieu des Ténèbres</u> [<u>The God That Failed</u>]. Paris: Calmann-Lévy, 1950, pp. 135-88.

    _____. In _____. Abridged ed. Paris: Séghers, Nouveaux Horizons, 1965, pp. 162-218.

56 "King Joe;" ["F. B. Eye Blues"] "Blues de F.B.I."; ["Red Clay Blues"] "Blues de la terre rouge." In "Les blues de Richard Wright." Translated by Michel Fabre. <u>Jazz Magazine</u>, no. 275 (May 1979), 42.

57 [<u>Lawd Today</u>] <u>Bon sang de bonsoir</u>. Translated and with a preface by Hélène Bokanowski. Paris: Mercure de France, 1965, 267 pp.

58 ["The Literature of the Negro in the United States"] "Littérature noire américaine." <u>Les Temps Modernes</u> 3, no. 35 (August 1948):193-220.
    Early version, never published in English.

59 ["Long Black Song"] "Complainte noire." Translated by Marcel Duhamel. <u>Samedi-Soir</u>, 1 June 1946, p. 3; 8 June 1946, p. 3.

60 [<u>The Long Dream</u>] <u>Fishbelly</u>. Translated by Hélène Bokanowski. With portrait by Monique Métrôt and an interview with Wright by Maurice Nadeau. Paris: Juillard, 1960, 436 pp.

61 [<u>The Long Dream</u> excerpt.] "Fishbelly." Translated by Hélène Bokanowski. <u>Pour l'art</u>, no. 72 (May-June 1960): 20-25.
    Excerpt from chapter 8.

Appendix I

62   [The Long Dream excerpt].   In Les Noirs Américains.   Edited by
      Michel Fabre. Paris: A. Colin, 1967, pp. 237-42.
      Dancing fire funeral.

63   ["The Man Who Killed a Shadow"] "L'homme qui tua une ombre."
      Les Lettres Françaises, 4 October 1946, pp. 1, 10.
      Preceded English publication.

64   ["The Man Who Lived Underground"] "L'homme qui vivait sous
      terre." Translated by Claude-Edmonde Magny. Les Temps
      Modernes 6, no. 69 (July 1950):1-43; no. 70 (August 1950):
      244-60.

65   The Man Who Lived Underground/L'homme qui vivait sous terre.
      Translated by Claude-Edmonde Magny. Edited and with an
      introduction and notes by Michel Fabre. Paris: Aubier-
      Flammarion, 1971, 192 pp.

66   [Native Son] Un Enfant du Pays. Translated by Hélène
      Bokanowski and Marcel Duhamel. Paris: Albin Michel,
      1947, 512 pp.

      [_____] _____. Paris: Le Club Français du Livre, 1950,
      448 pp.

      [_____] _____. Brussels: Club du Livre Sélectionné, 1954.

      [_____] _____. Paris: Livre de Poche, 1957, 493 pp.

67   [Native Son] "Un Enfant du Pays." Translated by Hélène
      Bokanowski and Marcel Duhamel. La Nouvelle République de
      Bordeaux et du Sud-Ouest, Summer-Fall 1949. Serial publi-
      cation. [Unverified]

68   [Native Son excerpt.] "Une chasse à l'homme" [Manhunt]. In
      Panorama de la littérature contemporaine aux Etats-Unis.
      Edited by John Brown. Paris: Gallimard, 1954, pp. 401-405.
      Bigger's flight on the roofs.

69   [Native Son excerpt.] "Un Enfant du Pays." La Gazette des
      Lettres (Paris), 23 August 1947, p. 4.
      The Killing of Mary, prepublication piece.

70   [Native Son excerpt.] In Les Noirs Américains. Edited by
      Michel Fabre. Paris: A. Colin, 1967, pp. 187-93.
      Killing the rat; Bigger fights Gus.

Appendix I

French

71 ["Note on Jim Crow Blues"] "Note sur les blues." Translated
by Madeleine Gauthier. La Revue du Jazz, no. 4 (April
1949):112.
Translation of liner note on Josh White's Keynote Album
no. 107, "Southern Exposure," 1941.

72 [The Outsider] Le Transfuge. Translated by Guy de Montlaur.
Paris: Gallimard, 1955, 493 pp.

73 [Pagan Spain] Espagne Païenne. Translated by Roger Giroux.
Paris: Buchet-Chastel-Corréa, 1958, 339 pp.

74 [Savage Holiday] Le Dieu de Mascarade. Translated by Jane
Fillion. Paris: Editions Del Duca, 1955, 272 pp.
New Title: Le Barbare du Septième Jour (Paris: Edi-
tions des Autres 1979).

75 [Uncle Tom's Children] Les Enfants de l'Oncle Tom. Translated
by Marcel Duhamel. With an introduction by Paul Robeson.
Paris: Albin Michel, 1947, 250 pp.
Includes "Le feu et la nuée" ["Fire and Cloud"], "Le
départ de Big Boy" ["Big Boy Leaves Home"], and "Long
chant noir" ["Long Black Song"].

76 [Uncle Tom's Children] Les Enfants de l'Oncle Tom. Translated
by Marcel Duhamel and Boris Vian. Paris: Albin Michel,
1957, 256 pp.
Same translation of same stories as 1947 edition, fol-
lowed by "Là-bas près de la rivière" ["Down by the Riverside"].

77 [White Man, Listen!] Ecoute, homme blanc! Translated by
Dominique Guillet. With "Avis au lecteur français"
written by Wright in February 1959. Paris: Calmann-Lévy,
1959, 229 pp.

78 [White Man, Listen! excerpt.] "Homme blanc, écoute!"
Lettres Nouvelles 6, no. 64 (October 1958), 338-53.

GEORGIAN

79 [Native Son] Syn Ameriki. Translated by N. Samukasvili and
G. Čikovani. Tbilisi: Nakaduli, 1971, 630 pp.

[_____] _____. Tbilisi: Merani, 1973, 702 pp.

Appendix I

80 [?] <u>Prisluga</u>. [Servant] Translated by G. Čikovani. Tbilisi:
    Nakaduli, 1967, 58 pp.

GERMAN

81 [Black Boy] <u>Ich Negerjunge</u>. Translated by Harry Rosbaud.
    Zürich: Steunberg Verlag, 1947, 306 pp. Reprinted:
    1966, 330 pp.

    [_____] _____. Frankfurt: Büchergilde Gutenberg, 1958,
    330 pp. Reprinted: 1964, 272 pp.

82 [Black Power] <u>Schwarze Macht</u>. Translated by Christian Ernst
    Lewalter and Werner von Grünau. Hamburg: Claassen, 1956,
    342 pp.

83 [<u>Black Power</u> excerpt.] "Ein Neger zum ersten Male in Afrika."
    <u>Die Woche</u> (Berlin) (October 1955):7-10.

84 [<u>Color Curtain</u> excerpt.] "Indonesisches Tagesbüch." <u>Der</u>
    <u>Monat</u> (Berlin) 7, no. 83 (August 1955):378-98; no. 84
    (September 1955):495-508.

85 [Eight Men] <u>Der Mann, der nach Chicago ging</u>. Translated by
    Enzio von Cramon and Erich Fried. Hamburg: Claassen,
    1962, 265 pp.

    [_____] _____. Frankfurt on the Main: Fischer Bücherei,
    1966, 235 pp.

86 ["I Tried to Be a Communist."] In <u>Ein Gott, der keiner war</u>
    [The God That Failed]. Constance: Europa Verlag, 1950,
    302 pp.

    [_____] _____. Zürich: Diana Verlag, 1950, 302 pp.

    [_____] _____. Cologne: Verlag Rote-Weissbücher, 1952,
    263 pp.

    [_____] _____. Vienna: Europa Verlag, 1952, 263 pp.

87 ["I Tried to Be a Communist" excerpt.] "Ein Gott hat ver-
    sagt." <u>Der Monat</u> (Berlin) 3, no. 25 (October 1950):55-83.

Appendix I

German

88 [The Long Dream] Der schwarze Traum. Translated by Werner von
    Grünau. Hamburg: Claassen, 1960, 448 pp.

    [_____] _____. Frankfurt on the Main: Büchergilde Gutenberg,
    1964, 464 pp.

    [_____] _____. With an afterword by Karl-Heinz Schönfelder.
    East Berlin: Volk und Welt, 1971, 485 pp. Reprinted:
    1973, 485 pp.

    [_____] _____. Zürich: Büchclub Ex Libris, 1963, 487 pp.

89 ["The Man Who Saw the Flood"] "Der Mann, der das Hochwasser
    sah." Die Deutsche Zeitung, 23-24 September 1961, p. 22.

    [_____] _____. Die Westphalische Rundschau, 12-13 May 1962,
    pp. 4-5. [Unverified]

90 [Native Son] Sohn dieses Landes. Translated by Klaus
    Lambrecht. Zürich: Humanitas Verlag, 1941, 503 pp.

    [_____] _____. Zürich: Diana Verlag, 1970, 461 pp.

91 [The Outsider] Der Mörder und die Schuldigen. Translated by
    Ruth Malchow-Huth. Hamburg: Claassen Verlag, 1966,
    486 pp.

    [_____] _____. Zürich: Neue Schweizer Bibliothek, 1969,
    468 pp.

92 [Pagan Spain] Heidnisches Spanien. Translated by Werner von
    Grünau. Hamburg: Claassen Verlag, 1958, 336 pp.

93 [Pagan Spain excerpt.] "Christ lebt im Untergrund" [On
    Protestantism in Spain]. Vorwarts (Bonn), 6 March 1959,
    pp. 7-8.

94 [Pagan Spain excerpt.] "Fallas in Valencia." Illuspress
    (January 1959):5 ff.
    From original MS; never published elsewhere.

95 [Pagan Spain excerpt.] "Das grüne Büch der rebellischen
    Fraulein Carmen." Die Zeit, 3 November 1958, pp. 21-24.

96 [Pagan Spain excerpt.] "Die politische Katechismus" [The
    Political Catechism]. Die Deutsche Post, 5 January 1960,
    pp. 18-19.

Appendix I

Indonesian

97   [Pagan Spain excerpt.] "Uralte Fastnachtsbrauche."
     Illuspress (May 1959):5.
     Unpublished chapter, "Las Fallas."

98   [Twelve Million Black Voices] Wir Neger in Amerika. Trans-
     lated by Anita Hüttenmoser. Zürich: Büchergilde Gutenberg,
     1948, 160 pp.
     New Title: Schwarz unter Weiss; Fern von Afrika
     (Frankfurt: Europaische Verl.-Anst., 1952), 147 pp.

99   [Uncle Tom's Children] Onkel Toms Kinder. Translated by
     H. Rosbaud. Zürich: Steinberg Verlag, 1949, 261 pp.

     [____] ____. East Berlin: Verlag Volk und Welt, 1967,
     274 pp.

100 [White Man, Listen! excerpt.] Die psychologische Lage unter-
     drückter Völker [The Psychological Reactions of Oppressed
     People]. Munich: Ner-Tamid Verlag, 1961, 45 pp.

                          HEBREW

101 [Black Boy] Ben-Kŭsim. Translated by Noah Stern. Tel-Aviv:
     Am 'Oved, 1948, 278 pp.
     New title: Ben Ha-Kushim (Tel-Aviv: Am 'Oved, 1961),
     240 pp.

102 ["I Tried to Be a Communist."] In Ha-el she-hikhziv [The God
     That Failed]. Translated by Efrayim Karlis. Tel-Aviv:
     Pales, 1953, 202 pp.

                          HUNGARIAN

103 [Black Boy] Feketék es Fehérek. Translated by Imre Köszegi.
     Budapest: Dante, 1949[?], 228 pp.

104 [Uncle Tom's Children] A Csiu-Csiangi Pokol. Translated by
     Gyorgy Buky. Budapest: Legrady, 1938, 159 pp.

                          INDONESIAN

105 ["I Tried to Be a Communist."] In Kegagalan Tuhan Komunis
     [The God That Failed]. Translated by L. E. Hakim.
     Bandung: Front Antikomunis, 1955, 49 pp.

205

Appendix I

Indonesian

[_____] _____. Djakarta: Timun Mas, 1956, 128 pp.

ITALIAN

106 [American Hunger] Fame Americana. Translated by Bruno Odera.
     Turin: Einaudi, 144 pp.

107 [Black Boy] Ragazzo Negro. Translated by Bruno Fonzi. Turin:
     Einaudi, 1948, 359 pp. Reprinted: 1969, 378 pp.

     [_____] _____. Milan: Mondadori, 1958, 272 pp. Reprinted:
     1959; 1965, 336 pp.; 1972, 339 pp.

108 [Black Power] Potenza nera. Translated by Quirino Maffi.
     Milan: Mondadori, 1957, 390 pp.

109 [Eight Men excerpt.] In Cinque uomini. Translated by
     Fernanda Pivano. Milan: Mondadori, 1951, 180 pp.
     Includes first five stories.

110 ["I Tried to Be a Communist."] In Testimonianze sul Comunismo
     (Il dio che è fallito) [The God That Failed]. Translated
     by M. V. Malvano, Giovanni Fei, Anita Rho, and Claudio
     Gorlier. Milan: Comunità, 1950, 382 pp. Reprinted:
     1957.

111 ["The Literature of the Negro in the United States"] "La
     letteratura negra negli Stati Uniti." Translated by Romano
     Rostan. Quaderni A. C. I. 4 (19 June 1951):41-72.

112 [The Long Dream] Il lungo sogno. Translated by Maria Luisa
     Cipriani Fagioli. Milan: Mondadori, 1962, 412 pp.

113 [Native Son] Paura. Translated by Camillo Pellizzi. Lugano,
     Switzerland: Ghilda del libro, 1948, 584 pp.

     [_____] _____. Milan: Bompiani, 1949, 427 pp. Reprinted:
     1959.

     [_____] _____. Milan: Mondadori, 1975, 423 pp.

114 [The Outsider] Ho bruciato la notte. Translated by Cesare
     Salmaggi. Milan: Mondadori, 1955, 438 pp.

115 [Pagan Spain] Spagna pagana. Translated by Giuliana De Carlo.
     Milan: Mondadori, 1962, 444 pp. Reprinted: 1964, 372 pp.

Appendix I

116 [Savage Holiday] Ma nel settimo giorno. Translated by Cesare
     Salmaggi. Milan: Mondadori, 1956, 235 pp.

117 [Uncle Tom's Children] I figli dello zio Tom. Translated by
     Fernanda Pivano. Turin: Einaudi, 1949, 318 pp.

     [_____] _____. Milan: Mondadori, 1960, 240 pp.

118 [White Man, Listen! excerpt.] In Razza: umana. Translated
     by Attilio Laudi. Milan: Il Saggiatore, 1959, 63 pp.
     "Tradition and Industrialization."

                    JAPANESE

119 [American Hunger] Amerika no ue. Translated by Masao
     Takahashi, 1978, 222 pp.
     Includes "Postface."

120 [Black Boy] Burakku Bôi. Translated by Masao Takahashi.
     Tokyo: Getsuyo Shobo, 1952, 287 pp.

     [_____] _____. Translated by Takashi Nozaki. 2 vols. Tokyo:
     Iwanami Shoten, 1962.

     [_____] _____. Translated by Kitamura Takao. Tokyo:
     Kenyusha Shuppan, 1976, 253 pp.

121 Black Boy; American Hunger. Japanese omnibus ed. World's
     Famous Classics no. 92. Kodan Sha. 1978, 428 pp.

122 ["Bright and Morning Star" and "Down by the Riverside"]
     Kagayaku ake no myôjô; Dakuryû. Translated by Kenji
     Kobayashi and Katsuji Takamura. Tokyo: Nan'un-dô, 1960,
     134 pp.

123 [Eight Men] 8 Nin No Otoko. Translated by Akamatsu Mitsuo and
     Tajima Tsuneo. Tokyo: Shobunsha, 1969, 341 pp.

124 [Native Son] Amerika no Musuko. Translated by Hashimoto
     Fukuo. 1972, 2 vols. Tokyo: Shinchô sha.

125 [The Outsider] Shitsuraku no Kodoku. Translated by Fukuo
     Hashimoto. 2 vols. Tokyo: Shinchosha, 1955, 660 pp.
     New title: Auto Saida, 2 vols., 1972.

Appendix I

Japanese

126 [Uncle Tom's Children] Ankuru Tom no Kodomotachi. Translated
     by Sôichi Minagawa. Tokyo: Shinchô sha, 1955, 266 pp.

127 [White Man, Listen!] Hakujin yo Kike. Translated by Kaiho
     Masao and Suzuki Chikara. Tokyo: Ogawa shuppan, 1969,
     250 pp.

KOREAN

128 [Black Boy] Heug'in Sonyeon. Translated by Jo Jeong-ho.
     Seoul: Bagyeongsa, 1960, 271 pp.

NORWEGIAN

129 [Black Boy] Svart Ungdom. Translated by Johan Borgen. Oslo:
     Gyldendal, 1947, 257 pp. Reprinted: 1958, 232 pp.; 1965,
     232 pp.

130 [Native Son] Nigger. Translated by Johan Borgen. Oslo:
     Gyldendal, 1947, 540 pp. Reprinted: 1951, 443 pp.; 1958,
     443 pp.

POLISH

131 [The Long Dream] Dlugi Sen. Translated by Zofia Klinger and
     Krzysztof Klinger. Warsaw: Czytelnik, 1966, 665 pp.

132 [Native Son] Syn Swego Kraju. Translated by Zofia Kerszys.
     Warsaw: Panstw. Instytut Wydawn, 1969, 461 pp.

PORTUGUESE

133 [Black Boy] Um Negro qui quis viver. Translated by Luisa
     Sampaio. Lisbon: Ulisseia, 1968, 417 pp.

134 ["I Tried to Be a Communist."] In O deus que falhou: uma
     confissao [The God That Failed]. Translated by Enéas
     Marzano. Brazil: Pongetti, 1952.

135 [Native Son] Filho Nativo. Translated by Monteiro Lobato.
     Lisbon: Arcadia, 1949.

Appendix I

[_____] _____. Translated by Monteiro Lobato. Sao Paulo: Cia. Edit. Nacional, 1966, 376 pp. New title: O Filho Nativo, translated by Daniel Gonçalves (Lisbon: Ulisseia, 1960), 493 pp.

136   [Uncle Tom's Children] Os Filhos do pai Tomas. Translated by Manuel de Seabra. Lisbon: Arcadia, 1958.

RUMANIAN

137   [Native Son] Domorodac. Translated by Bora Glišić. Subotica: Minerva, 1954, 441 pp.

[_____] _____. 2 vols. Sarajevo: Svjetlost, 1963.

138   [The Long Dream] Dugi San. Translated by Vladimir Ristic. Subotica: n.p., 1969, 404 pp. [Unverified]

RUSSIAN

139   ["Bright and Morning Star"] "Utrennyaya zvezda." Translated by N. Daruzes. Moscow: Pravda, 1938, 48 pp.

140   ["How Bigger Was Born"] "Kak rodilsya Bigger." Translated by Y. Kalashinkova. Internatsionalnaya Literatura, no. 3 (1941):145-56.

141   [Native Son] "Syn Ameriki." Translated by Y. Kalashinkova. Internatsionalnaya Literatura, no. 1 (1941):3-44; no. 2 (1941):4-153.

142   [?] Rasskazy. [Stories] Translated by D. Žukov. Moscow: Pravda, 1962, 64 pp.

143   ["Red Clay Blues"] "Pyesnya o krasnoi zemle." Translated by M. Zenkevitch. Internatsionalnaya Literatura, no. 1 (1940):86.

144   [Uncle Tom's Children] "Deti Djadi Toma": "Big Boy pokidayet dom" ["Big Boy Leaves Home"], translated by V. Toper; "Na beregu reki" ["Down by the Riverside"], translated by Y. Kalashinkova; "Tuchi y plamya" ["Fire and Cloud"], translated by T. Ozerkaya; "Utrennyaya zvezda" ["Bright and Morning Star"], translated by N. Daruzes. Internatsional-naya Literatura, no. 7 (1938):3-85.

Appendix I

Russian

145   [Uncle Tom's Children] Deti Djadi Toma. Translated by
      A. Snejdera. With an introduction by Isidor Schneidor.
      Moscow: Goslitizdat, 1939, 224 pp.

SERBO-CROATIAN

146   [Black Boy] Crni Djecak. Translated by Stana Oblak. Zagreb:
      Zora, 1951, 275 pp.

147   [Black Power] Crna Snaga. Translated by Ivan Slamnig.
      Zagreb: Zora, 1957, 328 pp.

SLOVENE

148   [Black Power] Crna Sila. Translated by Dusan Savnik.
      Ljubljana: Drzavna zalozba Slovenije, 1960, 342 pp.

149   [The Long Dream] Sanje Nekega Zivljenja. Translated by Mira
      Mihelic. Ljubljana: Cankarjeva zalozba, 1962, 463 pp.

150   [Uncle Tom's Children] Strica Otroci Strica Toma. Translated
      by Ciril Kosmac. Ljubljana: Mladinska Knjiga, 1956,
      207 pp.

SPANISH

151   [Black Boy] Mi Vida en Negro. Translated by Clara Diament.
      Buenos Aires: Sudamericana, 1946, 396 pp. Reprinted:
      1962, 229 pp.
      New title: El Negrito, translated by Enrique Pascual
      (Madrid: Afodisio Aguado, 1950).

152   [Color Curtain excerpts.] "De Sevilla a Bandung" [From
      Seville to Bandung]. Cuadernos, no. 15 (November-December
      1955):40-48. "Que representa Africa para mi?" ["What is
      Africa to Me?"]. Cuadernos, no. 10 (January-February
      1955):26-34.

153   [Eight Men] Ocho Hombres. Translated by León Mirlas. Buenos
      Aires: Sudamericana, 1962, 299 pp.

154   [Lawd Today!] ¡Qué día, Señor! Translated by León Mirlas.
      Buenos Aires: Sudamericana, 1964, 288 pp.

Appendix I

155 [Letter to Antonio Frasconi] "Una carta de Richard Wright a
     Antonio Frasconi." Marcha (Montevideo) 6, no. 269
     (2 February 1945):15.

156 [Letter to Antonio Frasconi] "Una carta de Richard Wright a
     Antonio Frasconi." Los Infrahumanos (Montevideo), (1945)
     2-3. [Unverified]

157 [The Long Dream] El largo sueño. Translated by Floreal Mazía.
     Buenos Aires: Sudamericana, 1960, 520 pp.

158 [Native Son] Sangre Negra. Translated by Pedro Lemona.
     Buenos Aires: Sudamericana, 1941, 572 pp.

     [____] _____. Condensed version in Omnibook (Buenos Aires)
     (February 1946):1-49.

159 [The Outsider] El Extraño. Translated by León Mirlas.
     Buenos Aires: Sudamericana, 1954, 620 pp. Reprinted:
     1955, 615 pp.

160 [Savage Holiday] De la inocencia a la pesadilla. Translated
     by León Mirlas. Buenos Aires: Sudamericana, 1956, 200 pp.

161 [Uncle Tom's Children] Los Hijos del Tio Tom. Buenos Aires:
     Sudamericana, 1950, 345 pp.

162 [White Man, Listen!] Eschucha, hombre blanco! Translated by
     Floreal Mazía. Buenos Aires: Sudamericana, 1959, 177 pp.

SWEDISH

163 [American Hunger] Hunger i Amerika. Translated by Caj.
     Lundgren. Stockholm: Wahlström and Widstrand, 1978,
     201 pp.

164 Black Boy. Translated by Nils Holmberg. Stockholm: Bonnier,
     1948, 256 pp. Reprinted: 1957.

     _____. Stockholm: Wahlström and Widstrand, 1974, 223 pp.

165 ["I Tried to Be a Communist."] In Vi trodde pa Kommunismen
     [The God That Failed]. Stockholm: Natur och Kultur,
     1950, 274 pp.

Appendix I

Swedish

166 [Lawd Today!] I Dag, Herre! Translated by Maj and Paul
Frisch. Stockholm: Rabén and Sjögren, 1965, 276 pp.
Introduction by translators.

167 [The Long Dream] Den Långa Drömmen. Translated by Pelle
Fritz-Crone. Stockholm: Bonnier, 1959, 441 pp. Reprinted: 1961, 476 pp.

168 [Native Son] Son av sitt land. Translated by Eric Palmqvist.
Stockholm: Bonnier, 1943, 285 pp. Reprinted: 1956,
415 pp. Serial publication in Frihet (Stockholm), July-
September 1956.

    [_____] _____. Translated by Gösta Olson. Stockholm:
Aldus/Bonnier, 1964, 378 pp.

169 [The Outsider] Utanför. Translated by Torsten Blomkvist.
Stockholm: Bonnier, 1954, 388 pp. Reprinted: 1956,
387 pp.

170 [Pagan Spain] Det Hedniska Spanien. Translated by Staffan
Andrae. Stockholm: Bonnier, 1958, 270 pp.

171 [Savage Holiday] Våldsam Weekend. Translated by Staffan
Andrae. Stockholm: Bonnier, 1962, 217 pp.

172 [Uncle Tom's Children] Onkel Toms Barn. Translated by Bertil
Lagerström. Stockholm: Bonnier, 1957, 238 pp.

TURKISH

173 [Black Boy] Kara Çocuk. Translated by Hasan Aslan. Istanbul:
Yaylacik Matbaasi, 1968, 274 pp.

    [_____] _____. Istanbul: Ahmet Sari Matbaasi, 1971, 248 pp.

174 [The Long Dream] Uzun düs. Translated by Leyla Ragip.
Istanbul: Üsler Matbaasi, 1974, 496 pp.

175 [Native Son] Vatan evladi. Translated by Leyla Ragip.
Istanbul: Bilmen Matbaasi, 1975, 461 pp.

212

Appendix II

Material by Others Related to Wright's Published Works

Black Boy

1   Karpman, Ben. [Psychological Studies of Native Son and Black
    Boy by Students of Dr. Ben Karpman.]

    One file box.
    Papers sent to Richard Wright for background information.
    JWJ Wright Karpman 1.

    _____. [Psychological Studies of Richard Wright's Native Son
    and Black Boy by Ben Karpman, MD, and His Students.]

    One file box.
    JWJ Wright Karpman 2.

2   Petrina, Tony. [Black Boy by Richard Wright: Screen Treat-
    ment.]

    Typescript (carbon): 1 leaf, 31 numb. leaves.
    Script of narrative and an outline of scenes.
    JWJ Wright American Hunger 17.

3   Rosenthal, Raymond. [Black Boy: Broadcast.]

    Mimeographed script: 1 leaf, 28 numb. leaves.
    Radio version, adapted for WMCA (New York) series "New
    World a Coming," 30 April 1946.
    JWJ Wright 16.

4   White, Ralph K. "Black Boy: A Value Analysis."

    Typescript (carbon): 3 leaves, 108 numb. leaves (1 leaf).
    JWJ Wright, MSS about Wright 15.

Black Power

Black Power

5 [Broadcast scripts featuring discussions of Richard Wright's
   Schwarze Macht, 22 October 1956-24 August 1958.]

   Two typescripts (carbon): 6 leaves.
   In German, on German translations of Black Power.
   JWJ Wright, MSS about Wright 2.

"Bright and Morning Star"

6 Ward, Theodore. "Bright and Morning Star: A Negro Tragedy in
   Three Acts."

   Typescript (carbon): 63 leaves.
   Adaptation of Richard Wright's short story.
   JWJ Wright 953.

Eight Men

7 [Broadcast scripts featuring discussion of Richard Wright's
   Der Mann, Der Nach Chicago Ging. 1 January-16 June 1962.]

   Two typescripts (mimeographed): 20 leaves.
   In German, on German translations of Eight Men.
   JWJ Wright, MSS about Wright 3.

"Fire and Cloud"

8 Goodman, Randolph G. ["Fire and Cloud": Introduction to
   Radio Play.]

   Typescript (original): 1 leaf.
   With MS additions. Introduction to Goodman's play adapted
   from "Fire and Cloud."
   JWJ Wright +959.

   _____. "Fire and Cloud."

   Typescript (carbon): 3 leaves, 52 numb. leaves.
   Adaptation of Richard Wright's prize-winning short story
   of the same name. Includes revised and unrevised versions
   of conclusion.
   JWJ Wright 960.

9 Lowe, Romona. "Fire and Cloud: A Dramatization of Richard
   Wright's Short Story."

   Typescript (carbon): 1 leaf, 16 numb. leaves.
   JWJ Wright 961.

Appendix II

The Long Dream

10   The Long Dream [play], by Ketti Frings.

Mimeographed typescript: 111 leaves.
A dramatization of the novel by Richard Wright. With a
few MS additions.
JWJ Wright 198.

Another copy: 111 leaves.
With some revisions.
JWJ Wright 199.

Another version (mimeographed): 101 leaves.
Her title: "Whippersnapper."
JWJ Wright 200.

Native Son

11   Belin, Rosa. Native Son [play].

Typescript (carbon): 1 leaf, 129 numb. leaves.
A free translation (into French) of Wright's play.
JWJ Wright 847.

Carbon of above.
JWJ Wright 848.

Another typescript (carbon): 107 leaves.
JWJ Wright 849.

Another typescript (original): 127 leaves.
Another version; a close translation derived, from intermediate draft of the play (folder 814[1-4].) With trans-
lator's MS corrections.
JWJ Wright 850.

12   [Broadcast scripts featuring discussion of Richard Wright's
Native Son, 4 March-15 July 1940.]

Five typescripts: 15 leaves.
JWJ Wright, MSS about Wright 4.

13   Wallfisch, Erwin. "Sohn Dieses Landes: Synopsis der Film-
handlung."

Typescript (carbon): 6 numb. leaves.
Synopsis of film of Richard Wright's Native Son.
JWJ +Wright, MSS by others.

Appendix II

The Outsider

The Outsider

14   [The Outsider] L'Intrus. French translation by Guy de
     Montlaur.

     Typescript (original): 1 leaf, 5 numb. leaves, 225 numb.
     leaves.
     Partial draft, with introduction and dedication and with
     extensive MS corrections.
     JWJ Wright 862.

Uncle Tom's Children

15   [Broadcast script featuring a discussion of Richard Wright's
     Onkel Tom's Kinder, 12 March 1961.]

     Typescript (mimeographed): 25 leaves.
     In German, on German translation of Uncle Tom's Children.
     JWJ Wright, MSS about Wright 5.

White Man, Listen!

16   Schrepfer, Margot. ["The Psychological Reactions of Oppressed
     People. . . ."] "Die Psychologishe Situation unterdrückter
     Völker. . . ."

     Typescript (carbon): 39 numb. leaves.
     Translation into German of text from chapters 1 and 2 of
     White Man, Listen! From a lecture given in October 1956
     at the University of Hamburg.
     JWJ Wright 1004.

Other

17   [American Theatre Association, Paris. Announcements and News-
     letter.]

     Mimeographed MS: 4 leaves.
     Announcing their production and a special reading of
     Richard Wright's Daddy Goodness. With a fundraising appeal
     by Fred Hare, director of the Association, 4 May 1959.
     Newsletters dated February and March 1959.
     JWJ Wright, MSS about Wright 1.

18   [Broadcast.]

     Typescript (original): 4 numb. leaves.
     Transcript of an interview in Swedish.
     JWJ Wright Misc. 333.

Appendix II

19   DeVaal, Hans. "Richard Wright--In Memoriam."

Typescript (original): 6 numb. leaves.
English translation of an article originally published in
Dutch in Litterair Paspoort. With DeVaal's typed letter,
signed, to Julia Wright enclosing article, 8 March 1961.
JWJ Wright, MSS about Wright 7.

20   "Helen Lund and Richard Wright."

Typescript (carbon): 1 leaf.
Statement quoting Wright's advice to a guest associate
editor of Mademoiselle.
JWJ Wright Misc. 405a.

21   "Letters from a Sharecropper."

Typescript (carbon): 70 numb. leaves.
Transcriptions of letters from a Negro union organizer for
the Louisiana Farmers Union to the Daily Worker, Harlem
Bureau, July 1936-23 April 1937.
JWJ Wright Misc. 461.

Another typescript (original): 15 numb. leaves.
Edited letters, with identifying names and places deleted.
JWJ Wright Misc. +462.

22   [Manuscripts by others--miscellaneous and unidentified.]

Typescript (original and carbon): 80 leaves.
JWJ +Wright, MSS by others.

23   Miller, Carl. "The American Writer in a Democratic Society."

Typescript (original): 7 numb. leaves.
Script of a broadcast interview of Wright by Carl Miller
for the Radio Division of the Federal Theatre's series
"Exploring the Arts and Sciences," WQXR (New York), 24 June
1938.
JWJ Wright Misc. 334.

Three mimeographed typescripts: 10 numb. leaves.
JWJ Wright Misc. 335-357.

24   [Miscellaneous MSS about Richard Wright by unidentified
authors.]

Two typescripts (carbon): 10 numb. leaves, 2 numb. leaves.
Contents: "Richard Wright." "How Richard Wright Found His
Editor" (1938?).
JWJ +Wright, MSS by others.

Other

25   [Plymouth Winter Lecture Series Lecture Announcement.]

Mimeograph typescript: 2 leaves.
Includes form-letter of invitation to Richard Wright to
speak on "Native Sons in Tomorrow's World," in their series
for 1944-1945.
JWJ Wright, MSS about Wright 9.

26   "Richard Wright--American People's Artist."

Typescript (carbon): 2 numb. leaves.
Outline for "a collective critique of the artist's work to
date, including a biography and an historical evaluation."
JWJ Wright, MSS about Wright 10.

27   Sapin, Louis. Papa Bon Dieu [play].

Mimeographed typescript: 2 leaves, 136 numb. leaves.
With MS notes for music and lyrics (laid in) for Richard
Wright's translation Daddy Goodness.
JWJ Wright, MSS about Wright 11.

28   [Second Blérancourt (France) Seminar: General information and
program.]

Typescript (mimeographed): 11 leaves.
Includes biographies of participants.
JWJ Wright, MSS about Wright 12.

Another copy: 10 leaves.
JWJ Wright, MSS about Wright 13.

29   Slochower, Harry. "In the Fascist Styx."

Typescript (carbon): 21 leaves.
With subtitle: "The Fate of Native Sons; from Remarque to
Richard Wright."
JWJ Wright, MSS about Wright 14.

Index

Note: Entries from the chapter on Wright's published works are prefixed with the year of publication. A "U" prefix indicates an entry from the chapter on unpublished works. I and II prefixes refer to the Appendixes. Only the first appearance of each title is indexed; see cross references in text.